CW00552356

PEDAL FOR YOUR LIFE
By Bicycle from the Baltic
to the Black Sea

Christopher Portway

The Lutterworth Press
Cambridge

To my son Paul, who also has the wanderlust.

The Lutterworth Press
P.O. Box 60
Cambridge
CB1 2NT

British Library Cataloguing in Publication Data:
A catalogue record is available from the British Library.

ISBN 0 7188 2946 8

Printed in Great Britain by Galliard (Printers) Ltd, Great Yarmouth

Contents

Acknowledgements

My most sincere appreciation is extended to a host of organisations, companies and individuals for their help and advice prior to, during and following the journey. Chief among the organisations is the Winston Churchill Memorial Trust whose trustees, led by Lady Soames, judged my project to be worthy of a Winston Churchill Fellowship.

Others included: Saga Group Ltd., coupled with the name of the chairman, Roger de Haan, and also Paul Bach.The Retirement Insurance Advisory Service, P.J. Hayman & Co Ltd., Travel Insurance Services, Vango (Scotland) Ltd., Tent manufacturers, Carradice of Nelson Ltd., Bicycle baggage manufacturers Burghaus and Peter Storm Ltd., Protective clothing manufacturers Rohan, outdoor clothing manufacturers Advance Textile Concepts, Grainger's International Ltd., waterproofing. M. & J. Cycles of Brighton, particularly its managing director Michael Robinson. British Rail, Eastern Region & Network South-east, Scandinavian Seaways, coupled with the name of Ray Hankin of Fleet Public Relations Ltd. Estlines, Eurolines, Stena Line, Austrian Railways, coupled with the name of Marien Tilsnig press officer of the Austrian National Tourist Office, London,German Rail/DB, coupled with the name of Juergen Schwarz of their London office. French Railways/SNCF, and especially Peter Mills, press manager. London,Swedish Tourist Board, London, and especially Barbro Hunter, director. Hilton International, and the Vienna Hilton, especially Michael Scheutzendorf, general manager. Tetley Tea Ltd., Youth Hostels Association, Royal Geographical Society, Natascha Scott-Stokes, Hazel Constance, Mike Gerrard, Harold Dennis-Jones, Hotel Laine, Riga, Latvia. His Excellency Mr Sergiu Celac, Romanian Ambassador in London. Cedok (London) Ltd., coupled with the name of Peter Brierly, then director. Polorbis Travel Ltd. London, coupled with the name of Stanislaw Stachura, director, Peter Easton of Peter Easton Associates. I am also greatly indebted to June Morrison for producing the index to this book.

And during the journey my heartfelt gratitude goes to many wonderful people in those countries through which we passed who, spontaneously and with little enough to offer, opened their hearts and homes to two passing strangers, especially: In Tallinn, Estonia, the Laansoo family. In Parnu, Estonia, the Kuningas family. In Kaunas, Lithuania, the Kuprys family. In Alytus, Lithuania, the Ambrazevicius family. In Cluj, Transylvania, Andras Kovacs, Dr Andras Bodor & family, and Romeo Ghircoiasiu. In Tirgu Mures, Transylvania, the Virag family, Zsuzsa Kiss, & Dr Zoltan Brassai & family. In Sfintu Gheorge, Transylvania, Albert Levante, plus others who offered help and kindness along the way.

Foreword
by Joanna Lumley

Just to look at the journey on the map makes your heart jump with excitement: from Estonia to Romania via Latvia, Lithuania, Poland and Transylvania, through Hungary to Vienna. Most keen travellers would be hunting out train timetables and checking the car's engine – Christopher, however, decided to celebrate threescore years' and ten by pedalling every foot of the way.

This was nearly insane; but at the same time the pulse quickens with envy. The prospect beckons: the open road, silences, vistas, birds, even the exhaustion and filth, and then the whisper starts in your head: he did it, I could do it, I shall do it. I am hugely impressed by his achievement, laudable by any reckoning; what makes it more remarkable is the other story which unfolds along the way, a tale of wartime imprisonment and escape, recapture, love and his eventual marriage to the Czechoslovakian Anna whose family had, at the risk of their lives offered him succor. It is as though he has pedalled back through his life leaving trackmarks on his memories: his humour and effortless prose are tucked alongside his readers in his saddlebag as we freewheel through fantastic times and lands. While our mechanised lives demand ever swifter journeys, and geography is reduced to airports and holiday resorts, Christopher's extraordinary and touching account urges us to slow down, reflect, observe and experience.

'. . . and the Elements / so mixed in him, that Nature might stand up / and say to all the world, "This was a man!"' This is a man, this great traveller through time and space.

Christopher Portway, I salute you with affection and admiration.

INTRODUCTION

The silly thing is that I'm not a cyclist at all, in either the professional or even the amateur sense. During my schooldays in Staffordshire, Essex and Herefordshire the landscape was either flatly convenient or scenically advantageous for cycling and most of us youngsters had bikes with which to escape at weekends the disciplinary rigours of boarding school. Came World War Two and multiple years in the army when no bicycle saddle ever graced my hindquarters, while, in the post-war years, any cycling experience was restricted to irregular pedalling of the four miles to and from work on the occasions I felt obliged to save on petrol.

It was only during my sixties that I have begun to look upon the bicycle as an occasional vehicle with which to investigate the charms of the lesser-known regions of my own British Isles as an adjunct to my vocation as a travel journalist. Thus I came to undertake, at rare intervals, perambulations along the rugged coasts of Donegal, Pembrokeshire and eastern Scotland. Until then my only other lengthy cycle ride resulted in unmitigated disaster. I had been persuaded, against my better judgement, to follow a route along the so-called East of England Heritage Trail between Norwich and Durham and, consequently, around the then newly designated Cumbria Cycle Way which circumnavigates the Lake District. From Norwich, on a bike handed to me minutes before departure, I endeavoured to keep up with an escort of cycling fanatics of the Norwich Cycling Club which included the Bishop of Norwich himself. Having seen me on my way these worthies peeled off at Fakenham, 26 miles on, with many verbal expressions of goodwill whereupon, round the first corner, I collapsed, exhausted, by the roadside, worn out before I had properly started. Ten days later, on the Cumbria circuit, I hit a Pennines blizzard east of Carlisle, ungratefully refused the proffered services of a hovering mountain-rescue helicopter, to arrive more dead than alive at my self-catering establishment destination near Talkin, only to discover it to be locked and barred, the owner having surmised that no cyclist in his right mind would or could reach it in such conditions.

And that was about the full extent of my bicycling experience before, in my seventieth year, my son Paul and I embarked upon the more ambitious pedal that forms the subject of this book.

Given the time we would have walked it. Paul uses his bicycle more than I do, mostly for the purpose of commuting between his lodgings and Swansea University (where he was learning Russian) though he, like me, has a good pair of walking legs on him. Both of us are, in fact, more walkers than cyclists.

My own two feet have carried my angular frame across far remoter and more difficult terrain than I shall ever accomplish on a bicycle, and assuredly walking is the best method of getting acquainted with a country and the countryside but the next best thing is cycling since, again, one's feet do the work and the same advantages apply. And yet whereas a walker is unlikely to exceed 20 miles a day, a cyclist of even my limited ability can cover 50 or more with still time to dally in places of interest.

Nor is a bicycle restricted to roads these days. The modern all-terrain machine can go virtually anywhere a walker can. Personally I'd prefer not to climb the highest peaks this way and the *raison d'être* of mountain bikes is not simply a novel method of surmounting the likes of the Matterhorn. I find their sturdiness, multi-gearing and resistance to punctures a boon on road, lane or track. It was barely a couple of years ago that I finally discarded my trusty (and rusty) Humber circa 1946, heavy, unwieldy and limping from puncture to puncture. On this my top speed was little faster than jogging pace while the saddle offered the equivalent discomfort to that of sitting astride an oscillating railway line.

For those who can recall the salad days of the Humber or the Rudge, the performance of modern bikes is a revelation. Far from being the no-frills transport of those who can't afford a car, modern cycles are symbols of affluence and independence, promoting fitness and, at the same time, doing the environment a power of good. For the green and caring 1990s bikes are suddenly desirable animals to possess.

These were but some of the considerations that prompted the use of a bicycle for my latest long-distance venture. And, since 1993 had been pronounced the European Year of the Elderly, here was a peg to hang it on, while, furthermore how could my choice of venue to mark it as well as my own seventieth year be anywhere but within Europe? I was going to have no truck with slavishly keeping to historic trails or the course of specific rivers; progressing from one sea to another by any route I chose to follow offered unlimited scope. Eastern Europe had long been my happy hunting ground so, for me, the journey could be something of a personal pilgrimage too; a peregrination down memory lane.

The itinerary I had planned for this latest encroachment lay across the three Baltic states of Estonia, Latvia and Lithuania – now independent nations once more, eastern Poland, Slovakia – which had sececded from the Czech Republic that very year, north-east Hungary and Romania, a different and more fragmented Europe than I had known before. Our proposed startpoint was to be Tallinn, primary seaport and capital of Estonia; our final destination the Romanian Black Sea port of Constanta, a city I had twice visited during the communist era. I could have knocked 400 miles off the route by commencing the ride from the Polish Baltic coast but, having long wanted to see something of Estonia, Latvia and Lithuania, here was the opportunity. I envisaged the total pedalling mileage to be somewhere around 1,700 though likely diversions could increase this figure to the 2000-mile mark. I had also considered the merits of undertaking the journey alone but the combination of a father and son appealed to me – particularly in this instance when Paul's bicycle maintenance and Slav linguistic skills were in advance of my own.

Images of crumbling communism re-flickered through my mind as the date of our departure approached. A young man attacking the Berlin Wall with a hammer, Hungarian soldiers dismantling barbed wire fences on the Austrian border, Lenin's statue crashing down from its pedestal, huge crowds filling the squares of the major cities. And because my wife and I – my wife more than I – had tasted the bitter fruit of twisted communism the excitement and unreality of those months of self-liberation had been, even from the sidelines, the headiest of potions. For East Europeans the first taste of freedom we take for granted had been like wine; an air of carnival pervaded the streets and cafes – anything and everything seemed possible. Today the East has a hangover, caught between a splitting headache and the desire to relive the drunken excitement of the night before. The question everybody asks is whether the aspirin is affordable.

The changes wrought since 1989-90 have been complex and unpredictable. On one hand, much of rural Eastern Europe remains dominated by peasants, farmers and centuries-old values with many villages still frozen in medieval time. More noticeable is the legacy of communism's ruthless industrialisation and 'modernisation' of urban districts still infested with sprawling out-of-date factories and crude housing blocks. The transformation now under way to bring the East into line with the West will take years to realise as will the attitudes and ideals that communism stood for and which it instilled into the captive minds of its subject masses. Entire generations were brought up to believe in the underlying veracity of the socialist state, and no amount of reform will convince hard-core believers that the communist era is extinct. Yet it's not only these hard-liners who point to a present situation in which unemployment has tripled, inflation skyrocketed and the standard of living for many dropped below what it was during the old era. In this sense, many East Europeans are more concerned about their future now than they were a decade and more ago.

In the meantime, Eastern Europe continues to struggle painfully forward, grappling with a future that is both promising and unsettling. After 45 years of communist domination, wherein most people's lives were lack-lustre but secure, there are many lessons to unlearn and numerous prejudices and fears to contend with before the countries of Eastern Europe can prosper. In the newly-named Czech Republic the people seemingly agree that underlying the apprehension is a strong sense of hope – a belief that Eastern Europe in general has gone too far along the road of reform ever to turn around and go back.

Prior to setting out I had read the manuscript of a proposed book, *The Amber Trail*, by a colleague of mine, Natasha Scott-Stokes, who, in 1992, had cycled across Eastern Europe with her husband, though on a more westerly course than mine. She had never been to the former Eastern Bloc countries before so had no first-hand experience of life there under either Nazism or communism against which to effect comparison. Her resulting impressions, therefore, had not been particularly happy ones. With both wartime and post-war observations and experiences beneath my belt I, at least, could conjure a yardstick so vital in assessing conditions in today's Eastern Europe.

I held no political or serious ecological aspirations so far as the seven differently affected countries through which I would be passing were concerned but I could not help but ponder upon the fact that my latest journey might offer a rather less familiar picture of Eastern Europe than I had hitherto absorbed.

Chapter 1
Baltic Beginning

The Baltic. There it was; grey, unenticing and polluted. Nine industrialised nations – Finland, Sweden, Denmark, Germany, Poland, Lithuania, Latvia, Estonia and Russia – share this shallow, brackish ocean. Within three short years and in one bold summer the careful equations that had governed business, diplomacy and military balance among them have been overturned. The former Soviet Union's share has been reduced when it spawned the rebirth of the three Baltic states while Eastern Germany – the former German Democratic Republic – has been swallowed by the West.

For long a buffer zone and a battleground between East and West since the days of the Vikings the Baltic has witnessed sea-faring tribes sacking each other in an endless cycle of cruelty and revenge. Only for a brief couple of centuries in the Middle Ages did a Baltic community unify under the Hanseatic League of prosperous cities that put trade before plunder. Since then, East and West have pursued their violence with the usual zest, culminating with Adolf Hitler and Joseph Stalin dividing people and nations between them. For more than two score years these Baltic waters became a chess-board for Cold War manoeuvres, patrols, provocative flight patterns and electronic surveillance, with each side monitoring the other into a kind of grudging stalemate that wasted millions of dollars, pounds and roubles.

Civilisation has washed its hands too long in this lake-like sea. Excesses of toxic waste, oil spill and the sewage of 70 million people pour into its waters. In response all the former nations of the Baltic community signed the Helsinki Convention of 1974, the world's first pact to protect an entire sea against pollution from every source. Since then a dramatic improvement has been registered. Was it imagination or simply wishful thinking but were those grey waters I gazed upon through the derricks of Stockholm harbour just a fraction less defiled than they were the last time I'd come this way?

Over the years I had made landfall on many a Baltic shore from the oft-frozen Gulf of Bothnia via Denmark's homely Bornholm Island, cheerful lively Copenhagen, the East German harbour of Sassnitz, and the Polish ports of Gdynia and Gdansk.

The first time I had gone this way, Helsinki had been my destination. Together with the full quartet of Scandinavian capitals it had formed a redoubt for a skirmish in the private cold war I was then waging against the totalitarian regimes of Eastern Europe in the 1950s. Thus my recollections of the Finnish capital had originally been tinged with a sombre hue eventually eclipsed by a more recent visitation made under happier circumstances.

It is, to me, something of a sombre city at the best of times. With its Leningrad architecture the place retains trappings of the days when Finland was a grand duchy of the Russian Empire – all samovars, borsch and the dark brocade of old restaurants. Yet it is a new city as European cities go, with much of its centre the work of the German architect Carl Ludwig Engel whose harmonious Senate Square fronting his Lutheran cathedral is one of the finest squares in northern Europe. From Helsinki I had gone north to the snowbound wastes of Lapland, to Rovaniemi and beyond, and to Oulu where the ice-channels in the Baltic bobbed with ice curds. Here I witnessed another aspect of this north European sea.

A summer sun had attempted to inject a little light relief into the uniform grey of its waters on a subsequent visit to the Baltic's opposite shore. The Polish coast rests on two urban-industrialised pillars – the Szczecin/Swinoujacie complex on the west and Gdynia/Gdansk on the east. Between them lies Pomerania, with its fields of white potato blossoms, tufts of dense forest, and seaside lagoons inhabited by wild swans. I had arrived at the Baltic's largest port, Gdynia, which had been no more than a hamlet when I was born. There is therefore nothing particularly historic or olde-worldly picturesque about the city, so its port grabs what limelight there is for its harbour containing a mix of sailing craft and old warships.

A tram-ride away lies Sopot – the one-time Prussian Zoppot before it became part of Poland in 1945 – its German influence still tangible. Chief resort of the so-called Polish Riviera – though don't expect temperatures and a degree of sophistication to match those of its Mediterranean counterparts – Sopot reminded me of a 1920s Bournemouth as depicted on one of those old sepia picture postcards. It is a fact, however, that the once graceful resort was the Cannes of this riviera and no more is this to be felt than in the noble pile of the Grand Hotel, ever-popular with Poles and Scandinavians.

Gdansk is another story. Known as Danzig to the Germans, pulverised by them in the Second World War, and the centre of momentous instances of history its past permeates this reborn and beautiful city. The first shots of the war were fired from Westerplatte, the promontory guarding the harbour entrance, but, for Westerners, Gdansk remains the most familiar city in Poland; the home of Lech Walesa and Solidarity, its images flashed across a decade of news bulletins. A heavily industrialised city too, a tall slender memorial rises from the former Lenin Shipyards to commemorate the workers killed in the 1970 uprising which was a precursor to the downfall of communism in Europe. The heart of Gdansk has been restored as carefully and lovingly as has Warsaw's Stare Miasto, the splendid Prussian and Hanseatic architecture again a delight to the eye and an icon to the soul of Poland.

It was from Stockholm, however, that Paul and I set sail to attain our forthcoming journey's point of departure. Cycling from the Central Station to the Estline quay, tucked away in an industrial suburb, gave little opportunity for the town to shine the brightest – which was a shame for many years had passed since I last cast my eyes upon it; Paul not at all. Such were the vicissitudes of the timetables of Scandinavian Seaways between Harwich and Gothenburg, and of Estline between Stockholm and Tallinn that it was necessary to dally for 48 hours in either Gothenburg or the Swedish capital. We had chosen Gothenburg as the less expensive option. At this most genial of port-cities on the Swedish North Sea coast we had been parted from our bicycles, they continuing onwards by train in advance of us; something I would have been exceedingly unhappy about had any railway system other than those of the super-efficient Scandinavian ones insisted upon the same procedure. To have lost – even temporarily – our bicycles on the outward leg of the journey would have been a far greater disaster than were this to occur on the way home. My experience of the cycle-carrying facilities on European railways was virtually nil but, on the journey from my Brighton home, via London, to Harwich, I was unable to fault British Rail who not only allowed us to keep our machines with us in off-peak hours on non-Intercity trains but made no charge for doing so.

Although I had carried out a certain amount of cycling training on the roads in and around Brighton I was unable to take possession of the machine loaned me for the project until less than a week prior to departure which gave little enough time to acquaint the various parts of my anatomy to its peculiarities. Only on one occasion did I load the bags and panniers with the object of sampling its handling characteristics under fully-laden conditions – and was not too happy with the result. Both Paul and I were of the opinion that two rear panniers each were adequate for our needs and that we could cut down on the luxuries of life accordingly. Additionally I was to carry a handlebar-fixed camera bag in which to stow my photographic equipment, though this item I soon discovered to be an infernal nuisance. Not only did its weight affect steering but, whenever I wanted to rest the bicycle against a wall, tree or post, the ballast on the handlebar pulled the front wheel around so that the machine would fall to the ground unless restrained.

And then, three days before leaving home, I was involved in a *contretemps* with a car outside my own front door while setting out on a training ride. The car stopped. The bike stopped. But I didn't. My dive over the handlebars ended when I hit the tarmac, my arms outstretched to protect my head. The bike suffered no more than scratched paint. I suffered a sprained wrist and a sprained elbow plus an assortment of cuts and bruises. Bandaged and plastered (in the medical sense) I never felt so averse to cycling anywhere than I did then. Even the ride to Brighton Station was fraught with calamitous possibilities, and crossing the City of London had me on the verge of a nervous breakdown, particularly when, outside the Bank of England, the serrated metal edge of the pedal caught my calf to send cascades of blood into my shoes. Those bikeless 48 hours in Gothenburg were a balm.

Aboard Estline's ferry *Estonia* [1], our bicycles tied to stanchions on the car deck, we made our introduction to the first country on our cycling itinerary. All the crew and most of the passengers were Estonians and Latvians spending money in the duty-free saloons as if there were no tomorrow. We had been given a berth

---

1. Tragically the *Estonia* was to founder in a storm a year later with the loss of 900 lives.

in the 'sump', down beneath the car deck, and, though perfectly adequate, it was considerably less palatial than had been our Scandinavian Seaways suite on the Harwich-Gothenburg crossing. Our bags and panniers, together with two rolls containing our bivouac and basic camping equipment, reposed with us.

Each pair of panniers were linked by a strap so that they could be carried across our shoulders when parted from the bicycles. The bivouac was small; just enough space for two if 'togetherness' is not too much of an imposition, and we carried no sleeping bags. In lieu we had equipped ourselves with Goretex bivi bags; in effect waterproof bags into which, normally, a sleeping bag proper would be inserted. But there was simply no room for everything. Our cooking gear consisted of no more than army-issued blocks of solid fuel, a crude solid fuel holder which served as cooker, an army-model mess tin we were to utilise as a container, frying pan and saucepan, two plastic mugs and the minimum of eating irons. Hardly the Boy Scout's complete outfit but, surprisingly, it sufficed.

Paul slept like the proverbial log that night, as he seems to do most nights and in any circumstance. But then he is young and possesses that envied ability to catch up on lost sleep whenever there is a pause in activities. Me, I'm hopeless at sleeping, though at my age I don't seem to need much. I lay awake pondering upon things to come and the sort of people we would be meeting in the morning on a new Baltic shore

All three Baltic states have a long and chequered history; Lithuania's is perhaps the most distinguished and is characterised by her ancient ties with Poland. Estonia and Latvia have for centuries been intermittently at the mercy of a variety of powerful neighbours – the Teutonic Knights, the Danes, the Poles, the Swedes, the Russian Czars and, finally, the USSR. They enjoyed a brief period of precarious independence between the two World Wars.

In many ways they are different from other former Soviet republics. They use the Latin alphabet; their traditions are completely Western, and their religions are Catholic and Protestant. Of the three, Estonia is the smallest, Latvia – the traditional 'workshop of the Baltic' – was an important industrial centre in Czarist times, while Lithuania – the 'Land of Amber' on the historic Amber Road that ran from the Baltic to the Mediterranean – has been a supplier of this rare product of the seashore from time immemorial. Until they gained their latest independence, the people of the Balkan states must have felt like American Indians - left with their dances and songs and languages but not much else. They had watched an immigration of Russians tip the population balance until Latvians lost the majority in their own nation and Estonians composed only 60 percent of theirs. Only Lithuania successfully kept its ethnic population at 80 percent. Of that much I was aware from my superficial researches. Soon, hopefully, I could be aware too of what it was like to be a Baltic states citizen today with 40 years of Soviet domination behind them.

I glanced at the name and address of our host family in Tallinn, one of four in Estonia and Lithuania. There is an organisation called 'People to People' wherein individuals in eastern Europe keen to meet Western visitors in their own homes register their particulars in a book (see bibliography) published in the USA and

Britain. I had obtained the edition covering the Baltic states and subsequently contacted a number of listed names which resulted in heartwarming pleas to accept their proffered hospitality. Though we only intended staying but a day and a night or so I felt this would be a most satisfactory method of learning how local people lived and felt about the new situation in their lands. On a more prosaic note it would also give us a welcome break from an envisaged heavy dose of primitive camping. We had notched up a further series of host families, with whom we might be briefly staying, in a trio of Romanian towns, but these contacts resulted from the good offices of a colleague of mine in Britain.

Came the dawn and, humping our panniers, bags and camping rolls up interminable flights of stairs (or are they companionways on ships?) we debauched on deck to behold the distant spires and steeples of Tallinn sparkling in a distinctly cool morning sunshine. Playfully and skilfully the seagulls circled in the wind as the ferry slowly pivoted amid the forest of cranes in the harbour.

Anne Lill's card read: 'Professor, the Chair of Classical Philology, University of Tartu, Department of Classical and Romance Languages', a daunting introductory disclosure to an ignoramus like me. But Anne struck me as being pleasurably unprofessor-like and very human as she met us on the quay in Tallinn harbour. A slight lady in, I suppose, her late 30s, she straightway took us under her wing to grapple with the problem of getting us and our bikes to her mother's flat some five kilometres out of town. It soon became apparent that Tallinn Corporation buses were averse to cramming loaded bicycles into their already well-loaded interiors even had we been able to get them through the automatic doors. Our suggestion of following her bus to the suburb in question met with no enthusiasm and the problem was eventually solved by her commandeering an empty van and bribing the driver to deliver us all to the Laansoo home among rows of Russian-built high-rise apartment blocks.

Anne's mother, Mai Laansoo, turned out to be a delightful lady very much in the mould of her daughter. Of any husbands there was no trace though both were or had been married. There was a son, however, a teenage lad with a pleasant manner who, the very next day, was due to leave for Oxford by coach with his fellow members of a Tallinn choir. To reach their flat we had to haul our bicycles up flights of stone stairs, an exercise we were to repeat umpteen times in the coming months. In contrast to the bare and shoddy exterior of the apartments, the interior of the Laansoo residence was warm and cosy. We were pressed to a late breakfast snack and, with Anne again, caught the bus – bikeless – back into town to be given a tour of the city.

And what a wonderfully preserved city of the old Hanseatic League Tallinn is. Its winding cobbled streets are made for walking; encouraging one to see what ancient fragment of the town lies around every next corner. The place is dominated by Toompea, the hill over which it has tumbled since the Middle Ages, and the Old Town is a jumble of medieval walls, turrets and spires, amongst them Fat Margaret – with its cannon – and Tall Hermann, affectionate names given to a couple of the 14th century bastions one of which – Tall Hermann – holds a special significance for today's Tallinn citizens. It was here, in August

1989, that began a human protest chain of two million Baltic people that stretched unbroken for 430 miles to Vilnius in Lithuania.

Tallinn – translated as 'Danish Castle' – was the Estonian name for Reval, the 13th century citadel of the Danish King Waldeman, set high on Toompea. The Danes subsequently sold it to German merchants who transformed the stronghold into a port for the Hanseatic League. Thereafter the region became a battleground as Swedes, Russians, Poles and Lithuanians fought over it, the Swedes finally taking control of the city. Under Peter the Great, Russia proceeded to smash Swedish influence during the Great Northern War of 1700 with the result that Estonia became part of yet another empire, that of Russia which abandoned it to the Germans in 1918. The Bolsheviks tried to win the lost territories back but were persuaded otherwise by the sabre-rattling of a British fleet. Independent but economically crippled the Estonian nation lasted only until 1939 when, once again, the country, together with its Baltic cousins, found themselves back in someone's empire, this time that of the Soviet Union from which they have only recently emerged.

I asked Anne what benefits she had felt the most from her country's new-found freedom.

"There are so many," she replied, "but besides the obvious ones such as being able to speak freely, read newspapers and books that are not just those passed as fit by communist authority, and have one's children educated without political brainwashing, the freedom that pleases me most is that of being able to visit countries other than those of the Soviet bloc. Look at my son going off to England tomorrow. And I'm expecting to attend an educational seminar in your country next month. None of this would have been possible a year or two ago. Alas, many Western countries make it nearly as difficult for us to enter their territory as the Soviets did when they were in control. Fortunately your country has done away with entry visas though there is still the currency barrier which, hopefully, will subside as our new currency becomes convertible."

"What about your Russian citizens? What do they think about suddenly finding themselves living in a foreign country?" I asked next.

"That's a problem to be sure," I was told, "but not all our Russian residents are pro-communist; far from it; many are willing to become Estonian citizens and integrate with the community. Equally there are a large number who don't and won't, who live a life apart from their neighbours, who refuse to learn Estonian or fit in with our way of life. Not that even many of these are pro-communist; they are just being – well, Russian." She smiled mirthlessly, throwing up her hand in a gesture of incomprehension.

Anne's English was good, as was that of her mother and son, which, to me, was surprising in a country where, for years, Russian was the priority language taught. I asked how this came about.

"Many Estonians speak a little English as well as, of course, Swedish, since Sweden is our nearest Western neighbour. For the last half dozen years our youngsters have become much more Western-orientated as restrictions imposed on contacts with the West have lessened, and learning English increasingly became all the rage. Though Russian was still taught in schools few took it seriously and

Russian lessons invariably became, in effect, English lessons."

With seemingly so many Estonians visiting Sweden and Finland I wondered how they managed in countries even more expensive than my own and was told that special provision was made for Estonians and Latvians while many such had suddenly discovered Swedish or Finnish-residing relatives. A recent 20 percent devaluation of the Swedish kroner had also helped matters.

Though goods in the shops showed a huge deficiency compared to those in Western Europe I was agreeably surprised to find a much wider choice than I expected. I was aware that Estonia was the most developed of the trio of Baltic states and that Tallinn, as a capital city, might inspire the best treatment but having been in Moscow only eighteen months previously and seen the pitifully-stocked shops and the shoddy goods on sale there – even in a top-rank capital – I had been prepared for the worst in an, until recently, obscure Soviet republic. Not at all, however, though everywhere I heard moans about the rising costs of everything. Estonia allegedly is the most expensive, as well as developed, of the Baltic states though prices were, to a Western visitor, ludicrously low.

We ascended Toompea, saluted Fat Margaret, circuited the spacious and cobbled Town Hall Square surrounded by fairytale houses, and gazed from the bastioned city wall over the red rooftops of the New Town which is not new at all, though, like everywhere in Tallinn, lovingly restored after wartime bombing. All around us the silhouette of domes, Baroque spires and steeples was unforgettable, stuccoed walls, sharp Gothic gables and steep red-tiled roofs presenting a stern face of Teutonic discipline. The sun flashed fire among the spires and gables, exploding against the tiles as if angry at being denied access to the narrow alleyways beneath. And, as we walked in Kadriorg Park, a woody untailored sort of park planted with lime, oak, ash, birch, chestnut and linden trees shading the gravel paths, mothers sat on benches rocking prams and old women scattered crumbs for the pigeons.

On the spire of the city hall the brass weather vane of the sentinel Vana Toomas – Old Thomas – stands guard. Anne told us the legend in which a wizened old man appeared each autumn during the town's construction to ask the same question: "Is the town finished yet?" and Vana Toomas replies "No, the town is by no means finished; it will take another year." So the old man mutters angrily to himself and departs. Should the sentinel's answer ever be yes, the old man will send the waters to destroy the city. And with the many buildings I saw being restored or awaiting restoration the sentinel could truthfully still be saying no today.

For a late lunch Paul and I were treated to a typical Estonian dish comprising Baltic herring and jellied meat bolstered by potatoes. Then, by bus and on foot, we explored more of Tallinn on our own before returning to the Laansoo homestead. The warm bright day with not a cloud in the sky boded well for our tomorrow's intended departure.

But our good hosts wouldn't hear of us leaving before midday and a further substantial refuelling following yet a further visit to the town centre this time to see off Anne's son on his Oxford-bound coach. Finally, our bikes reloaded and transported back to ground level, we were afforded a royal farewell as we pedalled off, slightly apprehensive, on the main road southwards. All of a sudden Constanta seemed an awfully long way away.

Chapter 2
Estonia, Latvia, Lithuania

Negotiating our way out of Tallinn was no problem whatsoever since the Laansoo apartment was not only on the edge of town but the very edge through which the Parnu road passed. And Parnu, 130 km south and still on the Baltic coast, was our next objective. Though the map indicated a sparsity of communities astride the route the fact that it was a trunk road suggested to us that provisions would be readily obtainable at frequent intervals. Which goes to show how green we were when it came to gauging rural Estonian amenities. The map showed four townships between Tallinn and Parnu, and Anne confidently predicted foraging facilities at Haiba, Marjamaa, Paadu and Parnu-Jaaguji though the first two were nowhere to be found.

In spite of an incessant headwind we made reasonable progress on sparsely used, smooth and dead-straight tarmac. The weather remained sunny and dry but it was only after several hours hard pedalling that I discerned that, in addition to the wind resistance, my front brake-drum was rubbing against the wheel. This rectified, our rate of knots improved considerably though hunger soon brought it down again. Resigned to the prospect of going supperless to bed we began searching for a suitable spot on which to raise our tent and thought we were being smart when we chose a couple of new-looking but discarded timber cabins as shelter for the night. Pleased at not having to bother with tent-erection we consumed our emergency tin of corned beef and stretched out on the hard floor having first removed sundry noxious substances from it. In the middle of the night it began to rain and it was then we discovered the reason for the abandonment of the cabins. Within minutes, water, with increasing fervour, found its way through the roof panels at multiple points. Dodging one deluge meant moving under another so we remained static and stuck things out, thankful for our waterproof bivi-bags. The smell of excrement, the noise of passing traffic, the unrepentant floor and the coldness of the night made sleep impossible – even for Paul – and the morning's verdict was that our first night 'in the field' had hardly been a resounding success.

A mess-tin of diluted marmite acted as breakfast barely had dawn raised the necessary illumination to enable us to heat the concoction and, thankfully vacating our treacherous refuge, we pedalled off along a river of a road, water spraying from our tyres.

Rain fell all morning as did our spirits. Lack of sleep and food had me insisting upon rest halts at ever-increasing intervals to swig water and mouthfuls of Dextrine tablets. Forests of dripping spruce hemmed us in on all sides giving that illusion of remoteness created by forests everywhere. But this wasn't altogether an illusion though the remoteness was lessened by the occasional passing of a car or lorry and the remorseless ribbon of the road. We stopped at a lonely farm to refill our waterbottles and the few moments of complicated conversation with the Russian occupants alleviated the sense of solitude. It was Sunday which could only mean that procurement of fodder would be all the more unlikely before arrival at Parnu.

And then the sun broke through the overcast sky and our spirits soared accordingly. I shall never cease to be amazed how a ray of sunshine or patch of blue sky can work such miracles of repair to damaged morale following spells of miserable conditions – though all too often the new optimism can be just as swiftly shattered. But not on this occasion. Within ten minutes there was not a raincloud in sight.

Then another miracle occurred. Some 40 kilometres from Parnu, approaching the village of Parnu-Jaaguji, we came upon a kiosk selling hot and cold snacks. What's more it was open for business on a Sunday morning and in the middle of nowhere. The good Lord above was being kind to us. We purchased microwave-heated hamburgers, Estonian chocolate and a bottle of Swedish beer, sat on the wet curb and wolfed the lot down. The bread must have been a week old and the beer was flat but no matter; it filled a void.

Refreshed, we pushed on, turning off the main road into Parnu-Jaaguji village for the purpose of telephoning our Parnu hosts to warn them of our imminent approach. "I'll meet you the further side of the bridge into town at 11 o'clock," I was told, and it wasn't until I had replaced the receiver that I realised he had given us but an hour to cover 38 km.

In the event we made it in an hour and a half which shows what even stale hamburgers and flat beer can do for one's physical well-being.

Kalle Kuningas was a lighting technician working at the town's theatre and we found him, together with his family, waiting in their car on the further side of the river bridge as arranged. Our new hosts were a young couple with a four-year-old daughter and they straightway took us for a light lunch in the theatre's canteen. I attempted to pay for the meal but they wouldn't hear of it. The nicest part of the meal was the natural apricot juice dispensed from a large glass container, and Paul and I were thirsty enough to crave gallons of the stuff so, while waiting for Kalle to take his wife and daughter home and return to show us around the town, we indulged our craving with gusto.

We rejoiced to see the Baltic again and at the prospect of following the coast all the way to Riga in neighbouring Latvia. Founded in 1251, Parnu became a small Hanseatic port and then a health resort at the mouth of the Parnu river; the mud dredged from the Gulf of Riga contained medicinal ingredients used in the town's sanatoria. On the broad promenade citizens strolled through shaded avenues, some no doubt tingling from the application of the therapeutic sludge.

Via the seventeenth-century Swedish-built Tallinn Gate and Parnu's largest park – the Rannapark – hosting a small run-down amusement complex we arrived at the 2-mile-long beach, now re-opened after long closure resulting from the high level of the sea's contamination.

"The crowds have been pretty thin for the last few summers," Kalle declared. "But it wasn't just the pollution that kept Russian visitors away; it was also us! They were just as afraid of the Estonian people as they were of our water!" I gazed at the shallow sea and the wind-driven white crests lapping at the beach and, though it was early July, felt disinclined to go in for a dip. Instead we downed a beer or two back in town while Kalle aired his views on Russians in general and communism in particular.

Though Estonia, it transpired, is attempting to stem the flow of would-be Russian immigrants along her border with Russia, Kalle was not averse to those Russian residents in Parnu prepared to integrate into Estonian society; he would welcome them in fact but he had nothing good to say about what he termed the hard-liners in their midst. He spoke vehemently against communists – both Russian and Estonian – still in power within Parnu's local government. "They continue to live in their big houses," he said with rising indignation, "and act like little Stalins trying to undo all many of us have done to achieve our freedom." He went on to explain how Estonia, with less than one percent of the Soviet population, held more than half the whole former USSR's joint-venture enterprises with the West. Private cooperatives such as coffee shops and snack bars had sprung up everywhere against the wishes of the Soviet regime. "We've earned our new liberty honestly and without bloodshed," he finished, "but the price has been taut nerves and constant stress. Even in my theatre we incurred official wrath by staging plays considered controversial, with all concerned – including simple lighting engineers like me – risking their jobs." Kalle drained his beer with a flourish.

But Kalle had not finished his tirade and the beer unleashed another fusillade of words. Nothing had been easy then or now, it appeared. Soviet capital had poured in for industry after the last war, but housing and services were left to wither. Living standards plummeted, and industrialisation created a demand for labour that could not be met by local people. Russian and other Slavic immigrants poured in in waves. There was, and still is, little social mixing, and the immigrants became ready scapegoats. Many of the immigrants are content with labouring jobs that Estonians avoid, even though wages were higher for the ditchdigger than for the doctor. But things are changing though many are uneasy about the backlash such changes could bring.

Kalle laughed mirthlessly as if pleased to have got things off his chest. We left the tavern and, following his car on our bikes, reached his home on the outskirts of town in an almost identical block of apartments to those of our previous hosts in Tallinn. There no hot water had been available and it was the same here in Parnu; we pampered Westerners would be hard put to accept such shortages and deficiencies as many Easterners currently have to suffer. "Maybe we *should* have had a dip in the briny after all," commented Paul ruefully, as he tried to remove cycle-chain oil from his hands in a basin of icy water.

Though dog-tired we sat talking well into the night and I kept nodding off in the comfortable armchair in which I had been placed. The Kuningas flat was small but, like most eastern Europeans, they had furnished it with taste and care completely at odds with the shabby concrete exterior so universal within the one-time Soviet empire. Our bikes were locked away inside Kalle's box-like garage in an adjoining car storage unit. Kissing the small daughter goodnight at the end of a meal equivalent to a British high tea I wished I could have followed the little girl's example and retired to my bed too.

We left soon after nine the next morning, Kalle leading us in his car again to ensure we found the Riga road. The weather remained fine but there was a wind blowing off the sea to push us into traffic coming from behind. Cycling along the coast gave us brief glimpses of a shoreline scrubbed by grey waves that foamed through the reeds into small inlets. The wind was cool but our exertions kept us warm and, where trees formed a wind-shield, the flat road made for easy cycling.

At Haademeeste, a couple of kilometres off the main road, we were prudent enough – having learnt our lesson – to stock up at the local supermarket where we purchased bread, beer, sausages and chocolate for the equivalent in Britain of 40 p. At the restaurant opposite we consumed a very passable early hot lunch washed down by a disgusting synthetic pear juice for a sum total that worked out at 60 p. By 1.30 p.m. we were at the Latvian border.

I never like changing money at border posts since the rates are usually less favourable than elsewhere but Riga was two days ride hence and there was little in the way of likely bank-possessing townships in between. If Estonia had confused me with its mixture of a newly printed currency together with the old Russian rouble still in circulation then Latvia made things no better with its old and newly-printed Lat. Changing £10 sterling plus the remainder of my Estonian crowns I lost track of the calculation and came away with a fistful of strange notes that might have been worth anything.

Latvia. A new country but, for us, little changed; even the language was no more comprehensible than Estonian. And, like Estonia, this beautiful land of which everyone sings in the reborn national anthem is at peace with itself. There are no mountains to climb, no racing rivers to conquer; just trees and more trees lining the highway to resemble a great crowd come out to greet a royal procession. We passed occasional breaks in the eternal forests where bog and marsh ruled over a few tiny acres snatched from the trees, then hard-won grainfields swept by the wind and hamlets huddled against proud churches of ageless stone, a land scarred and sacred with history. And so back into the trees again.

Outside Salacgrita we diverted into the township there to join an elderly toil-worn man for a beer. He chatted away in Russian and Paul's command of the language surprised and delighted me. It was to stand us in good stead within the Baltic states, less in eastern Poland but not at all thereafter. In the cramped bar, hazy with tobacco smoke, the man learnt of our journey's destination and method of reaching it. He shook his grizzled head in bewilderment. "Constanta! Constanta!" he kept repeating as if to ensure that he had heard correctly, then, shaking us by the hand, he shuffled off still shaking his head mumbling "Remarkable! remarkable!"

Additional to the bar Salacgrita could boast a hotel of quite respectable dimensions and, in need of the toilet, we went inside. Run-down the establishment might have been by Western standards but its one and only visible member of the clientele was a cut above the average, being none other than a retired brigadier – or so we were led to believe. What's more he spoke reasonable English.

Without preamble the man pointed at me and briskly proclaimed: "You are a soldier," then turning to Paul, added "And you are a scholar. Am I right?" He raised himself from an armchair and stood ramrod straight, still pointing.

"Not quite," I conceded, "but I used to be a soldier. What made you think that?"

"You look like a soldier."

I was surprised at this assertion for I never thought of myself as a military man or even of looking like one; certainly not at my age.

Paul offered the information that he too had been a soldier but that, indeed, he currently was a student.

"You see I was nearly right!"

The chap was swarthy with fleshy hands and a broad infectious grin. I felt it my turn to contribute to the guessing game.

"You too have been a soldier, I think," I vouchsafed.

"How did you know?"

"You, er, well you look soldierly," I replied appraising his upright stance and grey but well-trimmed hair. "Am I right?"

"You are," he replied, obviously pleased with my assumption, "I was a colonel general."

The British army possesses no colonel generals so I tabbed him as a brigadier.

"You were in the war, I presume?"

"Yes, I fought for everybody, Germany, Russia and Latvia," was the laconic reply. "Sit down," he ordered, "and I'll tell you about it."

And it was then that we learnt first hand of the conflicting loyalties and dilemmas faced by people of the Baltic States before, during and after the Second World War under German and Soviet domination. Together with Finland these nations had every reason to fight the invader of the territory whether they were German or Russian, the armies, in turn, occupying or re-occupying it with a high degree of brutality. As I well knew, having witnessed a fraction of it myself in 1945, the war in Eastern Europe was marked by destruction and massacre and a complete lack of common humanity on a scale that we of the West can barely perceive. In a mixture of English, Latvian, German and Russian our military friend gave us lurid accounts of battles fought against both enemies half a century ago.

We departed with much soldier-to-soldier hand-shaking and hugging. The bridge carrying the road over a river estuary was being widened, the traffic deflected on an 8km detour but pedestrians were picking their way across the excavated structure so we followed suit, wheeling our bikes to the other side with no great difficulty.

The straight road out of town was devoid of interest and I found myself ruminating upon the lives these Baltic peoples must have led over the past sixty or so years and of the disasters that had befallen them. How cosy were our British lives compared with them. I thought of our 'brigadier' and the twists and turns of his military life and then of my own youthful years and initial period in the British army.

Though I was born into a military-minded family – my father and uncle were colonels, the former winning a Military Cross in the First World War, and my younger brother consistently outranking me in later years – I never had the ambition to make an efficient soldier. Alas, I was the black sheep of the family – the runt of the litter, if you like – in other vocations too, but particularly when it came to matters military. I suppose a penchant for 'playing soldiers' and parading my toy army on the nursery table encouraged Father in his belief there might be a field-marshal's baton in his elder son's knapsack. As a schoolboy I had the choice of joining the Scouts or 'the Corps' (the Officer's Training Corps) but, of course, my choice had to be 'the Corps' and, quite honestly, I hated it. With the outbreak of war in 1939 I became a member of the LDV – Local Defence Volunteers, the forerunner of the Home Guard, today known as 'Dad's Army' – and this I enjoyed since most of its members were equally unsoldierlike.

My trouble too was that I was born at the wrong time with the second half of the war catching me just as I left school. Father was anxious I should be in his regiment – the Essex – so I was persuaded to volunteer, an act which offered the chance of joining the regiment of one's choice, and so found myself a raw recruit in an infantry training centre at Warley Barracks, Brentwood, of which Dad was second-in-command. This seemingly cosy arrangement was not a good idea at all since sundry sergeant-majors took it out on me for what they perceived as injustices perpetrated by him. And I could never get used to saluting my own father.

Pronounced a soldier after four months square-bashing, trying to hit a target with an assortment of weapons – some with vicious kicks – and throwing myself onto coils of concertina barbed-wire so that my colleagues could pass unhindered over my prostrate and bleeding body (a fiendish adjunct to the process) I was ready, aged 18, to kill my fellow men.

A sign indicating the 'Meleki Camping Place' broke the chain of my recollections and tempted us off the highway to investigate. At a pound a night the site was good value, close to the sea and equipped with ablutionary facilities which would have done us no harm at all. But there was still some hours of daylight remaining so we pushed on. The wind had dropped too and the smell of Riga was in our nostrils.

Dusk was made the darker by trees that crowded the road to offer alternate camping deep in a forest. Bloated with sausage and bread, we had our heads down well before darkness, and having put 130 km behind us since Parnu I should have slept well but didn't. Though comfortable enough, warm, snug and mosquito-proof, it was a case of not yet being acclimatised to the new environment of outdoor slumber.

We were up at 4.30 a.m. and reducing the final 60 km of the Baltic Highway to Riga by six. Breakfast was a shared tin of sardines and a mug of luke-warm tea without milk or sugar, and its deficiencies soon had us struggling hard. The road led through a string of small coastal towns but the hour was too early for any available source of further sustenance and Riga was a long time coming, the final 10 km a real pain. Joining the main Pskov-Riga highway in the outer suburbs we beheld a transport cafe serving early morning lorry drivers and here we tucked into very unbreakfastlike but none the less welcome fare.

Entering central Riga was an unpleasant experience; more so since it was the first of many negotiations of strange and sizeable cities to come. Pushed into the gutter by uncaring cars, lorries and – worse – trams and trolleybuses, ignored by pedestrians who acted as if we were invisible, attempting to avoid the worst of the pot-holes and open drains in unkempt streets, forced to a halt at traffic lights that switched straight from green to red, and not knowing where the hell we were going was just part of it. Our objective was the Laine Hotel in Skotas (School) Street which we hoped was near the city centre to which we were being pushed and chivvied anyway.

I had arranged in advance a night's lodging here for 'sometime during the first week of July' and the reply had been 'you'll be welcome any time'. And the Laine, when finally located, was as good as its word. The hotel was situated on the fourth floor of an office block approached by way of a courtyard with no more than a small wall plaque to announce its presence. The young manager, when I managed to unearth him from a pile of bricks on the third floor which was being transformed into a lounge and restaurant, suggested we keep our bikes in our room for safe-keeping. Cramming the machines into the tiny lift took a bit of doing but there was plenty of space for them in our room which contained four unmade beds and not a stick of anything else. But there was hot water available in a communal washroom and we made the most of it. Spruced up in our 'city best' – clean shirt and trousers – we emerged to explore the city.

When Latvian independence was self-proclaimed in 1918 the country had to be assembled like a jigsaw puzzle out of territory inhabited by Lett-speakers. These amounted to the Latgals, who occupied the eastern half of the country, together with the Zemgals in the west – but south of the Daugava river – and the Kurs from further west along the Baltic coast. Together with the Lithuanians and ancient Prussians, these peoples constituted a Baltic group who in the course of history – especially after the German conquest of Livonia (i.e. Latvia and Estonia, together) – fused into one racial and linguistic coalition.

To complicate matters further, Riga had hitherto been an independent city-state with an overwhelming alien population; a German city from the time it was founded in 1158 by a handful of Bremen merchants as a storehouse at the mouth of the Daugava. And so it had remained through all the vagaries of Polish, Swedish and Russian rule. About 1190 the Augustinian monk Meinhardt erected a monastery there and its Germanisation swiftly built up in co-operation with the Teutonic Knights.

The city is the largest and most vibrant of the Baltic states in spite of Tallinn's and Estonia's close proximity to the Western influence of Finland and Sweden. With a population of a million it seems too big for the country it heads; only twice that number live in the whole of Latvia. It is also the least ethnic of all the Baltic capitals; Russification of this cosmopolitan city was swift after the Second World War, and by the time of the country's recent independence a full 70 per cent was Russian. This is an even greater percentage than that of Latvia as a whole which, in 1989, was itself reduced to the barest majority of 51.8 per cent.

Whatever their ancestry the citizens of Riga appeared an exuberant bunch to us as they revelled in a metropolis now their very own. Its big city milieu became at once apparent though lacking the fairytale picturesqueness of Tallinn. The long-established German connections were likewise evident in church and shop while, whenever Paul and I wanted to converse with anyone, his Russian and our combined if limited German were entirely adequate.

It didn't take us long to encounter the exciting, edgy qualities of a place which is daily re-inventing itself from the virtually forgotten days of an early twentieth-century near-decadent past to what soon could be a near-decadent present. Its Soviet years are already half-forgotten as money flows in from Scandinavia and the West to change the face and mood of the city, bringing bad as well as good. Plain to see were the flashy new bars and restaurants already superimposing themselves upon the grid of traditional city life with high prices and a not-particularly-palatable cuisine mixing it with dingy, more earthy eating houses where the food is simple but wholesome. We made the mistake of lunching in one of the former and so learnt the reason for being its only clients.

The dead straight main street – Brivibar iela (Freedom Street) – led us down to the riverfront past the dour former Intourist high-rise hotel, the Latvije, around an equally Soviet-type structure, the monument to freedom, and into the car-free streets of the Old Town resplendent with rows of teutonic-looking edifices circa 17th century together with great slabs of antiquity such as the brick cathedral, Riga Castle and the two hefty churches of St Peter and St Jakab. More hefty than graceful is the October Bridge spanning the wide Daugava river.

St Peter once possessed the tallest wooden tower in Europe and Peter the Great took a special delight in climbing to the top; in fact he is reputed to have personally helped extinguish a fire when the tower was struck by lightning in 1721. What he saw as he looked down on the city is not too difficult to imagine today. Riga was, like Tallinn, a Hanseatic port with red brick fortifications and multi-storeyed merchant and store houses exquisite in form, decoration and colour, many displaying handsome façades, tall pointed gables and high-pitched roofs of red tiles. Pride of place among the jumble is the building of the Blackhead Brotherhood, an association that organised the city's social calendar in the thirteenth century and whose patron saint was the black Saint Mauritius who gave the brotherhood its name.

We lost ourselves frequently and revelled in doing so. At the massive university building we located a student-run tourism organisation whose enterprising staff gathered around us as eager to learn of our impressions of their country and capital as we were to learn more about them ourselves. In the station square, amongst street vendors selling hand-spun white candy floss and sachets of bright yellow lemonade, we purchased a picnic supper which we ate on a park seat. Tired but rewarded for our exertions we returned sore-footed to the hotel.

Mosquitoes did their best to spoil our night's sleep but a proper bed compensated. And breakfast was brought to us in bed. Well almost. With no restaurant breakfasts had to be conveyed to guest's rooms and ours arrived via a good-looking but sour young lady who pretended not to notice my nakedness as I searched for my clothes at the foot of the bed.

By 8.30 we were on the road again, crossing the bulky October Bridge and seeking a way out of the city in the general direction of Bauska. Barely had we left the suburbs when we found ourselves at the scene of a serious accident; both vehicles a heap of twisted metal. We had heard the impact and when we reached the scene quite a crowd were attempting to extract the unfortunate victims, though I would have thought it a wasted effort since no human was likely to have survived such a horrific collision. We pedalled by guiltily but there was little we could have done to help.

If nothing else the incident reinforced our own caution and for long we kept resolutely inside the white line border of the road that arrowed across the countryside. With Bauska hardly 70km away and the Latvian border but a further two dozen we expected to be well inside Lithuania by nightfall.

At Code we blew our remaining Latvian currency on two bottles of beer, a packet of biscuits and a clutch of Snickers chocolate bars, a Western 'delicacy' all the rage in the Baltic countries. We effected the transaction by the simple expedient of piling all our money on the counter and helping ourselves to the goodies until the good lady behind it said "diezgan!" which seemingly is the word for "enough."

Had we the inclination we might have detoured 11km from Bauska to ogle at the renowned palace at Rundale, a creation of the architect Bartolomeo Rastrelli who designed many of St Petersburg's most magnificent buildings including the Winter Palace. Instead we paused in Bauska itself, a small town of historic allure and a chunky fifteenth-century knightly castle which was being restored. A shower of rain had sent us scurrying for shelter earlier in the day but now the sun warmed the old brickwork of the town giving it a ruddy glow of contentment.

But no restaurant could we find to sustain our aim of one hot meal a day. "There's provisions at the border," maintained an all-knowing local and, foolishly, we believed him. Alas there was nothing – not even Snickers – to be had at the border, and no currency exchange either. "Where can we change money?" I asked a customs officer. "Panevezys," he replied, referring to Lithuania's fifth largest city a good 70km ahead. And then, just as we had cleared the border control buildings and their potential as shelter, we were struck by a violent downpour. We took refuge in a clump of trees and got as wet from their dripping foliage as from the rain itself. Welcome to Lithuania.

It was early evening and time to look for a camping place in the soaking, abruptly treeless countryside. Discarding the idea of a meal, hot or cold, we entered a village to espy a supermarket – or so a board outside the ramshackle wooden structure proclaimed. Hopes rose and then fell when we found it closed but a man caught sight of us pushing disconcertedly at the door and came to our aid. He introduced himself as the proprietor and, taking us inside the humble establishment, sold us a length of salami and a tin of chicken for two American dollars which was sheer robbery. But at least we would go to bed with more than Snickers lining our insides.

An overcast sky was dribbling rain as we raised the tent in the lee of a copse some 50 yards off the road. The grass was soft as well as wet and we were fortunate to have devoured our tinned chicken and struggled fully-clothed into our bivi-bags before the rain came down in earnest. We had accomplished well over 100km again which we were now classing as about an average rate of daily progress on these straight, flat and well-surfaced roads.

It rained on and off during the night and it was drizzling as we reluctantly emerged from our cocoons at 5.30 next morning. A sullen sky offered no comfort and it was belching water as we set off, our stomachs little appeased by unappetising salami, luke-warm marmite and the promise of hot food at Panevezis. Not only was it wet but distinctly chilly too and I wore everything warm and waterproof I had with me including gore-tex overtrousers. Intriguing-looking windmills loomed out of the murk at intervals but I felt too depressed to stop and take photographs; the light was not good enough anyway.

Occasionally we halted to munch stale Syrian-made biscuits in bus shelters, and in this desultory manner reached the suburbs of Panevezis which dragged on endlessly before debouching us into the centre. Surely here there would be no problems regarding currency exchange and the availability of hot meals?

At a main crossroads we spotted a sports equipment shop that also advertised itself as a change office. It was not due to open until 10.00 a.m. so we hung around for an hour watching the populace scurrying to work through the muddy street. The rain had ceased and, glory be, the sun appeared. At 10.00 I was first through the shop door but inside was no sign of a kiosk or change counter. "Change? We don't change money here. This is a sports shop," pointed out an assistant acidly – or at least that is what I presumed she said. An English-speaking lady came to the rescue. "Well why do they display 'Currency Exchange' in large letters outside their shop?" I asked with some irritation. The good lady was as perplexed as I but offered directions to a bank which, when we reached it, showed acute suspicion of my £10 sterling notes and refused even to consider Swedish kroner. The bank was heavily guarded by two uniformed officials touting kalashnikovs, and clients were only allowed to approach the single counter one at a time. I was aware that such establishments are well guarded in communist and Third World countries but here in seemingly law-abiding Panevezis it all seemed rather theatrical. However, at last possessed of another wad of strange banknotes, I was no longer a pauper in Lithuania.

Now for that hot meal we told ourselves gleefully. But though we scoured the town no restaurant could we find. I pushed Paul into asking for directions a score of times but we raised only shrugs. There were confectioneries and a baker or two as well as supermarkets containing the usual limited range of unsuitable foodstuff – and none of it hot. Queues were abundant. Finally, crouched on a refuse-littered building site, we picnicked on the ubiquitous salami, bread and bottled cherries. Panevezis, we decided, was a dead loss.

We left it, taking the Vilnius road, eventually turning off onto a lesser artery heading towards Kaunas. I was tempted to add the Lithuanian capital to our itinerary but it stood off our direct route and to include it would have involved at least another 100km. At that time I was not aware that, as luck would have it, we would be seeing the city later.

The weather remained cool, the fickle sunshine eclipsed only by the odd shower which we ignored. At first the road was almost devoid of traffic and we enjoyed the solitude. It was now well into the afternoon so we halted for 'tea' which consisted of a bottle of beer, dry bread and some solid cakes obtained from a roadside cabin manned by a Russian family who found us an amusing diversion from their boredom. The road, like those over which we had passed and those to come, were lined with kilometre stones, neatly posted. Useful though we found them they cruelly emphasised the distances and I tried to ignore them. But I found myself automatically counting every one, then doing arithmetic in my head, converting into miles the distance to the subsequent town before the next stone was reached and I could begin all over again. Distances in miles always sounded less than in kilometres.

By the time we reached the town of Kediniai we'd both had enough for the day. Unkindly I categorised the place as the 'usual scruffy Lithuanian town', not even bothering to stop and look for assuredly non-existent restaurants and shops holding anything remotely useful to buy. Such towns were little more than overgrown villages anyway; urban formality provided by a few neo-classical facades, a touch of grandeur by a chateau-like town hall, and ply-wood cabins labelled 'disco'. A fiendish wind had arisen which slowed us down as well as forcing us to exert double the energy.

Dead flat agricultural land with not a tree in sight paraded itself beyond Kediniai but with about 130km behind us we could go no further. Begging a refill for our waterbottles at a house on the outskirts we searched earnestly about for somewhere suitable to camp. There was little cover but, by walking our bikes along a farm track, we found a depression in the ground that provided shelter from the wind and partly screened the tent from the eyes of passers-by on the road.

In the event the site proved to be one of our more successful locations. A tractor growled by as we were going to bed but the driver never noticed us even though the tent and our prostrate bicycles were but yards away.

There were a number of reasons for this insistence on concealment when setting up camp for the night. One concerned the simple law of trespass; the possibility of raising the tent on private property though here in the Baltics most of the land was communal. Another was the possibility of robbery, particularly of our bikes which had to lie, albeit padlocked, outside the tent. And mountain bikes of the calibre of ours were a prize indeed for an east European; the attention we received from passers-by was aimed mostly at what we were riding. A third reason was the more childish one of our getting a kick out of surreptitiously locating a secret hiding place where nobody could see us – especially children who could hang around for hours handicapping our primitive culinary practices and delaying our early withdrawal to bed. As we progressed further south tales of attack and even murder by marauding bands assailed our ears to give our secrecy an added purpose though we always presumed the risks of this to be no greater than elsewhere in the world.

We were but 60 km from Kaunas and the home of the Kuprys family who had elected to be our next hosts. With no rain and only a mild head-wind we made Lithuania's second city by mid-day, covering the last 35 km on the hard shoulder of the Klaipeda-Kaunas motorway not shown on our maps. We wondered whether bicycles were permitted on Lithuanian motorways (this was the only one) and were comforted when we perceived other cyclists – many on the wrong side of the road – using it. In a village standing back from the highway we telephoned the Kuprys household to advise them of our proximity.

The family lived 5 km out on the opposite side of the city and we had one devil of a job locating their street, of which nobody had heard. Time and time again we pedalled down wrong roads as citizens either directed us wrongly or, more likely, we misunderstood the directions. Here Paul's knowledge of Russian was a godsend; I'd still be searching those Kaunas suburbs today if it hadn't been for him. However the search showed us something of this lovely city which we resolved to explore in more leisurely fashion later.

Running the Kuprys residence to earth on an unsurfaced road called Grybausko in a leafy outer suburb we took to the delightful family the moment we set eyes on them. Forty-year-old Povilas, the husband, described himself as a journalist and teacher, contributing to a regular column in the local newspaper as well as being an active member of the Lithuanian Teachers' Union. Later that year he was flying to America for a teachers' course and was bursting with enthusiasm at the idea of visiting a country outside of his own. Ruta, his less exuberant but essentially warm-hearted wife, was not so happy about his impending absence though ruefully acknowledging the benefits it could bring. The rest of the household comprised two happy and well-mannered children – a girl and a boy, a dog and a cat plus, for the first night we were there, another guest in the guise of a dishevelled young Australian. Their house was a sizeable one with garden to match in a tree-lined row of houses of similar calibre.

Povilas exhibited intense pride in his city as he conducted us around it that afternoon. Kaunas's population is more than 90 per cent Lithuanians; in fact Povilas put it higher with only seven percent being Russian and most of them willing to integrate with the locals, even sending their offspring to Lithuanian schools.

Standing at the confluence of the Nemunas and Neris rivers, the city is said to have been reduced to ashes thirteen times before World War Two which it came through relatively unscathed. Between the two world wars it was Lithuania's capital while Vilnius was in Polish hands, and more than any other Baltic city, has preserved its Lithuanian identity. Its heart is the Town Hall Square and though Kaunas was founded in the eleventh century most of the oldest surviving buildings here are fifteenth and sixteenth century German merchant's houses forming this picturesque and restored square. The fine white former town hall in the centre is now a 'wedding palace' and, the day we were there being a Saturday, was doing good business with wedding groups emerging with conveyer-belt regularity.

The hub of the town comprises the pedestrian precinct of Laisves aleja with shops and supermarkets well patronised by citizens searching out long-absent Western goods now rapidly re-appearing. When Povilas left us to our own devices we partook of a hot lunch in a recommended restaurant where the three courses were placed before us one after another without a word having to be spoken since there was no choice and therefore no need for discussion. The helpings were, again, insubstantial so we subsequently bolstered our intake with Lithuanian ice-cream.

Kaunas is a hive of churches; the former Russian Orthodox cathedral heads the Laisves aleja in Independence Square while, in Town Hall Square squats the huge St Vytaulas Church, biggest in Lithuania, together with an eighteenth-century twin-towered Jesuit edifice now back in religious use after years masquerading as a school. Here too was the single-towered Kaunas Cathedral and a clutch of further religious institutions from which a spire shaped like an arrow caught my eye. It rose from the square shaft of a belfry with four dwarf spires standing sentry at its base mimicking exactly the other's proportions and the little flourish of the eaves. It put me in mind of the Gothic spires of Prague on a tiny scale though deficient of the glory to be found in such Czech structures. On the very apex of the junction of the two rivers Kaunas castle displays an eleventh-century tower; probably all that remains of the original city.

Though guidebooks speak of Vilnius as a far more historic and interesting city, Paul and I were greatly impressed with Kaunas. It was made abundantly clear to us that there is much rivalry between the two cities and the fact that Vilnius holds the capitalship plainly rankles. We roamed the streets for hours poking our noses into other people's business and noting the strange carved figures on the facades of many buildings as well as the quaint old-fashioned telephone boxes.

In the early evening we returned to Grybausko Street on foot passing a Russian helicopter park where soldiers were loading military equipment onto railway trucks prior to a final evacuation of the Russian military forces. Paul, an aviation fanatic, insisted upon sneaking inside the wire fence for a better view of the helicopters and I had visions of him being taken for a spy but he returned unscathed. Near the botanical gardens we lost our way in the woods and were led to our destination by a garrulous Russian-speaking Lithuanian with whom Paul chatted enthusiastically.

Over supper Povilas spoke of his year as a lieutenant in the Soviet army and of how he hated to watch his Russian colleagues soil everything they touched and take whatever they wanted back to their homeland. "Though we were part of the Soviet Union we were treated like an occupied country," he told us, going on to explain how Lithuania maintained a low profile during the 40 years of Sovietisation. "But now the hated occupier is going home compensation is wanted for the enormous damage inflicted on our property as well as the theft of everything removable – even things like taps and baths – from their Lithuanian-owned bases. However, since our country is dependent on gas from St Petersburg, this gives the Russians the whip hand even as they depart – not that Russia could afford to pay compensation even had she been willing to do so."

The following day – a Sunday – we enjoyed a whole 24-hour period away from our bicycles, rising late and helping the family clean their small Lada car as well as involving ourselves in other homely chores. Paul made a big hit with the Kuprys children; he's always been much better with kids than I am. Later Povilas drove us into town together with the Australian who was catching a bus that day to Klaipeda; a somewhat nerve-racking drive since Povilas was clearly a novice at the wheel of a car. Involuntarily I closed my eyes as we crossed the busy, narrow, ugly and Russian-built bridge spanning the Nemunas river, the car hugging the centre of the road to the consternation of other drivers and Paul and I were greatly relieved to be set down safe and sound in the city centre.

With many of the supermarkets open on Sunday we occupied ourselves with stocking up on provisions and visiting the small park where a Lithuanian student had burnt himself to death as a protest against continued Soviet domination. We then returned home by bus to help Povilas polish off a bottle of Russian Stolychnaya before supper.

We left Kaunas and the Kuprys with sadness. Right from the start we had been treated as members of the family and had felt completely at home. Though we had known them for little more than a couple of days we felt as if they had been life-long friends – surely the very epitome of true hospitality.

By the main Kaunas-Suwalki road the Polish border was 90km away but we planned a detour to the town of Alytus where another Lithuanian home had been offered us. Thus with Alytus hardly more than 60km distant the day's cycling promised to be less than arduous. And so it proved with brilliant sunshine and an attractive terrain of undulating forested hills – the first rise in the landscape of the journey experienced so far – to add to the enjoyment.

All day the sun shone warm though, later, the inevitable wind arose. In the forests the sinuous, rhythmic movement of a myriad trees was like a slow-moving dance, directed by the wind – a mesmerisingly beautiful sight. Here and there stood carved notice boards bearing the name of a district or, maybe, particular forest, while in the clearings family groups hunted for berries or mushrooms. With time on our hands we nibbled at blackberries and wild raspberries ourselves and enjoyed prolonged rests ostensibly to study the map. By mid-morning the forest thinned to be replaced by grassland deeply cut in one place by the comely valley of the Nemunas river. An old man on a horse-pulled cart came by, enquiring of our destination and showing interest in our bikes. He told us he was 65 and when I told him I was approaching 70 he plainly disbelieved me.

The wind strengthened as the day wore on but we were pleased to dismount and walk though few of the hills were of the gradient to give reason for doing so. All of a sudden we were in Alytus when we least expected it. With time still to spare we dallied in the spaced-out town that put me in mind of Welwyn Garden City, its tidy industrial section giving way to a park-indented residential area. To pass another hour we toyed with a couple of beers in a supermarket cafeteria and licked at ice-cream from ever-open kiosks. We had arranged with our potential hosts to be with them after 4.00 p.m. and even by the time we had located their prosperous-looking and substantial home the far side of town we felt it expedient to hang around for a further hour.

Romualdas Ambrazevicius was a tour operator and travel agent and I had been put in touch with him by a fellow travel writer of my acquaintance. And since travel agents and travel writers have a natural affinity Rom – as we came to call him – was anxious to meet me.

In the event not only did he meet me but had to put up with Paul and me for all of three nights and two days. This came about through the phenomenon of a 72-hour downpour. But there was no inkling of this as we partook of a delicious supper – made memorable by cream cheese and home-made strawberry jam –

followed by wine and chat in a shrub-formed arbour in the garden.

That the Ambrazevicius family had struck oil was obvious the moment we entered the beautifully-timbered house garnered with expensive and eye-catching furnishings. It was home to a family of six with, additional to Rom and his handsome wife, four youngsters slightly older than those of the Kuprys brood and, I have to record, of less attraction. That they were spoilt rotten was obvious and I don't think either Paul or I managed one word with them – or they with us – during our whole stay. It took a little while for me to feel easy with Mrs A (I never did learn her christian name) but the warmth of her nature soon dispelled the chill. A mutual deficiency of our respective languages hardly made things easier though she had a better command of English than did Rom of whom we saw little through the pressures of his business.

By the next morning the downpour had commenced though not yet of the intensity to dissuade Paul and me from taking a walk in the town to find but another centre of near-empty shops and poorly stocked supermarkets. At midday Rom escaped from his office long enough to drive us to a local viewpoint that was the site of a castle overlooking the broad Nemunas river marking the one-time Lithuanian border. The view was obscured by driving rain but we could see the buttress of the great bridge that used to carry the Kaunas-Königsberg (now Kaliningrad) railway over the impressive valley and which was destroyed by the retreating Germans in World War Two, never to be replaced.

Though Rom could not be with us in the afternoon he thoughtfully arranged for his English-speaking lady assistant together with a driver to give us an excursion. The initial destination was Traku, the famed former capital founded by Gediminas in 1321 after that worthy's founding of the present capital, Vilnius. Of the two castles one is but a ruin. The other – Island Castle – has been effectively restored in red brick and, as its name implies, sits jauntily on a wooded island in one of Traku's many reed-bordered lakes. I found its exterior more impressive than the rather plain interior though only part of the edifice was open.

We were then in for a surprise. Rom had heard of my disappointment at having to miss out on the third Baltic state's capital and, since Trakai was 70km on the way to 96-km distant Vilnius, had suggested we continue on for a glimpse of the city.

And a glimpse is about all we got through the rain though, assuredly, this was better than nothing. Reputedly the greenest and most graceful of the Baltic capitals it lies on the Neris river and, in company with its fellows, has a ferocious history especially from the seventeenth century onwards, suffering fire, war, famine and plague. It was devastated again in World War One when the Germans occupied it for three and a half years and by subsequent Soviet, Polish and Lithuanian fighting. When the shooting died down, Vilnius found itself in Poland where it remained until 1939. It then became a major centre of Jewish culture, earning the title of 'Jerusalem of Lithuania' but, following another three-year occupation by Germans during World War Two, most of the Jewish inhabitants were exterminated either in the city's ghetto or the Paneriai death camp. Much of the place was wrecked again in the six-day battle by which the Soviet army recaptured it towards the end of that conflict.

How any of these large cities of central and eastern Europe bear any resemblance to what they were in the Middle Ages must be put down to the intensity of pride borne by their unconquerable citizens who, brick by brick, re-erect old structures almost as fast as they are knocked down. To me, on our three-hour visit, Vilnius appeared just as it must have looked before the seventeenth century. The winding cobbled streets of Old Vilnius were a pleasure to explore even in the rain and one could recognise the many reminders of the city's pivotal role in the campaign for Baltic independence. Its historical links with Roman Catholic Poland perhaps contribute to a less austere atmosphere than I found in Riga and I was to find direct evidence of the Polish connection in the many Roman Catholic churches into which we poked our heads. Most of the city is on the south bank of the river, its heart is Cathedral Square, scene of mass gatherings which ended in bloodshed during the country's recent efforts to rid itself of Russian domination. The square is the site of the weird Vilnius Cathedral separated from its bell tower which was once part of the city's defence system and looking for all the world like a Roman palace.

Because our good lady guide had once attended Vilnius University she had intimate knowledge of the ramifications of its scattered buildings so led us through a maze of austere and gloomy corridors of learning, my wet feet squelching on the cold stone flags. The back streets were littered with intriguing little cafes and restaurants of the sort to be found in university cities everywhere and I would have given much to have stopped for a cup of tea.

On the drive home an angry red sky gave false hint of a respite from the deluge, its treachery matching that recorded on a lonely stone by the roadside raised to the memory of a village destroyed by the Russians and blamed on the Germans, a war crime of lesser-known but similar nature to that of Katyn in the Ukraine. Lithuania, in company with most of the countries through which Paul and I would be travelling, was littered with such ghosts of the atrocities of not-so-many years gone by.

In spite of a momentarily-lighter sky the rain continued but the morning dawned no more than damp and grey. This notwithstanding we succumbed all too easily to the entreaties of the Ambrazevicius elders to stay on. We did so with misgivings. Not only did we feel that we were outstaying our welcome but found it difficult to resist the call of the open road. All of which made it oddly comforting when it began to rain again. To give Mrs A a respite from our presence we took ourselves off to a renowned cemetery in the forest. It rained on the way there and it rained on the way back while the cemetery itself, though a remarkable display of historic tombs, was not a destination calculated to raise depressed spirits, even in the sunniest of climes.

The third morning it wasn't actually raining, so when we awoke we hardened our resolve and decided to go. A gigantic breakfast steeled us for the fray and Rom, bringing out his own bicycle, insisted on guiding us onto the road to the border. We owe a great debt of gratitude to the Ambrazeviciuses for sheltering two strangers from the tempest; I don't know what we would have done without them.

Hardly had we cleared the town and climbed the hill out of it when down came the rain once more. We donned waterproofs and pedalled on miserably, feeling driblets of water sliding down our necks and soaking into our socks. My hands became so numb they could hardly operate the brakes and the cold pierced every garment we wore. Real cyclists would have taken more appropriate gear, I thought to myself as jets of water sprayed from un-mudguarded wheels to soak shoes and baggage. On the outskirts of Lazdijai we passed a restaurant. A *restaurant*! Such establishments existing in the middle of nowhere are not to be passed so we retraced our steps certain that it would be closed. But surprise, surprise, the place was open and, what's more, serving hot meals with even a choice of dishes. We were hardly starving but, on principle, chose the most expensive item on the menu hoping quality also meant quantity and were rewarded with quite a reasonable meat dish. There was nobody else in the room as we tucked into the fare, our clothes steaming from a warm radiator and dripping on the floor.

In the small border town we found a bank in which to change our Lithuanian currency into dollars and met with the same indifference, even veiled hostility, as we had in Panevezys, another tommy-gun toting cowboy escorting me through a locked door and standing over me as I conducted the transaction. Nobody smiled.

As we made our way the last 5km to the border a further climatic miracle occurred. The rain ceased, the dark clouds fragmented and shafts of sunshine sent spears of light towards a sodden earth.

Could this be an omen? We had been well-warned about the Lithuanian-Polish border. Back in Britain I had seen TV news bulletin pictures of miles-long queues of cars on both sides waiting to pass through a border inflicted by political squabbles between the two countries. Rom too had warned us about conditions, intimating that he had some influence there should we be turned back and have to return to Alytus. My heart sank as we blandly pedalled by the endless lines of vehicles, their inmates asleep or smoking in disconsolate groups in the road. There were no other cyclists in evidence. Would we be allowed through into a new country – our fourth – which, for me, held a myriad sombre memories our onward journey would assuredly unleash?

Chapter 3
North-eastern Poland

The third land frontier crossing of the journey degenerated into simple farce and a game of Snakes and Ladders. One by one we passed through a whole series of control points, their occupants wearing different uniforms so that I never knew which was Lithuanian and which was Polish. Proceeding through the controls like a dose of salts I could hardly believe it when we emerged from the process on Polish soil. But there was a catch. The last barrier was manned by the military and, in addition to sight of our passports, they wanted a piece of paper which we hadn't got. So it was back to square one to collect the deficient item which we bore triumphantly right through the same series of posts to the final barrier. "Yes," affirmed the soldier on duty, "but where are the stamps on it? You'll have to go back and get them." So back we went again to the great amusement of the driver of a stationary lorry, proffering in vain our pieces of paper to all and sundry until, finally, someone humoured us by stamping purple ink on them. Then back into Poland again to be told at the barrier that one stamp was not enough; there must be *four*. The lorry driver was now helpless with laughter as we once more retraced our steps on this occasion managing to procure two further purple ink marks on our papers which we none too confidently bore back to our unyielding soldier. "Would you settle for three?" we asked diffidently, waving our British passports in lieu of magic wands. But no. The soldier was adamant. The lorry driver was in a state of apoplexy as we yet again trudged by, wheeling our bikes. And at the nearest post we implored anyone with a rubber stamp to complete the quartet of imprints in our, by now, ragged squares of paper. Then, as we were again retracing our steps, a gust of wind snatched Paul's paper to bowl it along the ground, under cars and lorries, with us in hot pursuit to fall upon the offending item at the base of a barbed wire fence. Firmly anchored, we bore it victoriously to our soldier. The lorry driver was nowhere to be seen, having collapsed on to the floor of his cab. Even the soldier was unable to suppress a grin as he retrieved our crumpled offerings, tended a sardonic salute and raised the barrier. Welcome to Poland.

We had entered a region known as Masuria which, historically, has not been strongly Polish to say the least. Until the mid-thirteenth century it was inhabited by diverse pagan tribes but conquered by the ubiquitous Teutonic Knights during the second half of that century, its native inhabitants eliminated. The easternmost segment of Masuria, into which we rode, remained in the hands of the Knights and then under continued German influence until the outbreak of World War Two. It was Stalin who, after that war, arbitrarily sliced the region in half with a virtual straight-line east-west border, the southern part being given to Poland while the north, containing the strategic port of Kaliningrad (then Prussian Konigsberg) was annexed by the Soviet Union and today is cut off from its Russian motherland by Lithuania, Latvia and Belorussia.

The region around the towns of Suwalki and Augustow is one of the least visited of Poland; even for Poles anything beyond southern Masuria is still pretty much *terra incognita*. Because we had detoured to Alytus we were able to use a then newly opened border crossing south-east of the main Kaunas-Suwalki road crossing point and so were to by-pass Suwalki itself. Thus our first Polish urban landmark was Sejny which signposts repeatedly indicated but which never materialised. But we were firmly on the road to Augustow, that was for sure, and though political borders – particularly those forged by Stalin – are not drawn with geography much in mind, I do declare that hardly had we crossed this one when the countryside bucked itself into a series of hills of the like we'd never seen in Lithuania. But the preponderance of trees never changed and soon we were enshrouded by the Puszcza Augustowska – the Augustow Forest – that once extended deep into Lithuania. Small but enchanting lakes appeared amongst the great spread of trees yet few people were in evidence to enjoy them.

Beyond the twin villages of Giby and Fraki, the former boasting a fine wooden church, we wheeled our bikes up a track chosen at random and set up camp deep in the forest. The ground was pleasantly soft but the damp air brought out the mosquitoes. Our tent-raising had already become something of a drill with me preparing the frame and Paul carrying out the initial erecting followed by both of us 'pegging down'. Any cooking to be done I left to Paul, he being a better cook than I. Soup formed the principal ingredient of our meal that evening to compensate a little for the damping we had earlier received though our clothes were, by now, dry.

Between dusk and night we lay in our bivi-bags listening to the noises of the forest; the crack of a snapped twig and rustle of disturbed foliage. At intervals came the shriek of a distant train. I told myself how nice it was to be back in Poland, I remembered the first occasion I had sheltered among Polish trees.

Autumn 1944. The sky was devoid of stars and there was no moon. The sullen roar of multiple aero engines increased to a crescendo as the great bomber fleet processed overhead. For Gordon and I, sharing a seat in an end cabin of the odorous latrine of work camp E902, the throbbing thunder was music to our ears. Unwittingly the Royal Air Force had become a prop in our efforts to escape from German captivity.

Still in the Essex Regiment I had seen little of war for more than a year after joining the army though had done a great deal of preparing for it. I have vague memories of, among others, billets in such diverse locations as prim seaside villas in Leigh-on-Sea, and rusty Nissen huts in Hutton's Ambo, an extremely rural Yorkshire village. The war did intrude twice; in Leigh-on-Sea when Southend was bombed by the Luftwaffe and Dover when German long-range guns shelled it. And while on the Isle of Wight I can recollect nights atop Boniface Down waiting, with five rounds of ammunition, for German paratroops who never came. Two large-scale exercises, Spartan and Tiger, made unwelcome diversions, their discomfort and incident all too often being more lethal than actual combat. Particularly Tiger for part of which I became a very junior umpire. And just you try to stop a determined Canadian tank from crossing a 'blown' bridge if it wants to.

And then, as an NCO of the Dorset Regiment, came the Big Show – the real thing this time – and I found myself on a Normandy beach called 'Gold'. But the fruits of all that training could only blossom for a few weeks before my frontline duties as an infantryman came to an abrupt end with my capture by the counter-attacking SS panzer division which overran the position my unit had so recently taken.

To be made prisoner was at least a happier fate to that which befell most of my less fortunate companions whose broken bodies littered the nearby burning village. I stayed alive, though there had been occasions since then when I never expected to make it. Between the holding cages in France and Germany had been that dreadful rail journey when, for seven days and nights under constant Allied air attack, the train rumbled eastwards, the acrid, sickening stench of urine and excrement saturating the fetid air in the wagon with its freight of tightly-packed men driven crazy by lack of water. More dead than alive I had reached Poland, via a short sojourn at Stalag VIIIB near Tĕšín, to become a slave-worker in a Silesian coalmine.

Even given the best of circumstances coal-mining is not an occupation I would choose and right from the start I found it to be utterly detestable; made even worse in the knowledge that it could only further the Nazi war effort. It wouldn't have been quite so bad if they'd fed us a square meal once in a while but how we were expected to work (even had we felt so inclined) an eight – and sometimes ten – hour shift on an empty stomach beat me. To lie half-naked on one's back hacking at a seam's wet ceiling inches above, the loosened chunks of coal falling straight onto your face, was beyond a joke. Within very few weeks my ribs were protruding through the skin, every sore on my body turned septic and I'd had enough. It was time to go home.

In this endeavour I had found a like-minded colleague in Gordon of his name-sake regiment, the Gordon Highlanders. Our escape plan involved not only the unwitting co-operation of the RAF, the aircraft formations of which passed this way as regularly as clockwork, but also a pair of stolen wire-cutters, a home-made pulley device and a plank, these last two items for prizing apart the concertina wire that lay between the first and second fences of our prison compound.

Though I had been a prisoner for a number of months my earlier escape bids while in transit had been spur-of-the-moment affairs arousing the ire of assorted Wehrmacht soldiery. This time we had a concrete plan, tools for the *job, and a definite spur. We were not too happy about our intended objective of attaining the Russian lines then reportedly approaching eastern Poland but our own more congenial armies in the west were still on the other side of Germany.*

The nub of our plan evolved around the overnight antics of the RAF; their particular targets and route. Some nights the bomber streams passed too far to the north or south; not close enough for all the camp lights to be doused, nor, if they were, far enough away for the searchlights in the guardtowers not to compensate by sweeping the fences with their inquisitive beams. And our plan depended entirely upon an overhead flightpath and the extinguishing of all lights. . . .

One particular night our prayers were answered. And with a vengeance. Not only did the waves of aircraft pass directly overhead but they never stopped coming. And by the time the last wave thundered by the first waves started coming back.

Emerging from the latrines to crawl, dragging our apparatus, to the nearest segment of treble fencing, lying on our bellies – sweating with terror – we cut the lower barbed-wire strands of the first fence. There followed an interval as we spread-eagled ourselves – faces in the dirt – while the German patrol ambled by between the fences which it did about every ten minutes, then waiting only until the two soldiers were out of earshot, we prized apart the two coils of concertina wire by hauling up the lower section of the upper coil by means of our pulley device and pressing down the top of the lower concertina by resting the plank upon it. Spread-eagled again, but this time on the plank, I attacked the lower strands of the second fence and, with Gordon following, reached the cinder track used by the patrols. Straightway we attacked the third fence but its cable mesh defeated our combined strength and the cutters.

At this point terror gave way to blind panic. The droning of aircraft was dying away, another patrol was due and, at any moment, the lights would come on so that, transfixed by the beam of a searchlight, we could be legitimately shot dead. It was Gordon who saved the situation. With the strength of desperation he scaled the cable mesh at a point where it was affixed to a post doubling as a lamp standard. From atop the fence he reached down to pull me up after him and, as we squatted uncertainly balancing ourselves on the swaying mesh, the lights came on. Hesitating no longer we jumped into the allotment the other side and dived for cover among rows of brussel sprouts. A searchlight beam swept over us, its blue-tinged brilliance illuminating the vegetable patch, before passing on, leaving us in a blessed darkness only slightly diluted by the weaker illumination shed by the compound lights. No shouts or burst of machine-gun fire issued from the guardtowers.

But our immediate trials were not quite over. Creeping though the sprouts until out of range of the lights we took to our heels and ran full tilt into a battery of light anti-aircraft guns we had often heard thudding away ineffectively at night when Allied aircraft were in the vicinity. There was no secretiveness this time and we aroused a hornet's nest; guttural commands to "Halt! Halt!" ringing in our ears as we sheered away stumbling across an open meadow.

Neither of us was exactly equipped for being 'gentlemen of the road' in enemy territory, our work clothes conspicuously and ineradicably bestowed with big yellow 'K's' (for 'Kriegsgefangener' – Prisoner of War); our supplies no more than a few of the more durable items saved from Red Cross parcels that could be stowed in our pockets. With the impending dawn we proposed doing something about remedying these deficiencies.

Floundering about in the dark wasn't going to get us anywhere so, having put several miles between us and the prison camp, we searched about for somewhere to lay up for what was left of the night. By day-break our absence from both camp and work shift would be revealed and the security authorities alerted.

Though an industrial region there was ample agricultural countryside between each grimy coalmining town that soiled this part of Silesia, and it was with no great stroke of fortune that we chanced upon a sizeable copse where, among tangled undergrowth, we lay down side by side to rest and relax. The night became the cooler with the approach of dawn though my jangled nerves prevented any possibility of sleep. Over one hurdle, we now faced another in the guise of travelling hundreds of miles over alien territory equipped with no money, no identity papers, no disguise of any sort and very little food or command of the German language. The prospects were daunting to say the least

Even the weather turned against us by starting to drizzle and I burrowed under Gordon who had insensibly managed to fall asleep. He awoke an hour later to berate me for keeping dry at his expense but more serious matters were now to occupy our attentions. A grey luminosity showed through the trees so rising from our damp resting place we cautiously made our way to the edge of the copse and into the eery half darkness of a waking world. To rectify at least some of our shortcomings as fugitives we would have to resort to simple robbery and, oddly, the notion of a short spell of a life of crime failed to dismay me. Might even be quite fun. Somewhere in the far distance came the shriek of a train.

For Paul and I our night in Augustow Forest was enlivened by no more than the usual bane caused by stifling the need for a pee; evacuation of bivi-bag and bivouac in the darkness being a disturbing business. The rain held off until we were clear of the forest but at the approaches of Augustow town it fell in torrents.

An early-opening supermarket gave shelter and an introduction to the comparative profusion of goods even in this remote corner of Poland. We loaded ourselves with edible goodies in spite of everything being considerably more expensive and the presumption that hot meals shouldn't be so hard to come by in a country with a healthier economy. For the best part of an hour we idled in the bus station tucking into pastries and chocolate then, with no hope of an early improvement in the weather, donned waterproofs, mounted our bikes and pushed on through the curtain of water. There was nothing to keep us in Augustow though, on a fine bright day, its lakes and forests could provide great attraction.

For a while we were stuck with the main Warsaw road stricken with heavy freight traffic that threw up plumes of water and hit us with their slipstreams. Providentially, Highway 19 rescued us by diverting due south towards Bialystok and beyond to, eventually, Rzeszow near the Slovak border. A road sign indicated Rzeszow as 600km, which failed to add to our joy. However, Road 19 was to become something of a constant companion as, with diversions, we pedalled stoically across eastern Poland.

It rained all morning and well into the afternoon but the well-paved road and low density of traffic made the going not so unpleasant. The countryside was flat and uninteresting; any vestiges of a hill or two left behind at the Lithuanian border. Nearly every village had its resident nest of storks precariously balanced on chimney or telegraph pole, the birds themselves staring morosely at passers-by below. Herons flapped lazily into the air from streams and marshes. The odd dead cat or dog marked the verges almost as regularly as did the kilometre stones.

At the village of Sztabin we halted for a beer at a well-patronised off-licence masquerading as a pub. On a seat outside we lightened our load by eating some of our provisions only to come upon a restaurant hardly had we moved off again. While sheltering from yet another downpour we were treated to a gratis cabaret enacted by a pair of elderly drunks who, hilariously, fell over each other as they danced, musicless, together. Most drunken scenes lack any comic element but this was an exception. One of the pair was middle-aged with a ruddy face and drooping black moustaches. His partner was bald as a coot except for a bunch of woolly grey hair behind each ear. Even sober their appearance alone would have made them a fortune as a music hall act.

Before we left home, Polorbis, The Polish State Hotel Agency, had recommended a detour to Tykocin, directly west of Bialystok. We were not sure what attraction the small town held and I was suspicious of non-cyclist's recommended destinations which were 'just off your route.' So many people think in terms of the automobile when gauging distance, not appreciating that, for us, every extra kilometre had to be paid for in sweat and tears. However a look at the map showed the place to be not too far out of our way and a return along the main Warsaw-Biazlystok highway meant we would not have to retrace our steps. So at Korycin we turned off 19 onto a delightfully switchback lane virtually devoid of any traffic at all.

From Augustow onward we were in for a heavy dose of camping punctuated by just five overnight hotel sojourns; one each in the trio of eastern Poland's major cities courtesy of Polorbis and one each in the two easternmost cities of Slovakia provided by Cedok, the equivilant Czech agency. There would be no more scheduled indoor stayovers at least until Transylvania and even then these would be dependent upon circumstances ruling at the time of our arrival there.

Our ensuing encampment was again among trees; in this case a copse close to the road and one well endowed with raspberries and blackberries to go with our hot soup and sausage. The verges and meadows alongside the little road were a riot of poppies and wild flowers; a serene landscape scattered about with woods and pastures cut up by rectangles of maize and stubble.

Though short bursts of rain had swept through the copse that night the morning was fine and bright, encouraging our progress in the early hours along a valley where peasants were making hay. At one point we rested, our backs to a tree, watching women in wide skirts as they bent to sweep the hay into rows with their long rakes, or moved down the rows and turned the hay to dry it. Others, with a twist of the rake, raised bundles of hay onto miniature stacks that were skewered about a central pole. Each movement flowed into the next, the rounded figures working in unison. At the edge of the field stood their wagon, and the horse contentedly grazing. It was a scene that had been enacted without change over the centuries.

We stopped again to fill our waterbottles from a pump in a large village called Knyszyn where a middle-aged man wished us God speed and a safe journey. Outside the gateways of their houses, women sat spinning, their daughters and grand-daughters seated beside them. The women were the workers here in the Podlasie countryside as this region is known. Snowstorms of geese whitened the fields as we pedalled by a series of goose-farms to enter Tykocin across a girder bridge spanning the river Narew.

The palace-like Holy Trinity church, more a cathedral than a mere church, gave promise of drama to come in the sleepy little town but, alas, not a lot in the spectacular mould materialised. However, Tykocin's size and present stature belies its historical significance. As well as having been a stronghold of the dukes of Masuria, it also contains one of the best-restored synagogues in the country, a reminder that this was once home to an important Jewish community.

For centuries there has been a strong Jewish element in Poland, ever since the eleventh century in fact, when Jews converged upon this then most tolerant of countries, fleeing from political and economic persecution elsewhere. The Roman Catholic Church was ambivalent towards them for, although the Jews in general remained strictly true to their faith, the Polish culture was enriched by specific Jewish characteristics. They made major contributions to scientific development and frequently occupied leading positions in medicine, mathematics and astronomy as well as in cultural realms such as architecture and painting. But their very separateness and success proved to be their undoing. During the Second Republic of 1818 to 1939, the National Democratic Party, which held strong right-wing leanings, became increasingly radical in their attitudes towards the Jewish population and it became fashionable to make the Jews responsible for every social evil. After 1939, as we all know, the Nazis took things a step further.

The synagogue in Tykocin is a Baroque building, recently restored to house a museum of Jewish artefacts including a beautifully embroidered cloth in memory of murdered Jews. Their cemetery lies at the end of the town and we walked there, wheeling our bikes through cobbled streets bordered by rows of cottages built of brick or wood looking warm and cosy in spite of the simplicity. In a field we came upon chunks of broken tombstones laying at drunken angles, their inscriptions no longer legible; a sad forgotten corner seldom visited.

In the miniscule town square surrounded on three sides by nineteenth-century wooden houses we enquired the whereabouts of a restaurant only to find that, contrary to expectation, Tykocin could raise no more than a juke-box-blaring snack bar. But our enquiries were overheard by a smartly-suited young man who led us to a building behind the synagogue that turned out to be the town's night club. Unlocking a series of doors he took us down a flight of stairs to an underground bar furnished with tables and chairs. Seating us, he prepared a tasty meal of meat and vegetables bolstered by ice-cream, beer and tea.

"People don't usually want lunch this early," he remarked as we settled the bill and only then did we realise it was but 9 o'clock in the morning and not 10 o'clock as supposed. We had gained an hour at the Lithuanian border three days before and had remained unaware of it.

With an hour in hand we cycled out of Tykocin and all too soon hit the traffic-snarled Warsaw-Bialystok main road. It had been our intention to spend another night of camping before sampling the urban delights of this chief city of north-east Poland. But the suburbs reached out to us well before midday so we continued into the city, only to discover that the Lesny Hotel, into which Polorbis had kindly booked us for a night, was situated in the western outskirts through which we had already passed.

Of the three Polorbis hotels we were to experience we rated the Lesny the fewest stars though this is not to say that its modest offerings were not appreciated. A real bed is always welcome after even a few nights of rough living and though the water was cold we happily immersed ourselves and our clothes in bath and basin (repeating the performance later when the hot water came on).

Leaving our bikes in the hotel cloakroom we trekked the couple of kilometres into the city centre, glad to use our legs in the manner their Maker presumably intended. It is a big brute of a place, not in the least orientated towards the conception of tourism though its mix of Polish and Belorussian cultures give it a feel not found in other Polish cities.

Founded in the sixteenth century, Bialystok's real development began two centuries later. This was when Jan Klemens Branicki, chief of the armed forces and owner of vast estates, established his residence here, building a mighty palace for himself. Restored following destruction by the retreating German army in 1944, it remains today a horseshoe-shaped Baroque edifice – once known as the Versailles of the North – and the seat of the Academy of Medicine. Startling more than beautiful, it is the city's one structure of note. The main thoroughfare of the city, ul. Lipowa, we found to be a handsome street with the Branicki Palace and its park at one end and the dominating St Nicholas Orthodox Church at the other, the latter's double-barrel cross on high shining bright against a rare blue sky.

Becoming the largest textile manufacturing centre after Lodz, Bialystok attracted entrepreneurs of different ethnic groups, including Poles, Jews, Russians, Belorussians and Germans, who pushed out its boundaries in a spontaneous and chaotic manner until 1939. World War Two brought this to an abrupt end, the Nazis murdering about half the population, destroying the industry and razing the city centre. Post-war reconstruction concentrated on tangible issues such as the recovery of industry and providing the surviving inhabitants with the basic necessities. Thus one can hardly expect this comparatively new and tragically-treated town to exhibit much of a picturesque nature though its sturdy citizens today bear no rancour. Referring to the hideous events of 1944 one elderly Pole told me with a shrug of the shoulders "It was the luck of the draw." Poland is too often viewed as a tragic country whose fate is ever to be conquered and partitioned. Yet the tragedies apply to only about a quarter of the nation's story which, for the most part, was significant, heroic and glorious.

Poland saved Europe from the Tartars early in the Middle Ages and from Islam at the end of the seventeenth century when King Jan Sobieski raised the

Turkish siege of Vienna with an expeditionary force of Polish cavalry. Indeed, to a considerable extent, 'Christian Europe' owes its survival to Polish feats of arms. Even in 1921 Lenin had to revise his strategy for world revolution after Polish cavalry defeated an advancing Red Army on the Vistula river.

After the union with Lithuania in the fifteenth century, Poland became a huge kingdom and commonwealth stretching from the Baltic to the Black Sea and encompassing large tracts of Belorussia and the Ukraine. It is these episodes of their history which give Poles the pride and power to overcome their very real – but nevertheless subordinate – sufferings.

Our washed clothes were virtually dry when we got back to the hotel. Our socks had been wet for a week and, speaking for myself, this had been the first time I had taken them off during that period since I persisted in the erroneous idea they would dry on my feet at night. We had turned our bedroom itself into a drying room for the tent which, each morning, we had had to stow away, wet from rain or dew.

Highway 19 beckoned us towards Lublin, our next city destination, but we had discovered a smaller, more rural forest-lined road that could lead us initially and more evocatively to Bielk Podlaski where, 50km later, we would be reunited with 19. And indeed the smaller artery made a most pleasing run through leafy villages of houses crowded together within old fortifications, their flaking stucco, and steep red roofs often dominated by lofty churches sporting bulbous green belfries and ribbon-decorated crucifixes. But, for our spurning of the larger road, there was a forfeit.

With no warning the tarmac gave way to cobblestones, pushing us onto the sand verges where other cyclists had forged rutted tracks that trapped our wheels and had me grinding to a halt every time my lame wrist was unable to correct the steering. Cobbles are uncomfortable enough for vehicles but impossible for bicycles and it was a considerable relief when they finally petered out at the junction of Highway 19.

Our chosen route out of Bialystok had by-passed Zabludow which was the junction of 19 for the Puzcza Bialowieska. Polorbis had strongly recommended this most unspoilt forest in Europe that runs along the Belorussian border and was once the hunting ground of Lithuanian princes, Polish kings and Russian Czars. Here the primeval bison may still be seen roaming free. Wild boar, horses, reindeer, red deer and wolves are also to be found, but to effect a worthwhile visit would entail a number of days. Bielsk Podlaski lay level with the forest some 20km away but we resisted the temptation of its proximity.

The small city's main street was being excavated but the detour in the back streets found us an inexpensive restaurant serving a substantial meal of *bigos* (sauerkraut with meat and sausage) and *flaki* (entrails) which, I have to say, offered us more inner strength than would have sight of the celebrated cathedral that we missed in the city centre.

Out of the cities and towns – and sometimes even in them – I gained the feeling of having stepped back in time. The Poland I knew a half century ago was not only here but accentuated. The same black earth turning after rain into glutinous mud, the same bright green farmland spotted with woods, small herds of cows, tumble-down cottages, fruit trees, wayside shrines invariably decorated by fresh flowers, mushrooms hiding by forest tracks. And in the villages rough drinking dens where unwashed men smoked and quarrelled, and tiny cafes serving potato soup and gherkins. Here too was the eternal peasant with small sharp eyes stuck in a solid fleshy face; his wife thick and powerful, wearing a faded head cloth. And the rosy-cheeked children always ready to bandy words with the passing stranger, country carts pulled by steaming brown horses, garish street kiosks selling newspapers, tobacco, combs and shoe-laces.

And the dogs. Sheepdogs trained to kill intruders in rural areas are one thing; I had come across this sort in Peru and elsewhere, but even the yappy, harmless kind can be lethal in a different way. We were to experience their sudden charges from hidden gateways, their high-pitched barking causing an involuntary swerve into the middle of the road and consequential risk of being mown down by traffic. It was while passing through a hamlet in the vicinity of Dzladkowice that I experienced my nastiest canine encounter. A large monster with white foam dripping from a heavily fanged mouth came at me with obvious hostile intent, its growling of the intensity which showed it meant business. The piece of meat that was its target was my bare left leg which kicked out violently to catch the beast on the nose, an act that halted it in its tracks. My own growl seemed to surprise the animal too for it failed to chase me as I sped hastily on. I called a warning to Paul, following in my wake, but the dog had had enough.

As we'd learnt in Riga, cyclists bring out the worst in this north-east portion of Europe. Apart from an easily endured loss of status (that is until the quality of one's bike is revealed) there are other impediments to progress such as broken glass, hot liquid tar, cobblestones, pedestrians who walk on the road and not on the verge, live dogs as we have seen, dead dogs and cats, and anti-cyclist truck drivers taking pleasure in steering their huge vehicles as close as is possible without actual physical contact being made. Garages too despise cyclists. Attempting to buy oil with which to lubricate our chains and axles we met with but shrugs and indifference so helped ourselves to the dregs of oil remaining in discarded cans. This actually proved advantageous as it cost nothing.

We camped the next night in a forest 17km north of the industrial town of Siemiatycze, taking care to avoid several highly active ants'-nests. We were awoken by the ominous sound of cracking twigs and what we thought was heavy breathing but though we repeatedly peered out of the tent into the darkness there was nothing to be seen. I can only assume it to have been deer, of which we had earlier glimpsed some fine specimens in the vicinity.

Sleeping in forests has the drawback of confounding the daylight though on this occasion it confounded the reading of my watch; hence we rose an hour too early and were away before the dawn. But the error was to allow us to achieve our highest daily mileage of the journey, putting something in excess of 150km behind us by dusk. Real cyclists will not be impressed but, with our loaded bikes and lack of proper sleep, it nearly crippled me while Paul too was drained at the end of it. During the course of the ride Highway 19 had led us through the towns of Siemiatycze, Sarnak, Losice, Miedzyrzec Podlaski – replete with palace about which nobody could tell us or, if they did, the explanation foundered in incomprehension – Kock and Lubertow – with another palace about which we were then in no fit state to enquire. 8km on and just 24 short of Lublin we staggered into an over-populated wood but were too tired to care as we struggled to raise the tent.

The final 24km into Lublin were abruptly hilly but in spite of walking – somewhat stiffly – for much of the way we were in the city before the morning rush hour. Another night's accommodation had been arranged here and, though we were three days ahead of schedule, the Unia Hotel – the best pad in town – made no complaint. There was room at the inn. Once more we were advised to keep our bikes with us in our room and to reach it had to push them up the grand staircase much to the astonishment of smart-suited businessmen descending it. And at the top I failed to resist the childish temptation of cycling down the long plush corridors – something I've always secretly felt like doing in such establishments. And here surely, was the perfect opportunity for so doing! A huge bathroom together with luxuries like shampoo, bath foam, trouser press and hair-drier were all brought into play with wild abandon as we immersed ourselves and our clothes in bathfuls of piping hot water.

Passing through the suburbs of this capital city of eastern Poland had presented the all too familiar ambivalence, sprawling high-rises and Stalinist smokestacks obscuring a historic heart. Once in the centre we were amongst cobbled streets and dilapidated mansions – a wishful reminder of Lublin's past glories. Here, unlike in Warsaw and elsewhere, the fabric of the old quarter came through World War Two relatively unscathed, though years of post-war neglect have left it in a pitiful condition.

For almost a millennium Lublin was one of the most important of Poland's cities. It grew from a sixth-century settlement into a significant outpost protecting the country from the east. Predictably it was repeatedly destroyed by Tartars and Lithuanians but with the expansion of the Polish kingdom following the uniting of Poland and Lithuania the city became a vital trading centre, continuing to develop until the early seventeenth century. Thereafter the glorious times ended and Lublin fell into decline but revived before World War One. In 1918 a Roman Catholic university – the only one in eastern Europe – was established here, managing to survive throughout the communist era. The Jewish community increased from the mid-fourteenth century and grew so rapidly that, 200 years later, the town had the third largest Jewish population in Poland. Alas, World War Two put an end to that, the fate of those unfortunate people being today commemorated by the memorial that is the site of Majdanek Death Camp.

Paul and I spent much of the day wandering about the city, exploring the narrow alleys of the Old Town under a persistent drizzle. Though a few enterprising souls have introduced tearooms and an 'English pub' (incongruously selling Guinness) into the compact Old Town it remains a spiritless square mile; the street called Rynek lined with old burghers' houses that would be sensational given some restoration and a lick of paint. At the northern end stands the castle that is not a castle, the original fourteenth century structure being almost totally destroyed. What can be seen today is actually a prison built in the 1820s and utilised as such until 1944 when, in that year alone, 100,000 people passed through its grim walls en route to Majdanek.

As soon as the rain began in earnest the atmosphere of Lublin became melancholy indeed, the flooded streets, the poor shops and shabby citizens untypical of Poland in general. Standing on a mound behind the uninspiring cathedral we looked down upon the infamous Street of the Tormented (Droga Meczenikow) along which doomed wretches in their thousands were driven to the death camp three kilometres away in the suburb called Majdanek. They were watched, we were told, by the whole town as they trudged along the road with their bundles and their children, the Jews from Lublin Ghetto walking by their own familiar houses. Then, like the Pied Piper's flock, they vanished. But instead of being sucked up by a magic cloud they were stripped naked, suffocated in a black tomb, the gold fillings and dentures wrenched from their mouths, and the bodies incinerated; their hair baled, weighed, packed, invoiced and sold for profit.

We asked an English-speaking student how far the camp site was but though he thought it was five or seven kilometres away he didn't really know. And he found it odd that we should want to go there. "Anyway, it's much too far to walk," he pronounced. So we walked.

A colossal block of concrete raised as a memorial stone looms by the entrance to a large grassy meadow. The block put me in mind of a rotten cheese, cracked and pitted in symbolism of death and hopelessness and the excrement of evil. In the distance we could see a dome – the mausoleum – and walked the long straight path to it under a sudden burst of sunshine. Only a few of the old prison hutments have been left standing but the barbed wire fences, the guard towers and the gates are intact. The dome is suspended over a circular pit filled with compacted pulverised human bone. Nearby is a crematorium above which rises a squat brick chimney. We entered to find a clinically-clean set of furnaces, tidily labelled in three languages. The atmosphere was antiseptic, unreal.

We walked across the empty camp to a row of huts. One was crammed with mouldy prison shoes, another with striped prison uniforms patched and threadbare; yet another was filled to the roof with prison caps. Other exhibits included countless bundles of human hair and sets of gas containers. Wall photographs illustrated the insane perfectionism and methodical callousness of the Nazi extermination machine. There were copies of prison records, personal documents, enlarged pictures of execution scenes and of corpses being flung onto a pyre, all exuding that air of unreality, detachment; a statement taken out of context.

The years had swept away the stench of burning flesh, the last echoes of the screams of the dying and the hideous sight of waxwork naked bodies rotting in pits. All that was left were relics durable and respectable enough to be turned into a showpiece for weekend sightseers. All that remained of 350,000 human beings were some old clothes, hair, bones and a mound of human ash.

We had been in the camp all afternoon and had seen only half a dozen fellow-visitors; few it seemed today bother to walk around these sombre acres. The sun grew warmer as we trudged around the fences. They say that birds no longer sing in such places as this but they do, they do, even if the ones I saw were but black hooded crows perched on the wire screeching like demented SS thugs.

My mind had, inevitably, slipped back again to the year 1944. Though fortunate enough not to have experienced such suffering as occurred here I was, later that year and into 1945, to witness a bestiality that has never been erased from my soul. I watched Paul enthusiastically examining every exhibit in a detached manner but I just wanted to go from this awful place. On the road outside the camp a stall was selling coca cola and blackcurrant ice-cream to a crowd probably larger than the Majdanek Death Camp can muster in a week.

Autumn 1944. Basking, albeit damply and irascibly, in our new-found freedom wasn't going to get us anywhere and the urge to put distance between our former captors and ourselves was strong. Since our camp boasted no refinements such as escape organisations providing the likes of Gordon and me with natty civilian outfits, forged papers, compasses, maps and the like, it was going to be up to us to acquire what we could from outside sources.

Thus came the moment we felt obliged to enter upon a life of crime and in this Gordon set a far less conscious-stricken example than I. The farmhouse of our initial attentions lay conveniently close to the wood in which we had spent the last hours of our first night of freedom; it was remote and we were able to observe the occupants departing for work in the surrounding fields. A chained dog was barking incessantly which suited our purpose admirably since its bark of real alarm would be ignored. Sauntering into the yard with an air – we hoped – of casual labourers looking for a job we reached the door and found it unlocked so pushed inside to stand uncertainly in an untidy kitchen-cum-living room. It was devoid of occupants except for a cat that fled. As if he had done it all before Gordon scooped up several jackets and assorted garments that lay across an ancient sewing machine while I contented myself with a loaf of bread from the table. My companion then swooped on a peaked cap from a hook behind the door and I had to dissuade him from nicking the family silver as well. Clasping our booty we withdrew, ignoring paroxysms of enraged barking, to share our spoils between us, discarding a woman's apron that had come with the bundle. Then, arraying ourselves in our new attire with, I regret to say, some levity, we consigned our tell-tale working clothes to a ditch and, fortified by hunks of bread, issued forth in search of liberty.

We had experienced the folly of moving on foot by night so resolved to make daytime use of minor roads and tracks as well as open fields so long as we could maintain an easterly direction. We did posses a map of sorts; a sketch provided by a sympathetic miner, indicating a line of towns through or near which we would have to pass en route to Cracow, the first major city of our intended route. At the time of these events Silesia was part of Germany, populated by a Silesian people as well as ethnic Germans, all of whom we had to class as enemy. In Poland proper we might expect a measure of assistance from the local populace.

Over the flat landscape towns and villages were easy to pick out, their gaunt pithead shafts better landmarks than church towers. We felt obliged to enter one town if only for the purpose of finding out where we were and this we did, though not without some hesitation. The place selected was of depressing uniformity; rows of workers' houses, a scattering of dingy shops and a deserted church. The exercise was not wasted, however, for, at a cross-roads, a yellow signpost made most helpful reading by indicating the road to Chyzanow, on the route to Cracow, and marked on our sketch map. Our bravado proved something else too. Though few people were in the streets those that were showed not the slightest interest in us. Passing a crowded beerhouse, a gaggle of German soldiers ejected onto the pavement in front of us. One of them, a corporal, asked for a light for his cigarette and Gordon unhesitatingly obliged, babbling away idiotically in Gaelic to which the soldier turned not a hair. With occupied Europe awash with uprooted nationalities any language with the possible exception of English passed muster even if not understood. On the spur of the moment I nipped into the smoke-filled tap room, removed the shoddiest cap from the crowded coat rack and returned. Now I too could cover my blonde locks with a headgear that is virtually a uniform in these parts. Had we possessed any funds we might have dared to purchase basic provisions but acquiring money by theft was not going to be so simple as rummaging around people's kitchens for the odd loaf of bread; cash was usually locked away somewhere. And simple bank robbery had such a pursuit-raising quality about it.

Heartened by our reception – or lack of it – from the good citizens we made our way along the road towards Chrzanow, leaving the mean streets with undisguised relief. However, we shied away from the road as soon as we were clear of houses, for it was a well-utilised artery only needing some nosy minion of authority to be travelling along it. Instead, therefore, we attempted a parallel route but this proved to be a tiring, frustrating business, detouring around fences, farms and teams of workers in the fields. On the bank of a stream we bathed our feet in cold, rust-coloured water. Long-unaccustomed walking had produced blisters on our heels and worn holes in our socks but the water treatment cooled the throbbing and raised morale. The road we were trying to follow became erratic, running straight for a mile or two and then taking a corkscrew route to serve half a dozen townships. Sometimes we found ourselves on the road itself and fell to the temptation of its firm surface but the sound of approaching vehicles would send us scurrying into the fields again. At the edge of one such field we chanced upon the hot embers of a fire in which we baked potatoes gathered from a handy clump, the one time we found food and the means of cooking it in the same place.

The autumn dusk arrived all too early and we cast about for shelter for the night. A barn held more attraction than the depths of a wood; it could offer both a roof and the warmth of hay or straw, and within an hour we found one. It was locked but an open window at the rear invited us inside to bed down atop a stack of clover-scented hay that shared the floor-space with sundry agricultural implements. Through cracks in the brick and timber wall we studied a neighbouring house, noticing the thin plume of smoke issuing from its chimney. Eagerly we consumed our meagre fare of the rest of the bread together with cold, burnt potato.

We slept well, disturbed only by the activities of the wildlife in the hay, activities that were a lot less unpleasant than had been the lice and bed-bugs that were the scourge back at camp. Awakening early we lay listening uneasily to rough unintelligible voices but the sound of a cart being driven away released the tension. Descending to the ground we found a heap of swedes, yellow and half-rotten, which we cut into portions and tried to eat. But they proved course and fibrous and raised a thirst we were unable to assuage. In disgust we flung the bits away.

Another scrutiny of the house revealed no further sign of life except for the wisp of smoke so we prepared ourselves for another forced entry. Aware that bold confrontation paid dividends we made straight for the back door, gently pushed it open an inch or two, and listened. All was quiet; not even a dog barked, so we crept into another kitchen and, our ears strained for sounds from the yard or inner regions of the house, searched for food of any description. From a bread bin I removed a whole loaf and half a cake which I bundled into a sack brought along from the barn for the purpose, while Gordon rummaged through a handbag. But we got no further as voices and approaching footsteps sent us into inglorious retreat, Gordon still clasping the handbag. We sped across the yard keeping to the lee of a wall and away into the fields.

Assured of no pursuit we undertook a thorough search of the bag and unearthed the equivalent of £8 in Reichmarks. Burying everything except the money and munching bread we moved on feeling rather pleased with ourselves. Even I was becoming inured to the profession of burglary.

There was not a stir in the crystal stillness as we climbed down a slope, broke through a hedge and returned to the road there to descend with it into a shallow valley. Two men appeared before we could take evasive action so we carried on walking, mumbling a reply to their greeting and feeling their eyes boring into our backs.

The second day we made better progress in spite of blisters and objecting calf-muscles but our general weakness from months of semi-starvation and neglect was plainly telling. Pauses for rests became more frequent and, as the day wore on, we found ourselves becoming increasingly light-headed and careless, walking straight through villages instead of detouring around them. Covered mounds by the roadside turned out to be potato clamps, so we dug several potatoes out, putting them in the sack with the idea of risking a fire or, as a last resort, eating them raw. We also came across an unguarded bicycle propped outside a shop. We could easily have stolen it, but what use was one between the two of us?

The town of Mystowice we likewise tramped straight through without a care and were surprised at its size. We felt safer in the larger centres and far more anonymous than was the case in villages where strangers – even legitimate ones – were objects of scrutiny. A town centre signpost indicated 'Oswiecim 21 kms' and 'Chrzanow 24 kms' and it was only because we had designated Chrzanow as being a route-mark on the way to Cracow that we chose the more easterly road. The alternative would not have been a good idea – though at the time we were not to know that the German word for Oswiecim was Auschwitz.

Soldiers and elderly uniformed men of the Volksturm (Home Guard) were among the dowdy civilians in the streets but none appeared to be on duty. We remained in dread of the sudden materialisation of a patrol or road block where *identity papers would be needed. But our luck held. Being under German authority, there was no strong reason for supposing the Silesian population to be anything but pro-Nazi. Crossing into a not entirely subdued Poland proper could produce mixed blessings; the hand of friendship as well as the arm of repression.*

A lone barn provided a third night's lodging, this one rotting and stagnant and far from any human habitation. The straw was musty and smelt of manure but was dry, so dry in fact we utilised some as fuel for a fire, filling the place with smoke. The stuff made a poor heat source so we dined that evening on luke-warm potatoes as hard as unripe apples.

The ensuing days were ones of increasing pain and grief as we slowly, oh so slowly, reduced those kilometres to Chrzanow, reproving ourselves for our snail's rate of progress; surely 20-year-olds could do better than that. But our physical condition was such that bouts of nausea and vomiting ensued whenever we ate something that disagreed with long ill-treated stomachs or when we pushed ourselves too far. We didn't much like the look of Jaworzno so tried to detour round the considerable town only to get lost in allotments and hostile suburbs. Twice we were chased out of gardens and on one occasion had to make a real run for it when Gordon, hunger getting the better of his judgement, lunged at a skinny chicken. Barns continued to provide shelter – the single plus-element of that excruciating walk – but our further efforts to steal were lamentably futile. Urban shops held so little there was barely anything worth stealing or buying, our one shop-lifting venture netting us a couple of hard pears and a tin of spam that tasted like dog-meat – and probably was. We did at last catch a chicken, the wretched bird's squawkings being drowned by a dog's barking. To celebrate this event we lit a fire among trees and toasted the limbs, one by one, on the flames but the smoke drew a couple of boys to the fireside. Their curiosity became too belligerent for our peace of mind so we eventually had to stamp out the fire and move on, stuffing half-cooked drumsticks into our pockets.

We could see Chrzanow long before we reached it; the villages and townships becoming fewer and spread further apart. Cracow, we estimated, would be at least another 45km. And we could think of nothing after Cracow. There we would be amongst staunch Poles and in a land where people universally hated Germans. Anything could happen once we were there. All that our minds could grapple with was the pain of walking. We evolved great longings for not only a decent meal, but a modicum of comfort in an environment where not everybody wanted you dead.

It was about this time that the 'train plan' was born. We had discussed the idea of using trains before our escape but had discarded it as too risky; virtually impossible in fact without the possession of identity documents. But we had not delved so deeply into the concept of freight train travel; securing ourselves away in a railway truck where no questions need be asked or papers demanded. However, this form of transit was fraught with difficulties, complications and not a little danger but, out here in the sticks getting nowhere except weaker all the time, the prospects appeared less daunting. Stowed away in a bed of hay on the sixth night, we agreed to have a go.

Chrzanow, we knew, was on a railway and the line was part of a network that served Cracow. We were also aware that it was a junction which meant that trains emanating from the town could go in three directions only one of which could suit our purpose. Snooping about in the freight yards trying to decipher dispatch cards clamped to wagonsides would hardly pay dividends even if we weren't caught by militia or railway workers. No, we'd have to look for a stretch of track outside the town that fitted the circumstances of the situation; a spot where we could lie in wait for a train going eastwards, that was suitably remote, the topography of the terrain raising a gradient and need for a curve of the line both to slow the train and foil vigilance from personnel already aboard it. Freight trains, we had learnt, carried armed guards as a precaution against sabotage. These were usually placed at the rear and with the locomotive crew at the front. Thus it was imperative they remained ignorant of what we were proposing to do in the middle.

Again we took the road straight into town, this time intent upon locating the railway station and then following the correct set of tracks out of the place. Our stomachs ached for food and rumbled audibly as we tramped the pot-holed tarmac but our spirits had risen with the prospect of new action. Intricately designed lamp standards accompanied us into a maze of awakening streets and we wondered if we dared enter a bakery and buy a loaf of bread. Citizens, muffled against the cold mist that heralded winter, scuttled along pavements made uneven by subsidence. A policeman directed desultory traffic at an intersection and a horse-drawn wagon full of soldiers clattered over ill-laid cobbles. One of the soldiers bore a remarkable resemblance to an unsavoury camp guard we knew as 'Snotty Nose' and I looked away hurriedly though assuredly it wasn't him.

We located the station with no difficulty. The freight yards adjoined it, the entrance, as half expected, manned by a civilian wearing an armband and shouldering a rifle. Any lingering ideas we harboured of investigating freight yards faded.

Following the eastbound line out of the town but finding no junction we were forced to the conclusion after several miles that the bifurcation of the track must have occurred on the other side of the station. What we had here was a double track keeping firmly to a single route. Disinclined to walk the trackside path itself we retained the railway in view from the parallel road though this too had become too much of a main artery for comfort.

Both road and rail entered a spruce forest and, losing sight of the tracks, we moved through the trees to stand upon the line. With nobody in sight in either direction we now felt bold enough to walk alongside the rails, they being close enough to the trees to make a run for their cover if necessary. In this manner we made reasonable progress, the only interruption being an oncoming two-coach local passenger train which sent us helter-skelter for shelter.

From an embankment we watched the thing rattle by, noting its speed which was much too high for our purpose. Continuing, we located a curve in the line – not as sharp as we would have liked but adequate – and rested here for a couple of hours to observe more trains in both directions but, again, we gauged their speeds to be too great.

For much of the day we followed the tracks resting up at likely points and watching the passing of rail traffic but only as the trees were thinning by late afternoon did we come upon a curve sharp enough to offer hope of providing the circumstances for which we craved.

It had rained in the morning but ceased after midday leaving the undergrowth wet and soggy with a steady litany of drips from sodden trees. We were in a clearing; the lineside row of spruce and fir having receded to leave the railway naked of close cover. The spot was far from perfect but would have to suffice; hunger and exhaustion were making walking difficult again as well as affecting our judgement. We waited, crouched in a hollow.

A heavy goods train jangled into view and we dashed for the trees again, aware that the dusk was not dense enough to conceal us in the open. An overworked locomotive engulfed in a sweat of steam headed a long line of wagons that rattled and jerked against each other as if the driver was applying his air-brakes. We could see the driver and his mate leaning out of the cab and surmised that some obstruction ahead was causing a speed restriction. The pace of the train was perfect now but the thing was going the wrong way damn it. I cursed our luck but then it came to me that the obstruction – if indeed there was one – might work for trains coming from the opposite direction too; those that had already been slowed but had not yet had time to pick up speed. We watched the brake van disappear into the murk but could discern no occupants.

Darkness was not complete when the sound of a train from the direction of Chrzanow lured us from cover, hearts thumping against our ribs. A headlamp pushed a yellow antenna ahead of another large locomotive, its stack belching spark-infested brown smoke. We waited a few seconds to allow the engine to pass, then sprinted for the track, confident that the darkness would be intense enough to hide our running figures. Crouching close against the passing wagons, we watched for hand holds projecting from the dark mass looming above us, and as we ran, keeping pace with the train, tried to avoid too close contact with the iron wheels, cruel and menacing.

My eyes were also trying to watch for signal cables and other lineside impediments. Behind me I heard Gordon pounding at my heels, swearing with the exertion. A lever on a wagon caught my eye and I lunged at it, clutching the cold metal and holding on. It dragged me along the ballast and I envisaged a terrible fear that my legs might become enmeshed in those grinding, relentless wheels. Trying to swing them outwards and into the air at the same time, my other hand fastened upon another protrusion. My feet dropped again, the toes of my boots bumping along the line but with my two hands firmly anchored I was able to draw myself upwards though the effort took every ounce of my remaining strength. A red mist curtained my eyes as I fought to raise my body to the flank of the wagon, my right foot searching desperately for a toe-hold above the wheels. And then it was all over as, with a final heave, I reached the couplings between two wagons.

Gordon was already atop the high sides and was working his way along the rim to join me. For a moment I cogitated upon the falseness of movies I'd seen where the hero nips smartly up into such a train as this to a musical accompaniment from a philharmonic orchestra. My hollow laugh was lost on Gordon as we turned our attention to the interior of the wagon. To our dismay it was empty, bare of anything except a scattering of coal-begrimed sacks; an empty floor surrounded by four cold, damp walls.

Attempting to stand up against the swaying motion we explored our new domain. There were enough sacks to superficially conceal our forms in the event of a cursory examination by railway staff but that was all. We shook the coaldust out of some of the damp bags and gingerly sat down on them. The train rolled on making no effort to pick up speed.

It was pitch black outside now; only the sparks from the locomotive made dancing illumination up ahead but we could detect that the area was clear of the forest. By climbing the walls of the wagon we observed our progress but this told us nothing of where we were going. Chinks of light from houses occasionally slashed the night.

Abruptly the train screeched to a halt, the wagon couplings reverberating. No town showed but we nevertheless covered ourselves in sacks in case of a search. We listened to the wheezing of the locomotive and the sound of a shouted exchange followed by a prolonged banshee whistle. The train jerked into motion again – but in the opposite direction.

I glanced at Gordon. He glanced at me. We flung the sacks aside in a gesture of exasperation, our white faces smeared with coaldust. The train rolled on, still quite slowly and we debated whether or not to bale out. But, after the effort of boarding it, the inability to believe that our efforts might have been in vain ensured we stayed put. Maybe they were shunting the trucks onto another line? Perhaps there was a junction this side of Chrzanow after all? By the time we had exhausted the unlikely possibilities our minds had been made up for us when the train picked up speed, blocking any attempt to leave.

A glow ahead intensified, indicating a return to Chrzanow so we took cover once more but the train never slackened pace for an instant as we rattled across a complex of points and crossovers, roared through the station – lights stabbing the darkness – and out into the countryside again. The cold night air whipped our faces as we clung to the sides of what had now become our new prison. Which line had we taken? The question had arisen for, with Chrzanow passed, going at this pace would have us back in the Katowice industrial region within the hour. We might as well drop off at the gates of the camp and give ourselves up. Bleak despair engulfed us.

An hour passed and the train sped on but no urban lights or pit workings showed. Maybe we had taken another line? We blundered through one biggish town but though aglow with light we were unable to make out its name.

It must have been in the very early hours when we began to slow with ponderous deliberation. Still there was no industry just as there were no stars in the sky. The faint outline of houses drew nearer the tracks. We waited, clutching wet sacks, uncertain what action to take.

With a final hiss of steam we drew to a halt in a small siding. Dawn bruised the sky and a handful of early morning workers were about their business; indistinct figures whistling in the semi-darkness. Furtively we clambered out of the wagon and dropped to the ground. Ensuring nobody was near we ran to the fence that bordered the yard, clambered over it and melted into a deserted backstreet.

A lane led away from the village, small town or whatever it was, and we took it, having no desire to be seen at this hour of the morning. Clear of the last house we lay down, shivering and apprehensive, on a low mound of stalks and twigs amongst a patch of undergrowth. That we slept for a time was a measure of our exhaustion.

It was the cold that awoke us, that and the noise of people on the road. Broad daylight showed us our surroundings in rude clarity; flat agricultural terrain similar to that through which we had been passing the past six days – or was it weeks? Jumping about to restore a sluggish circulation we surveyed the methods open to us of retracing our steps for plainly we had allowed ourselves to be transported deeper into enemy territory. The very fact that a train had brought us this far raised the possibility that a train might be induced to take us back. And to make sure we knew where we were going on this occasion a passenger train offered a much more positive means of doing so. Walking was now completely out of the question; we were fast starving to death, while jumping non-public transport vehicles was getting us only from the frying pan into the fire. We thought we had adequate funds to finance such a journey if the neighbouring township could raise a station as it had a goods yard. Neither of us much cared for the idea of loitering around such establishments – anathema to escaped prisoners – but we concluded a small one would be unlikely to raise all that number of nasties. Another method of evasion discarded at the planning stage had, all of a sudden, become infinitely appealing.

Straightway we went to work tidying ourselves up as best we could, removing the coaldust from neck and face with the help of roadside puddles. If we were going to travel in style we would have to appear a little less like fugitives on the run from the law.

By mid-morning we had re-entered the township and located the station. Signposts showed Breslau (the Polish Wroclaw) and Opole on their westward-pointing arms, the former as something under 100km, so at least we had some idea where we were. The station held more positive promise with Cracow as a direct eastbound destination; a train going there was scheduled for shortly after midday. Having elicited all the information we could want except for the fare our nerves gave way so we slunk out of the station and out of town into the concealing countryside to await events and our further destiny.

We might not have been quite so pleased with ourselves had we known the fate Cracow held for us.

Chapter 4
South-eastern Poland

Though unaware of it we had seen the last of Highway 19; our allegiance transferred to a road number 17 that was to carry us between Lublin and Zamosc on a more substantial detour than the previous one. Polorbis had rapturously enthused upon the glories of not only Zamosc but a scattering of historic villages and townships north-east of Rzeszow, the last of our Polish city trio. With time in hand we could afford the indirect route.

Luxuriating in our beds at the Unia Hotel we had listened with mixed feelings to a growling thunderstorm and accompanying downpour during the night, happy to have avoided it yet ominously aware the deluge could persist through the morning. But the worst was over as we debouched onto Lublin's watery streets to encounter the city's rush hour and its attendant antagonistic drivers. Sprayed with dirty water by lorries, hooted at by cars, clanged at by trolley buses and ignored by road-crossing pedestrians we cleared the suburbs and rejoiced to be once more on the open road. And for a while fate smiled upon us by enticing sunshine to break through the grey cloud ceiling.

Highway 17 proved to be a road afflicted by a seeming need to climb every rise in the land that geography had bestowed upon an otherwise flat landscape. This it did with long straight sweeps up and down over a series of ridges, the route ahead arrowing into infinity. Atop one ridge we halted at a picnic site to partake of a snack lunch of bread, marmite and cheese which, having made pigs of ourselves at the hotel buffet breakfast, we deemed adequate. This however was reduced to bread and marmite when it was discovered we'd left the purchased cheese in the Lublin shop. But we did find a discarded bottle of lemonade on one of the picnic tables though the reason for its abandonment became all too apparent upon our first swig.

Our map showed we were in the Chelm region and approaching the Ukraine. To the north, close to the border, lay the site of another one-time Nazi death camp – Sobibor, scene of a desperate breakout by its inmates pushed beyond endurance by the cruelty of their jailers. And as if death lay heavy on this tortured land I was myself this very day to come as close to my own extinction as I have ever been.

The incident occurred at the one point that Highway 17 deviated from its usual pattern, dropping into and climbing out of a gully in a series of zig-zags, the carriageway narrowing in the process and providing little in the way of a verge. Paul was following me though a substantial gap separated us.

The two heavy articulated lorries approached at high speed from behind, their drivers racing one another neck and neck, encouraged to do so, no doubt, by the absence of other vehicles and the earlier straight road. They might also have been drunk. Paul managed to take evasive action by riding into an opportune gateway and shouted a warning to me which I never heard. But I did hear the approach of the lorries. The first sharp bend and abrupt descent of the road into the gully took the drivers by surprise and, with the high-pitched squeal of brakes, I sensed the peril hurtling, out of control, towards me. But there was no gateway or flat verge to provide refuge; only a near vertical bank that held me to the road.

Aware of the situation, I stood hard on my pedals, driving the bike forward with all the fervour and strength I could muster, desperate to outdistance the nearside steel monster, its brakes locked, from overwhelming me. But it was only by the grace of God that I was saved from certain death. Paul told me afterwards that it was the closest to a fatal accident he had ever witnessed.

Shaken by the incident we took violent evasive action at the approach of every motorised vehicle that came our way, a precaution soon discarded as time wore on and our fears subsided.

In the town of Krasnystaw we wheeled our bikes into a grimy bar-restaurant since to leave them, even padlocked, outside and out of view was inviting theft. Though we had carried out this procedure before with no objection raised, this time we were brusquely ordered off the premises by a rotund and disapproving matron who was not going to have lowly bicycles in *her* establishment. Confronted by this apparition we tried to turn the bikes in the confined space only to collide with tables and chairs as we attempted to flee. The clientele of gruff male citizens found the spectacle hilarious and the little cafe rang with laughter. Back in the street a hamburger joint provided alternative sustenance and we played safe by devouring our meal in the gutter.

By mid-afternoon we were in Zamosc to behold a sensational little city, its charm not apparent until arrival at the market square. The place was founded during the Renaissance as a fortress able to resist the attacks of both the Cossacks and the Swedes, the fortified palace with its thick walls presenting a gloomy barrack-like atmosphere in spite of the pleasant parkland that surrounds it. The market square, however, is where the true glory of Zamosc is revealed. Pearl of the Renaissance, Padua of the North, Town of Arcades are all descriptions applied to it and they are assuredly justified.

The square is bordered by former town houses of the mercantile bourgeoisie and dominated by an impressive town hall approached by a sweeping double stairway. The character of the vividly-painted houses may have changed through countless renovations but they still remain a wondrous spectacle. What is to be seen today is one of Europe's best-preserved Renaissance town centres classified by UNESCO as an outstanding historical monument.

Inside the town hall there is a room commemorating local citizen and socialist theologist Rosa Luxemburg, though the staff don't rush to open it for visitors. In World War Two the town was spared destruction, but not its people of whom 8,000 were executed by the Germans. Odiously renamed Himmlerstadt, Zamosc and its region was made the target for a brutal 'relocation' scheme for German settlers – part of Hitler's plan to create an Aryan eastern bulwark of the Third Reich. The town's earlier history is the more inspiring, it being not only one of the few places to withstand the seventeenth-century 'Swedish Deluge' but also scene of the Red Army's repulse in the Polish-Russian War of 1919-20. Not bad for a town that started life as a model urban centre by a sixteenth-century chancellor with grandiose ideas and a more than avid taste for vodka.

Our way out of Zamosc led, via a series of smaller roads, through the Puszcza Solska – Solska Forest – to tongue-twisting Szezebrzeszyn – an endless industrial town, Bilgraj and Tarnogrod in the general direction of Rzeszow, Highway 17 having sheered off towards Lvov, the former Polish city now regional capital of Western Ukraine. Between Szezebrzeszyn and Bilgraj we camped in a wood plentifully endowed with raspberries which we collected by the mugful, more than the usual density of mosquitoes, and a colony of polecats, these curious little creatures watching us intently from the trees. The weather had stayed fine and dry since Lublin but a cloudburst caught us as we emerged to make breakfast following a night enlivened by the rumble of goods trains and the clattering of amorous storks.

Provisioning ourselves in Bilgoraj while sheltering from the rain we lunched well at a 'citizens' restaurant' in Tarnogrod, where we mistook the number of noughts on our tendered zloty notes – another currency that drove me barmy with an exchange rate then in excess of 24,000 to the pound sterling – but were saved from short-changing ourselves by the honesty of the proprietor.

At the innocuous village of Sieniawa we visited the recently restored palace of the Czartonyski family, now a sensational hotel. Escorted through palatial chamber after chamber, and boudoir after boudoir – they could hardly be described as mere rooms – the prospect of our forthcoming night in our humble bivouac became distinctly anticlimactic.

We were now in the region of Malopolska, well provided with treasures of basilicas, palaces, cloisters and bulwarks, confusing in their profusion. We missed Lezajsk and its unique Baroque basilica but, following another wet night's camping in a dripping wood, came upon medieval Lancut and its magnificent palace, former residence of the noble families of Lubomirski and Potocki. Originally a fortress it was transformed by Stanislaw Lubomirski, with the help of the Princess Elzbieta Lubomirski – a stunning-looking lady by all accounts and renowned throughout the courts of Europe – into a residential palace at the beginning of the nineteenth century.

Our route had taken us through the provincial capital of Przemysl, just 10km from the Ukrainian border, and a historic border town that has been a melting pot of cultures and traditions since the seventh century. The heavily wooded and hilly Pogorze Przemyski stretched away south of the city towards the Carpathians to which we would be heading after our sojourn in Rzeszow. Przemysl is a hauntingly beautiful town of winding narrow streets, the oldest city in southern Poland after Cracow.

The last 35km to Rzeszow was, alas, on the busy E40 international highway. We had joined it at Przeworsk, an urban complex containing fragments of old walls, a Bernardine cloister and a lesser palace also owned by the Lubomirski family who, it can be said, were never short of real estate.

Rain again fell at night as we camped in yet another wood but neither the dripping foliage nor the all-night traffic on the E40 bothered us; had there been complete tranquillity we would probably not have slept a wink. Paul suffered a dose of the 'runs' in the evening but happily this cleared by morning, as did the rain, though it was under threatening clouds that we pedalled the final 30km against a wintry wind into Rzeszow early enough to avoid the heaviest concentration of traffic.

Though this unremarkable – some would say soulless – city holds an eighteenth-century palace that had been yet another piece of Lubomirski property and started life as a Ruthenian settlement as far back as the thirteenth century, there is little to show for it. Following World War Two, when its considerable Jewish population was, as usual, decimated, the post-war government attempted to revive the area by cramming the place with industry. The handful of surviving antiquities were further reduced by new buildings so that today Stalinist monstrosities make uneasy bedfellows with crumbling edifices of a bygone age.

One of the monstrosities was the multi-storey Rzeszow Hotel in the city centre and I am ashamed to say that its architectural shortcomings dismayed Paul and me not at all that cold damp morning. Within its concrete heart lay a cosy bed for the night and blessed shelter from a 24-hour downpour that struck hardly had we wheeled our bikes into the foyer.

For the last 35km our direction of travel had been west but from now on it would swing due south again. Had we continued on the original axis we would have reached a metropolis that claims a corner of my soul – that of the old Royal Polish capital city of Cracow.

My knowledge of and fluency in the German language is probably worse than anybody who professes to the very minimum of linguistic ability – with the possible exception of my partner-in-crime, Gordon, though his Scottish accent together with a smattering of Gaelic offers certain similar guttural overtones. While waiting for our Cracow-bound train in the concealing thicket we practised our lines, repeating to ourselves over and over again the German phrase we intended using at the station ticket office window. 'Eine Fahrkarte erster Klasse nach Krakau, bitte' – 'A first class ticket to Cracow, please' – and the reason we chose to travel first class was two-fold. Not only did 'erster' trip easier off the tongue than the German equivalents to 'second' or 'third' but, by travelling first class we hoped to raise a little more respect from a universally class-conscious authority and any minion of that authority to whom we were likely to be subjected. Close to midday, under a weak sunshine, we made our way back to the station.

Our timing was perfect and, in company with half a dozen members of the commuting public, we lined up at the ticket office exhibiting what we hoped was an air of having done all this before.

At the window Gordon, clearing his throat, spoke the magic formula and received a hard look from a Germanic lady behind the grill. But with the look came a ticket. Swiftly I added "Ich auch" – I too – and the deed was done. We even got change from the total sum of moneys tendered. On the platform a train indicator announced the next service as the Personenzug to Strumien, though where Strumien was we had no idea. But it was obviously the destination of everyone else for when the two-coach train arrived it scooped up all and sundry leaving us loitering in the station; just the occurrence we had hoped to avoid. To hide our nervousness we stalked around the platform and so came upon a stall that sold frankfurter-type sausages. Before I could intervene, Gordon had purchased half the stock.

Seldom has food had such impact. The sausage may have been horse or dog-meat but it filled a void. We sat on a bench and munched away, oblivious to any eyes that may have fastened upon us.

An hour and a half went by before our train steamed in 70 minutes late. It was a four-coach affair and this time was ironically classed as a Schnellzug. Only half of one of the coaches was reserved for first class ticket-holders and in one of the four empty compartments we settled ourselves, side by side, adjacent to the corridor and facing the engine.

The train gathered speed to bound along the single track over flat terrain that, by little stretch of the imagination, could have been rural Essex; small fields, woods and rural villages with un-Essex-like onion-domed churches. Gordon broke into a laugh and I too felt strangely light-headed.

The door slid open and we stopped laughing. The ticket inspector stood in the opening staring at us questioningly. His "Fahrkarte, bitte" was laced with sarcasm and impending wrath as if we had been caught in a higher class of travel than that for which our tickets were validated. The man was short and tubby but authoritative in his Reichsbahn uniform and was plainly taken aback when we produced the appropriate tickets. Slamming the door he moved on, shaking his head, and we hoped he wasn't going to air his misgivings to more potent authority.

Over the next hour came a number of halts at wayside stations. Few people joined the train; equally few alighted and none invaded our exalted portion of the coach. We stopped for a longer period at a larger, busier station. Its name was Oswiecim, one we'd seen on a signpost several days earlier. People – soldiers displaying the double lightning strike of the SS on their sleeves among them – joined the train but, again, we were left in peace.

The ticket inspector padded down the corridor at intervals glaring disapprovingly through the glass as he went by but taking no further action. The train bowled on, rocking from side to side.

Another prolonged halt occurred at Chrzanow, and here our luck faded. Two officers – a naval lieutenant and a Wehrmacht captain – entered, stowed their briefcases on the rack and sat down opposite us. We feigned sleep for all we were worth.

I felt the newcomers' eyes resting upon us, sizing up our un-first class looks and attire. It was a hard penetrating gaze, loaded with query and, though I shifted my position thus proclaiming a doze rather than deep slumber, I felt myself weakening; unable to ignore the stare which I had glimpsed through my fingers. Just for a second I opened my eyes wide and was caught. The smiling *captain nodded, seemingly eager to chat.*

I nodded back, whereupon he enquired, in German, of our nationality. We were ready for this one so I mumbled "Ungarish," a nationality we had 'borrowed' for just such an event, it being unlikely that anyone hereabouts could speak or understand Hungarian. Gordon too had abruptly 'awakened' and proceeded to enter the conversational gambit. The two Germans were handsome young fellows putting me in mind, for some reason, of fresh-faced American university students.

"I've never been to Budapest, more's the pity. A lovely city I believe." observed the captain. I felt this needed more than a nod in reply so launched, in halting German – supported by Gordon – into a description of Bristol having not, at that time, visited the Hungarian capital. Unfortunately Gordon had Glasgow as his yardstick which didn't help. Our German was atrocious and words of English kept intruding. But the captain seemed satisfied.

The Navy entered the exchange. "What do you do?" I heard the word 'arbeit' so caught on. "We work in a hospital," I said quickly, before Gordon could come up with something sardonic. "In Krakau?" I nodded, hoping he wasn't going to ask which hospital. We'd only hit upon that occupation because it was comfortably vague, smelt of useful war-work and 'Krankenhaus' and 'Lazaret' – 'hospital' – were German words we both knew. I tried explaining that we had been working on a farm in the country over the weekend but got bogged down through lack of the right words and also because I suddenly realised that I didn't know when the weekend was.

Gordon fortuitously interrupted. "Fahren sie nach Krakau?" The two men nodded and mentioned some barracks or office of which we'd never heard but pretended we had.

Our feigned sleep had ensured we'd missed the location where we had made our ill-fated boarding of the freight train but judged the city to be close. At all costs we'd have to leave the train before the station which would be a big one – a Hauptbahnhof – lousy with police, Gestapo, military gendarmerie and other abominations. I stared out of the window attempting to pick out tell-tale signs of an imminent conurbation but the terrain remained obstinately rural.

The captain rose to his feet, took down his briefcase and sat down again. He then opened the case with a snapping of catches and produced a bunch of black grapes in the manner of a conjurer producing a rabbit from a top hat. Plainly grapes were a rarity in wartime Greater Germany even for privileged German officers and they certainly were for the likes of us. Breaking the bunch into four parts he distributed largess to everyone.

"Vielen Dank," gushed Gordon and I with unfettered enthusiasm, wondering what the two would think if they knew they were bestowing comfort upon the enemy. Gordon began wolfing down his portion, stalks, pips and all so I kicked him surreptitiously, trying to indicate that he should eat in a manner befitting a first class ticket holder.

"Fünf minuten nach Krakau," vouchsafed the lieutenant thereby helpfully supplying the answer to what we wanted to know. Outside, the countryside began to sprout a rash of houses.

I mumbled something about being late for work as an excuse to leave the compartment and, with Gordon at my heels, slid open the door. "Vielen Dank und auf Wiedersehen," we enthused, employing a large chunk of our German vocabulary and flashing our brightest smiles. We moved to the exit at the head of the coach, hoping nobody else would be in an hurry to alight.

The corridor remained empty giving us a clear and unobserved chance to make an unorthodox departure which we proposed to effect as soon as the speed of the train permitted it. The ticket inspector was nowhere in sight.

The brakes came on with a squeal and we felt the slowing motion of the train. I unfastened the door, leaning out of the window; my eyes scanning the ground for an obstacle-free landing pad. At any moment passengers would start issuing from their compartments.

Gingerly I climbed down onto the first outside step, hanging on to the hand rail and restraining the door from swinging too wide. The wind was fresh in my face. I spied a heap of clinker and cinders – the spot where locomotives had their boilers raked out – coming up. "Here we go!" I whispered urgently to Gordon who was breathing down my neck.

I landed with a crunch, Gordon virtually on top of me and, together, we rolled away from the moving train. The clinker was sharp, scouring my hands as well as back even through the clothing I wore. Hardly had we risen to our feet when we heard voices further down the track and beheld a knot of passengers from an adjacent coach who had made a similar exit. I wondered what their reasons for doing so were; simple ticket-evasion or perhaps they too were allergic to heavily watched railway stations. I remembered we were now in Poland proper.

We climbed over a substantial fence and found ourselves amidst rows of lorries. Under the cover of the cab of the nearest vehicle we took stock of our surroundings.

It appeared we had landed ourselves in the middle of a military freight depot with soldiers loading crated machinery onto flat trucks. There was only one entry point to the depot so far as we could see and it was blocked by soldiers. The high timber fence, made from old railway sleepers, enclosed the yard, that lay in full view not only of the soldiers but of anyone at the windows of the houses overlooking it. We made our way to a derelict wagon quite close to the wall; a perfect refuge in which to lay up until nightfall or departure of the working parties; whichever came soonest.

We waited through the rest of the afternoon and into the night. More troops arrived; cheerful fellows in overalls, and a convoy of further lorries. A group of youngsters took time off for a smoke very close to our hideaway, forcing us to remain very quiet indeed. With nightfall, powerful arc lamps came on and the work resumed under artificial light. Cramped and cold we continued waiting.

It must have been well after midnight when work finally ceased. The troops marched off, the main gate slammed shut and the depot was plunged into darkness. An eery silence was confounded only by the sullen rumble of a living city.

Stiffly we moved to the timber wall, helped each other over it and jumped down the other side onto a road. Not a car, not a soul was to be seen or heard and the windows of the houses were no more than blind eyes. Even for so late an hour the emptiness was uncanny.

Proceeding cautiously along the pavement, trying to muffle the thump of our hob-nailed boots, we made our way towards the glow in the sky that marked the city centre, not quite certain what we were going to do when we got there. A delicious aroma of baking assailed our nostrils, deflecting us into a dark alley.

In it we could just make out a bakery, the smell issuing from a vent above the locked door. I played with the idea of knocking, revealing our identities and asking outright for succour since we were amongst a generally sympathetic populace. But Gordon had other ideas.

Some of yesterday's bread was displayed behind a glass frame that formed an adjustable window. Picking up a rusted metal hinge that lay in the gutter, Gordon went to work in an attempt to prize it open. In this endeavour he was only too successful, the whole frame falling outwards with a tremendous crash of breaking glass. We each grabbed a loaf, turned on our heels and fled.

It was just our luck that a military foot patrol should choose that moment to materialise from around the corner where the alley joined the larger road. Even had the four steel-helmeted soldiers not heard the breaking glass, the sight of a couple of ruffians, loaves of bread in their hands, sprinting for dear life down the middle of the road, told its own story. A gruff authoritative voice shouted "Halt oder wir schiessen!" Swiftly we came to heel to stare into the muzzles of three rifles and a Schmeiser. Devious though we had become our combined cunning could not worm us out of this one. Resignedly we raised our hands.

The soldiers, upon learning of our nationality and intentions, became exceedingly friendly. "You were lucky," they told us, "we have strict orders to shoot on sight anyone who breaks the curfew." The curfew! We'd clean overlooked this scourge of the occupied territories.

An indignant Polish baker appeared on the scene, having discovered the damage to his property. A big florid man wearing a white flour-dusted apron, he took in the situation at a glance and invited all six of us back to the bakery.

And there we were plied with all the fresh warm bread we could cram into our stomachs to the detriment of our digestive systems if not our hunger. The patrol-leader, a sergeant, encouraged us to eat all we could and then gave the reason.

Shame-faced, he told us that his orders were that all curfew-breakers had to be handed over to the Gestapo and there was nothing he could do to alter the situation. The man spoke a little English and was so sincere with his apologies I felt quite sorry for him.

Our pockets stuffed with still-steaming bread we reached the centre of Cracow though hardly in the circumstances envisaged. As we tramped the cobbled streets of the lovely old town, I ruefully appraised the sum of our accomplishment. It had taken ten days and more than 200km to cover 80 km towards liberation; no cause for much sense of achievement there. And the fact we had been at large for all that time with no identity papers or evasion aids save stolen clothing and money was no more than the luck of the devil. But not all was negative. Hadn't we successfully avoided ten days and more of slave labour down our hated *coalmine? That alone had been worth the effort.*

It was still night when we were led through a side door of a tall block quite close to the cloistered Market Square of the city with the Town Hall Tower rearing up as a dark mass against the lesser darkness of the sky. A black-uniformed Gestapo clerk glared at us before signing a receipt and dismissing our escort. The soldiers scurried down the steps without a further word as if all the hounds of hell were at their heels. I would have given much to have followed them. For Gordon and myself the fun was over; now came the settlement of the account.

Taken into a bare concrete-walled room we were questioned thoroughly by a vile little man wearing civilian clothes, thin-framed spectacles perched on his nose. The thrust of his questions was aimed at the identity of Poles he was certain had helped us on our illicit journey. Because nobody had helped us we were only telling the truth when we both said so. But this was not the answer wanted so each time it was proffered he nodded to the pair of thugs who stood on either side of us. They promptly knocked us to the floor. And as we lay there, mute and passive, we were kicked to our feet again, the unrewarding process being repeated until, presumably, our statement was believed. Our jackets had been removed, searched, and the remaining Reichsmarks revealed, which led to accusations of robbery. This we, falsely, denied saying we had acquired it from our camp guards. And when it came to giving details of the camp from which we had absconded we resolutely insisted, by pre-arrangement, that it was Stalag VIIIB at Těšín on the Czech-Polish border which had been a cushy number compared with the rigours of working camp E902. Between the bouts of being knocked down and picking ourselves up our bare arms were burnt with lighted cigarette ends which hurt abominably. Twice I had to whisper urgently to Gordon whose Scottish temper was such that he might otherwise have thrown himself at his tormentors; the result of so doing assuredly being lethal.

We were then moved to a row of underground and windowless cells, each about ten feet square and containing no furniture whatsoever; not even a blanket to shade our eyes from the eternal glare of the single grid-protected light bulb in the centre of the ceiling.

So far as I was able to calculate we remained there three days and nights with not a scrap of food being given us. I blessed the Wehrmacht patrol for insisting upon us filling our bellies with bread for, otherwise, we would have been in a bad way. I also castigated Gordon for his rash action that brought about our downfall, but saw no future in rupturing our relationship at a time we needed it most. With nothing to do we spent the time scratching rude epithets on the already epithet-crowded walls and pretending to ourselves we hadn't noticed the obscene stink of sweat and blood that permeated the block nor heard the occasional scream issuing from the corridor.

Came the moment when the cell door was opened and for a few blessed minutes we could imbibe gulps of fresh air before being hustled into the back of a military truck reeking of petrol fumes. I was sick twice, much to the disgust of our escort, on the hour-and-a-half-long journey out of town to I knew not where, for the back was totally enclosed.

And to this day I cannot be certain of the situation of the fenced compound in which we were to be incarcerated. But, thankfully, there were no further Gestapo interrogations to endure; instead our guards were sullen SS louts who never spoke a word. We had a bunk on which to lay, a thin blanket to cover us, and the compound in which to exercise. Food in the guise of a watery gruel was issued once a day. Otherwise we were left severely alone.

That we were upon the threshold of somewhere unspeakably evil was not lost upon us however. Other compounds, very much more inhabited, stretched away in all directions, their inmates in a pitiable condition. Our own bodies were emaciated but theirs were no more than skeletons.

But a pinnacle of horror became evident one day when I was to witness a scene that I have, ever since, attempted to keep to the far depths of my mind. The population of the neighbouring compound were Mongolians and I was to see a dozen men around the corpse of a woman who had been brought into the compound and raped to death. The men were laughing as they awaited their turn to vent their lust upon her dead body. I turned away, engulfed by a tide of revulsion. Yet the evil was understandable for those Mongolians, together with their Russian and other colleagues, had been transformed by the Germans into something lower than the most obnoxious of animals by prolonged brutalisation.

We departed from this hellish abode in the not unpleasant company of two elderly stalag guards who had been sent to collect us from a camp from which we had never escaped. This said little for teutonic efficiency, but our joy at the turn of events was palpable as we made our way to a railway station the name of which I never noticed. Our guards were reluctant to talk about the establishment in which we had been held though one of them mentioned a name that sounded like 'Birkenau'.

The rain was still falling as we descended to breakfast next morning feeling strangely clean and well-laundered following a series of hot baths and clothes-washing sessions. Alas, the meal was not the help-yourself variety wherein we could stuff ourselves as well as pockets with well-filled rolls, hard-boiled eggs and Danish pastries, but miraculously the rain ceased the moment we wheeled our bikes out of the hotel foyer.

In spite of the downpour we had seen all there was to see of Rzeszow town so felt no compulsion to linger in it. A signpost in the square directed us onto road number 9 to Barwinek on the Slovak border 100km distant while another arm pronounced Cracow as 149km to the west. I would have liked to have shown Paul this city of Polish kings for it is a striking place. On my last visit there – in the communist era – I had persuaded my minder to enquire of the whereabouts of the former Gestapo headquarters and this he did. And there, beneath a present-day supermarket, I had been led down the concrete steps to the row of cells and, in particular, to number 3 in which I had briefly resided. A blood-red ribbon had been stretched across the open doorways; each cell left intact as a memorial. I was invited to enter number 3 there to discern my wall-scratched exhortation as to what the Gestapo could do to itself. But I was unable to dally longer. I don't suffer from claustrophobia but the loathsome smell of blood and sweat taunted my imagination to the extent of my feeling physically sick. From former Gestapo headquarters I had been delivered to the city hall there to have my name inscribed in the huge Book of Honour, a distinction which gives me considerable pride.

Right from the start road 9, narrow and rural, had one thing going for it. Except for infrequent convoys of concrete brick-carrying lorries, the route was devoid of heavy traffic and, beyond the junction for Krosno, we had the road virtually to ourselves. Soon after the suburbs of Rzeszow had faded the land began to change, imperceptively at first, bucking itself into gentle but definite hills while the villages took on alpine tendencies, the houses becoming substantial with wide overhanging eaves under which firewood was neatly stacked.

Thickly wooded as well as hilly the landscape hardly gave an impression of being oil-bearing. And, perched on a hill, the town of Krosno looked nothing like the petroleum capital of Poland which it undoubtedly is. However, for the time-being its mineral resources are under-exploited; the deposits small so it remains more rooted in the past than expectant of future riches. Not that Krosno's past is all that exciting. Founded in the fourteenth century and prospering during the Renaissance golden age – when it was sometimes referred to as 'Little Krakow' – it slid into decline before reviving in the mid-nineteenth century with the development of the oil industry. We only saw the place from a distance but could make out the town's historic core atop the hill, a remnant of its prosperous beginnings.

We were looking forward to being in the Carpathians. In fact I longed to be among hills and mountains after so much flatness where the occasional promise of a few hills was broken time and time again. The Carpathians were supposed to be the most mysterious mountains in Europe; the bulk of their ranges today falling within the borders of Romania, but, hopefully, these last kilometres in Poland and those across the eastern neck of Slovakia would be enlivened by something more than mere hills. The way into Slovakia was via the Dukla Pass which sounded encouraging.

After Krosno the road became trapped in a series of valleys. On either side soft green hills came closer, humped with dark patches of deciduous woods; up ahead the hills were blue and long-backed. The air was clear and cold after the prolonged rains and spasmodic sunshine varnished the broad blades of the maize leaves.

The region in which we found ourselves was known as the Beskid Niski, or Low Beskid, a hilly range stretching for some 85km along the Slovak frontier. Its people, like those further west in the Tatra ranges, are called *gorale, gora* meaning 'mountain'. Moulded by their harsh environment, the *gorale* are fiercely loyal to the land that nourishes them poorly but which gave them their roots and their pride. Tourism in the Tatras has, superficially at least, tamed the *gorale* and commercialism tainted their way of life but here in the Low Beskid the pride and individuality assumes, to foreign travellers like ourselves, the guise of hostility. Few Western visitors come this way.

Wooden villages with their small wooden Orthodox and Uniate churches are to be found in the region, though the ones we were to see stood on Slovak territory.

We found the township of Dukla to be a windy and somewhat bleak place – every bit the frontier town with its eerily half-deserted stage-set square.

Strategically located close to the Dukla Pass, the lowest and most easily accessible passage over the Western Carpathians, the town's situation brought it prosperity in the sixteenth century when it became a centre of the wine trade on the route from Hungary to the Baltic. But in the winter of 1944 Dukla's location ensured its destruction after one of the fiercest battles of World War Two in which the combined Soviet and Czechoslovak armies finally crushed the fanatical German defences, leaving a total of 100,000 soldiers dead.

Our road had been rising steadily for many miles though at Dukla, where we spent our last zlotys on provisions and ice-cream, there was still 17km to the top of the pass and the Slovak border. We camped in the forest 6km short of it, an uncomfortable site on sloping rock-impregnated ground with the inevitable rain returning with the dawn.

On both flanks of the summit were memorials and cemeteries together with Russian military hardware mounted on concrete plinths, so that this quietly beautiful area reeked of war and death. Alas, Poland in general is a country scarred by the cruelty of conflict, but it was sad that our last hours on Polish territory should be marred by these souvenirs and – for me – new memories of that terrible winter of 1944-45.

It took the German military authorities a month to discover that Gordon and I were not authorised inmates of Stalag VIIIB, during which time we took full advantage of the comparatively relaxed conditions. Our previous short spell there had been terminated by assignment to the work camp and now came the day when we were once again escorted by train to the purgatory of the mine. First, however, as punishment for our sins, we were subjected to two weeks solitary confinement on bread and water which was still more palatable than hacking coal out of the bowels of the earth. We served our sentence in a nearby Russian POW camp, the good inmates of which, though far worse off than their British counterparts, regularly passed us crusts of bread through the ventilation slits of our cells to supplement our punishment ration.

Our notoriety as escapees earned us the exclusive grade of 'dangerous characters' upon our return to the colliery; we having to display bright yellow distinguishing stripes on our clothing which singled us out for the meanest attentions and tasks. When an epidemic of diphtheria laid me low in the camp hospital I deemed it a blessing, of which Gordon was insanely jealous. However, when a crate of German beer was found under my bed I was straightway consigned back to work though hardly able to stand for which I was to wreak revenge with an act of sabotage to celebrate my 21st birthday. Christmas Day was a double – 16-hour – work shift at the coal face, and 1944 ended with the evacuation of Camp E902 and the participation of its personnel in what became known as 'The Death March'.

Here arose perhaps the most horrific episode in the whole of World War Two. The titanic sledgehammer of the Soviet armies had smashed westwards through eastern Poland pushing ahead phalanxes of human flotsam fleeing from unspeakable cruelties or driven by fanatical German authority away from potential liberation. No one could tell how many millions had fled. Even rough estimates were impossible in the general confusion. One could only guess at the scope of the migration of nations by looking at the roads of Silesia, Pomerania, East Prussia and much of Poland as caravan upon caravan, convoy upon convoy of refugees, prisoners, concentration camp victims and broken Wehrmacht units, haggard with exhaustion, wound through the intense cold and blinding snow in search of refuge.

The civilian population of these eastern nations did not commence its flight until the German front line had been shattered and the retreating columns of their rear echelons came racing through the towns and villages collecting in their wake a panic-stricken civilian army of despair spilling onto every road and highway to mingle with the beaten troops. Behind the raging battles this human tide rolled west and south in columns of tens of thousands, many to vanish without trace in the maelstrom of the collapse and the severe snow-storms that swept the countryside throughout the month of January; the uncountable swarms still growing larger from day to day.

This catastrophe, unparalleled in history, developed into a race against the Russian spearheads. From the end of December the icy storms – the worst for nearly a century – that had afflicted East Prussia gathered in strength and swept south into Poland and Silesia. Snowdrifts blocked the roads, temperatures plummeted to many degrees below freezing and the piercing cold numbed the senses. The white roads were black with treks of wagons, people and cattle moving at a snail's pace and, whenever the snow clouds lifted, made easy prey for Russian fighter aircraft that roamed the skies, as the endless treks crawled from village to village, from farm to farm vainly seeking succour. Those who died along the way – the old, the sick, the lame and the young – stayed where they fell, their frozen carcasses soon mercifully hidden by snow. In the villages the bodies of old men, women and babies lay on the streets frozen together in a final embrace.

We of Camp E902 were just one tiny fragment of this cataclysm. Escape would have been easy but death by freezing the certain reward, our stiffened corpses simply adding to the myriad others that, literally, made stepping stones through that snow-bound hell.

Thus, for us too, began a terrible time of mass wandering with those who looked upon the Oder river as the great divide beyond which lay comparative safety.

The hunger was appalling. We dug for edible scraps in villages half destroyed by maddened mobs desperate to find food among the houses and farms. Not even the cemeteries had been spared; their gravestones toppled over, the graves themselves dug into. We were fast becoming accustomed to horror yet were aghast at the spectacle of hunger-maddened crowds fighting for the exhumed portions of bodies amidst the litter of discarded clothing.

In our column alone, thousands-strong, we were a mixture of nationalities, chiefly British, Canadian and Russian. The Russian prisoners were treated with horrendous bestiality; they died in droves of starvation, cruelty and cold. Many had old rags tied round their feet in lieu of boots, their tattered overcoats held together with paper string. We did what we could to keep these poor ragged wretches moving, for stragglers were arbitrarily shot or bayoneted to death by the SS execution squad that formed the rear of every column. But we too were weak from malnutrition and, all too often, our weakness prevailed as we dragged along those pitiful wrecks, exhorting them to greater efforts in a tongue they couldn't understand. One by one we were forced to leave them to their fate, an act that nourished a fierce hatred for our captors and an ineffable sadness; the silent tears freezing to our faces.

To the east, Marshal Koniev's Red Army legions advanced remorselessly, sweeping aside the attempted delaying actions of the retreating German army. The reports I heard of the conduct of the victorious multitude amounted to uncontrolled savagery which could only spur on the tidal waves of humanity before them. These reports – many undoubtedly true – were of murder, rape, looting and deportation on a titanic scale. The columns were strangely silent, and this made them unutterably sad. Villagers, uncomprehending, stood in front of their houses, stiff with fright, watching the ghostly procession of shuffling, misery-laden people.

Occasionally we were overtaken by remnants of disciplined units of the Wehrmacht, their faces as grey as their uniforms; mere ghosts rather than men. There were also refugee-soldiers amongst our shambling ranks; soldiers without rifles, without ammunition, without hope; worn out and despondent, having been pursued by forces outnumbering them fifteen to one.

In the early stages of the huge evacuation the prisoner columns were marched through the night, the Germans being anxious to get their charges west of the Oder. Thereafter came irregular overnight halts at commandeered farms where prisoners found what shelter they could in farm buildings. Food remained virtually non-existent and many a time we were forced to resort to rooting in the mud of pigsties for remnants of sugarbeet or swede spurned by the long-gone pigs themselves. As more and more men succumbed to the elements so hand-pulled carts were utilised to carry them. But such bone-shaking transportation had to be a last resort since the risk of hypothermia was as high as that of being eliminated by the end-of-column executioners. At one point I suffered a bad attack of dysentery that was within a hair's-breadth of causing my extinction. With the onset of each successive attack I would attempt to increase speed to position myself as near the head of the column as possible, then move aside to squat in the snow there to drop my guts while watching for the tail. Whether I had completed my business or not there was no alternative but to rise and, with bare legs streaming with liquid excrement, pull up my trousers and rejoin the ranks. Once I nearly left things too late, seeing an SS trooper unsling and cock his rifle and make towards me. At least I might have rated a shot in the neck or head; for many of my fellow-trekkers their end was not even deemed to be worth a bullet.

Brutality was commonplace as we dragged our footsteps across the last kilometres of Polish soil; beatings with rifle butts, shootings and bayonetings rife. But another climax of nausea for me was something I witnessed outside the town of Raciborz where victims of the concentration camp there deemed too weak to be evacuated were being systematically exterminated. Our column, miles long, was held up at the Oder bridge as Russian aircraft vainly strafed it and, together with others, I found myself standing opposite a yard of the camp. In batches of about fifty, lines of human beings, naked in the snow, unrecognisable as men or women, tottered like mechanical dolls before a bullet-scarred wall there to stand in resigned silence to be mown down by machine-guns. The faces of those poor wretches will remain etched in my mind to my own dying day, each devoid of any human emotion whatsoever. And as one line fell, another shuffled forward to take its place. If any emotion did momentarily flicker across those withered faces it must have been simple relief that the suffering was at an end. I turned away from the dreadful sight to perceive our German sergeant major – a veteran of the Eastern Front – retching in the ditch. Scores of my fellow-compatriots had been witness to the scene and their anger spread through the column like a forest fire, the growl of an uncontrollable fury rising among them. The guards were quick to appreciate the danger and hurried us on.

By the end of February the worst excesses of the hideous exodus were behind us and the survivors of our columns dragged themselves onto the soil of Czechoslovakia in their countless thousands.

Chapter 5
Eastern Slovakia and North-eastern Hungary

One inalienable factor about topography is that what goes up must come down, and it was exuberantly, freewheeling down the other side of the Dukla Pass on the soil of Slovakia, a newly independent country which, six months before, had been the easternmost province of Czechoslovakia.

Though there were queues of cars on both sides of the border even at this early hour Paul and I on our bicycles were waved straight through both sets of control posts with no more than a glance at our passports. Massed clouds, bruised purple and yellow as if by weight of snow, advanced across the ridges of the surrounding hills and spots of rain together with an ice-cold wind welcomed us into the Carpathians.

At the Ruthenian village of Vys Komarnik, a couple of kilometres inside the border, we paused to investigate its wooden church which, sadly, was firmly closed. I went in search of a key I thought might have been in the hands of the owners of the nearest of a line of timber houses, but nobody was at home. Poles and Slovaks call this type of house *chalupa*; it is sculpted from spruce and fir logs and held together by no more than a superb fit. Curiosity overcoming my reticence, I squinted through the windows and so gained an insight into the layout of the house made up of a hall, a back room for everyday living and, as in many British houses, a front room used for social occasions, this one dominated by an outsize bed piled high with embroidered pillows. Neighbouring houses displayed carved beams, pegged doorways, and little crosses of some probable mystical meaning. The area here is dotted with such Ruthenian villages, their inhabitants forming a considerable minority in the far east of Slovakia, Ruthenia itself having been forcibly incorporated into the Soviet Union in 1945.

We had entered a strange corner of eastern Europe that sees few visitors. Its roots are jumbled with the destinies of neighbouring states and long-dead empires to a bewildering degree. The Czechs and Slovaks were once controlled by the Austro-Hungarian Empire, a Western power, even though many of its people to the east held a separate cultural heritage. The Czechs and Slovaks however are Slavs while the Hungarians are Magyars, with an entirely different ancestry and linguistic background to any other central and eastern European nation. On the other hand, the Polish and Czech Crown were once the same, under Wenceslas II, and even Hungary was briefly added to his family's domain when Wenceslas's son was offered the Hungarian crown in 1301. Ruthenia itself had been Hungarian, Czechoslovak, Russian and, now, Ukrainian. For just 24 hours it was an independent nation before Germany authorised annexation by Hungary in 1939.

Since Prešov, our next urban centre that promised a hotel bed, was but 112 kilometres away and we had no need or desire to reach it until the following morning, there was ample time to dawdle. This gave Paul opportunity to inspect and speculate upon every T34 tank, fighter aircraft and artillery piece that rusted away among the cornflowers and primroses. But the cold and an enticing highway bright with white-painted lane markings upon its smooth tarmac – probably to impress arriving Poles – encouraged us onwards.

Much as we had been looking forward to mountainous terrain the long downhill proceeded to degenerate into a fitful spasm of ascent and descent which our uncomfortable night and lack of proper sleep made exceedingly trying. Usually I was only too glad to dismount and walk but some of the sharp inclines experienced here, and in later Carpathian terrain made pushing a heavily laden bike exhausting. Bursts of driving rain made things no easier.

At Svidnik we made efforts to acquire some local currency but could find no bank though a hotel, which would accept no Western currency except dollars, produced old Czech notes overstamped with the Slovak imprint, forerunner of the new paper currency. Giraltovce, the next township, excelled with a fine lunch in spite of everything closing down on the stroke of midday as we arrived there. It was a Saturday and the early closing of supermarkets, restaurants and shops irks many people in the Czech and Slovak lands, and it certainly irked us. Drowning our sorrows in a bar we were bemoaning our luck to the barman when a young man approached and offered to find us a meal. Paying for our beer, he led us to the best restaurant in town, unlocked the door, sat us at one of the empty tables and proceeded to cook us a substantial lunch of unlimited soup and Wiener Schnitzel with potatoes all for the equivalent of about £1.25. Other potential diners watched enviously outside the door but failed to gain admission.

Under storm clouds and intermittent showers we pushed our heavy bikes up an interminable hill outside the town and, a few kilometres short of Kapusany, espied a sizeable wood we deemed suitable for overnight camping though to reach it necessitated an uncomfortable struggle across muddy and water-logged meadows. All around was engaging mini-alpine scenery of tree-clad hills looking sadly dismal under the prevailing weather.

A leaf-mould padded ground and no more than a few drops of rain contributed to a better night's sleep, the dawn generating a damp mist together with a promise of sunshine to come. And the promise held. At Kapusany we were stopped in our tracks by the sight of a dramatic castle floating in the air, the hill on which it stood being hidden by a band of mist that matched the departing morning cloud.

The suburbs of Prešov early on that Sunday morning offered the impression of a ghost-town; no traffic, no people and deserted tramlines. Paul's eyes were only for a Czech Air Force graveyard of derelict MIGs and other military aircraft lined up as if on parade, a sure reflection of the collapse of the Cold War.

Even the centre was devoid of life when we reached it and we had to wait several hours for our room at Cedok's Dukla Hotel to become vacant. But our bikes were taken into store leaving us free to explore this most agreeable little city.

Slowly the place awoke with knots of citizens – mostly family groups – in their Sunday best, making their way to the three main churches. In our none-too-clean shorts we felt the heathens we were, preferring to patronise one of those stand-up 'bufets', so popular in central Europe, there to assuage our appetites with a hot meal of *knedliky* (dumplings), meat and sauerkraut which, with a pint of good Slovak beer, cost us all of 60 pence.

The historic heart of Prešov contains many fine ecclesiastical buildings including the late Gothic St Nicholas Church, the lovely fifteenth-century Renaissance Orthodox Church and the Baroque Evangelical Church of a later period. All were full to overflowing with fervent worshippers, many kneeling on the gravel outside. And this notwithstanding the fact that the three churches represented three different Christian sects. A very much more religious crowd are the Slovaks compared to their Moravian and Bohemian neighbours.

The compact city is the centre of Ukrainian culture in Slovakia, the Ukraine itself being little more than 100km to the east. Its other claim to fame is somewhat controversial now that the communists have been ousted from power. It was here, in 1919, that enthusiastic comrades first established their own Slovak Soviet Republic, just 17 months after the Bolshevik Revolution in Russia. This early attempt at communism lasted only three weeks, however, being in fact a method by the Hungarian Red Army under the notorious Bela Kun to win back Slovakia from the newly formed Czechoslovak Republic. Although the black wrought-iron balcony from which the clench-fisted firebrands harangued the crowds is still ceremoniously flood-lit at night the name of the street was changed from Slovak Soviet Republic to an uncontroversial Main Street in 1990. Interestingly, the museum nearby still tells the tale of the SSR from a heavily Marxist perspective, old habits dying hard in a town where remnants of communism had not quite expired.

The Dukla Hotel, an unlovely oblong block of a building, was better than its appearance denoted, our bedroom balcony catching the full blast of a brilliant sun set in an impossibly blue sky. Another scrubbing session of selves and garments undertaken, our laundry was put out to dry on the balcony railings no doubt shocking further the God-fearing burghers of Prešov promenading in the modern opera-house square below.

Late in the afternoon we were invited for an orangeade by a student who was keen to practise his English on two rare British visitors. Beneath the striped awning of the open-air cafe we asked his opinion of the separation of his country from what has since become the Czech Republic. In company with many of his countrymen he was strongly against the undertaking, expressing the view that it would bring disaster in its wake. "We were not even asked whether we wanted the split; it was just imposed upon us by our new government in spite of the fact that many of us are against it," was his bitter comment.

"Why didn't you all make your views known?" I asked. "I don't remember reading about any demonstrations against the decision."

The student shrugged. "We are a peaceful easy-going people," he replied, "we would never stoop to violence. Anyway demonstrating is something we've never been allowed to do these last 40 years so we're unaccustomed to it. And there are powerful people amongst us who *do* want independence and who have good arguments to support it for, over the years, the Czechs *have* treated us as the poor relation both morally and economically. But now with threats of further splits within the country – our considerable Hungarian minority wanting their own nationhood for instance – we just won't be able to go it alone. And look at our out-of-date Soviet-built factories, lack of raw materials and even our geographical location stuck deep into eastern Europe far from the influence of – and maybe help from – the West."

Separated from the Czech lands by history, language and culture the new republic walks an uncertain line between one-time province and newly born nation. Controlled by Hungary since the tenth century, the Slav peasantry here was long dominated by the Hungarian nobility. Only with the birth of a Slav nationalist movement in the nineteenth century and with the redrawing of the map of central Europe following World War One did Slovakia come to be linked with Bohemia and Moravia. Briefly independent under a puppet government after Hitler's annexation of the western two-thirds of Czechoslovakia, the region experienced rapid development during the decades of communist rule. With most of the Jewish population 'removed' by the Nazis, there remains a mixed population of not only Slovaks but Czechs, Germans, Hungarians, Ruthenians and Gypsies, not a community exhibiting a high degree of mutual brotherly love.

But for me Slovakia, together with the Czech Republic, will always remain a nation I have known as 'Czechoslovakia', and for more than half a century my destiny has been inexorably linked with it.

By the end of February 1945 the worse excesses of the horrendous exodus were behind us and the magic of spring was in the air. The snows had receded and we had entered a land whose populace looked upon us with infinite compassion. Our German overseers beheld a solution to the almost unsurmountable supply problem and permitted Czech bread and soup, in restricted quantities, to be distributed as the columns ground westwards. Overnight accommodation in the larger Czech farms with their easily guarded and spacious barns became a regular feature of the 'Death March', their hay and straw storage greatly appreciated for the warmth and snug comfort it generated.

With the improvement in conditions Gordon and I began re-assessing the practicalities of another escape. The daily marching stint of 15 to 20 miles remained a gruelling ordeal for our wasted frames, its only heartening aspect being that every step was taking us closer to the Allied armies now on the western frontiers of Germany. We were also aware that our route would eventually lead us out of Czech territory onto that of Germany and an assured renewed deterioration in our treatment. Thus the attraction of remaining on Czechoslovak soil was strong.

The execution of another escape, however, was not going to be so easy. The guards had become more watchful and in the flat, open countryside of Moravia and Bohemia there was little hope of a sudden dash from the column. This left the alternative of a breakout from or self-concealment within, a farm; one or other action we proposed to take as soon as the opportunity arose. Initially the circumstances required for both refused to materialise. Either the Germans were too skilful with the placing of their guards or the props of concealment were too poor. To secrete ourselves in the hay or straw storage of a barn was an obvious method – though it would be equally obvious to the Germans. And time and time again the size of a storage stack failed to meet our exacting specifications.

Until, that is, suddenly there it was, a barn and its contents meeting all our requirements. Within minutes, several hundred captive soldiers turned the solidly constructed building into a seething ant-heap of tired and irritable humanity staking claims to bed-space. Gordon and I, with mounting excitement, threw ourselves down upon the springy hay well content with the dimensions of the stack and resolved to dig our way deep in to its core before the subsequent dawn. To undertake this task necessitated the help and trust of a third party and, in this, we were lucky to enlist the services of a Durham Light Infantry corporal, a farmer's lad no less.

And so it transpired that, when the others had descended to the ground to acquire the meagre issue of bread and acorn 'coffee', the sole food for the day, we burrowed down into the musty interior of the stack close to the slatted timber barn walls so as to extract what little extra air we could. Our colleague then stamped wads of hay down on top of us so that the composition at the surface would remain uniform.

Judging our depth to be adequate and out of range of the long bayonets with which the German search party would probe the stack following discovery of our absence, we waited, our hearts palpitating with the effort, anticipation and lack of air. From the outside came muffled sounds of movement as our compatriots prepared for yet another day of trudging.

Hours later – or so it seemed – I heard a door crash open and disjointed voices with no words percolated through to our ears. Then a pause, a prolonged pause. Were our jailers giving up the search already? There came vibrations as heavy boots scaled a ladder. More voices, closer now and distinguishable as German, and the thud of feet above our heads coupled with a slight vibration of the stack. A shouted warning and the scything motion of jabbing bayonets began. Obeying a reflex reaction we squeezed into balls to make smaller targets of ourselves.

Fear had me within an ace of giving up and scrabbling to the surface but the knowledge that I would be betraying my companion became the stronger emotion. Above and around us the long knives prodded deep and methodically.

The new vibration made by a descent of the ladder was sweet music in our ears. I whispered encouragingly to Gordon. The barn doors closed indicating the departure of the search party but we were taking no chances – the ruse by which searchers would pretend to leave but actually remain behind was known to us. We lay motionless, determined to stick things out for another hour or two even after the sound of multiple tramping feet had faded into the distance.

In the event our caution was misplaced. We were on the point of scrambling to the surface when an unholy uproar broke out. The barn doors crashed open again to herald the rustle and shudder of numerous bodies mounting the stack. We froze, perplexed and worried. Words drifted to us; words which were not German nor English, but which, having listened hard, I concluded were Serbo-Croat. The realisation struck. Another column of prisoners had arrived to take over the farm for the night. Alarm was tempered with relief. At least Yugoslavs were allies; we had nothing to fear from them.

The expression on the face of the Serbian sergeant as we emerged, two hay-covered figures, from beneath his nose was one of incredulity. Recovering, he swiftly came to terms with the situation and within the hour he and his colleagues were feeding us morsels of food from their German-issued rations. To be released from our stifling confinement was a welcome respite, even though, in theory, we had become captives again. But the new set of German guards were oblivious of the fact that they had gained a couple of prisoners and we ensured it stayed that way. For the rest of the day and over the following night we remained firmly atop the stack, moving no further than the wall to answer the calls of nature.

In the morning we re-buried ourselves. There was no need to go deep; just enough to allay the suspicions of any checking guard. And there we waited for the noisy departure of our hosts, determined to delay our final getaway no longer than necessary in case the next visitation was Russian.

Twenty minutes we allowed ourselves, then again surfaced. All was quiet within the familiar confines of the building as we descended to the ground and tiptoed to the open door. So accustomed were we to crowds that our initial sensation was of a peculiar loneliness. The farmyard too was deserted. Sunshine bathed the peaceful countryside, mottled with unmelted snow, in a gentle warmth. The hum of a distant tractor reminded me of home.

This time round our evasion tactics were likely to run a different course since we were on the territory of a sympathetic populace though aware of the terrible risks it ran by offering succour to the likes of us. In Poland we had had an objective: the Russian lines. Here in Bohemia all liberating agencies were out of reach. Gordon strongly favoured making for Prague, barely 30 miles distant, with the notion that contact with the partisan movement would be easier in the city. I was for sticking to rural climes. To finish the war with a Czech resistance group seemed a worthwhile pursuit; on that we were firmly in agreement. All along I had been making the decisions so felt it time to give Gordon his head. The loneliness still persisted as we set out for the Czech capital.

The two weeks that followed were, to some extent, fruitless in endeavour, but were to mark a milestone in my life. We reached the city with little difficulty, keeping away from main roads and knocking on the doors of houses to request bread whenever the pangs of hunger became unbearable.

What remained of our uniforms was hardly recognisable as such though our regulation boots, stained and grubby battledress trousers, and the identity discs around our necks could save us from a firing squad in the event of recapture. We both wore thick pullovers, removed, weeks before, from bodies whose need of them had long ceased. They too were liberally soiled; the most unmilitary of garments.

Usually our appearance on the doorstep of a Czech home produced consternation but seldom were we to leave without a hunk of bread or slice of cake being thrust into our hands by the occupants even though their fright was painful to behold. In one habitation, however, a farm labourer was bold enough to invite us inside for a steaming plate of dumplings which we devoured greedily, clumsily wielding unaccustomed knives and forks. Watching our performance, the man's wife, composed and distant earlier, abruptly broke down and wept as she perceived our hunger and condition, imploring us to sleep on the sofa after the meal. But the awful danger of German retribution was foremost in our minds, sending us hurrying away.

The urban spread of Prague reached out to us the second day. Another barn, into which we had broken, provided a familiar night's shelter and in the morning we had run full tilt into the owner as we departed. A large burly fellow, he first upbraided us for trespassing and then, upon learning our identity, for not having asked him for a bed. We tried to explain the risks but he would have none of it. In compensation he insisted we come into his house for a bath and breakfast — and in that order. I hadn't realised we smelt so high.

For the final kilometres into the city proper we followed the Vltava river which provided a good navigational aid. Progress through a maze of building estates and allotments became tortuous, though once accustomed again to walking openly in crowded streets, we discovered genuine enjoyment. I had not forgotten the events that led to the termination of our previous bout of freedom. As in Cracow, there would be a curfew imposed in the city after dark so we would have to be off the streets by dusk.

In the centre the drab office buildings and grimy historic edifices hemmed us in; the people, equally drab, hurried by. We seemed to be the only dawdlers and therefore likely to be the more conspicuous but nobody, not even the German soldiery we saw, took the slightest notice of us. There was little traffic, with most of it military, and the peculiar smell of low-octane petrol mixed with that of boiled cabbage assailed our nostrils as it had in Poland. Crowded trams lurched and clattered by at irregular intervals.

Having attained Prague, the next move became obscure. Though Gordon had been the instigator of our going there, he now was even less certain what to do than I. To cover his own confusion he brought matters to a head by selecting a house virtually at random at which to apply for assistance.

The middle-aged lady who answered the summons gave no hint of surprise or fear even when we revealed our nationality. I had been ready to run for it had she started yelling blue murder but, instead, she ushered us into the house without a word. In the gloom I jumped at the silent presence of a tall, soldierly-looking man who stood against the wall and who had, so the notion struck me, vetted us before allowing his wife to let us in.

Over a decanter of red wine we told our story. Our hosts listened attentively; both could understand and speak English. They were obviously a well-to-do couple but I knew better than to ask for details of their lives. For their part they were not slow to offer advice as to what we ought to do, making it plain that we should get out of Prague fast since it was a hotbed of Gestapo agents and informers. The man suggested we make our way due west towards the industrial region of Kladno, a reputed centre of resistance to the German occupation. Against our better judgement we accepted the couple's invitation to remain with them overnight; the prospect of a real bed was too much to resist. And anyway, with the curfew hour approaching, what was the alternative?

The night was memorable for soft clean linen, and fortified next morning by a giant cooked breakfast we took our leave of a nameless man and woman who had risked their lives for two strangers knocking at their door.

We had been given a map which offered invaluable information once we had cleared the central districts of the city and, swinging south, had taken once more to the open fields. The provision of food for the day was no problem since our good benefactors had supplied us with thick cheese sandwiches, but we nearly came unstuck that night when trying to locate shelter in what turned out to be a village police station. The law must have been as taken aback as we were and it is quite possible it would have been willing to find us the night's shelter we craved. But we were taking no chances. Beating a hasty retreat we finished up by breaking into another barn.

The next day found us hovering around the perimeter of a neighbourhood of smoking chimneys our map confirmed as Kladno, but it gave no inkling of the fact that I was upon the threshold of the incident that was to change the course of my life.

It began to rain about mid-morning. It spat in my face, never continuous but like bursts of misdirected cold gunfire before the wind blew it away. The sky was low with grey cloud and it seemed to me, as the two of us walked between the tall featureless houses, the whole of Kladno was closing in on us like a trap. Walking there in the rain I felt again that extraordinary loneliness, a loneliness that exaggerated the hopelessness and frustration within me so that it was as if the wind, the cold whip of rain and the dismal streets were combining against us. I caught the whiff and sound, as we drew near the industrial sector of the town, from a locomotive shunting wagons within the compound of a steel works.

Beside me Gordon cursed the weather in his expressive London-Scottish brogue. The hostility of the streets merged into a single heavy nausea that was like a sickness – a sickness to be home, in England, safe, away from it all. I longed bitterly to be out of the mess we had got ourselves into, out of Czechoslovakia, out of an environment in which you never knew if a fellow-human was a friend or foe. But England was but a tiny speck of light a long way down the tunnel. If we stayed alive we'd make it eventually but the war could drag on for months and the present alternative to this ridiculous evasion exercise was simply a return to the endless trudging along the destinationless road of central Europe.

We stalked through the centre of the uninviting town, skirting the grey slag-heaps to veer off to the north seeing small hope of succour among the lines of mean houses. Clear of the urban clutter we received a glass of milk and a hunk of dry bread from a frightened householder in a lone cottage. Increasingly we hated ourselves for having to compromise these decent people but, other than a resort to open robbery in a friendly country, there was nothing else we could do.

By evening we were close to a village called Smecno and, failing to break into one of its barns, spent a miserable night in a damp ditch. The night was a repetition of the day, wet, squally and cold, all of which sped us on our way by dawn. On our way to what? A road tried to entice us towards the town of Slaný but we had had our fill of towns so declined its appeal to find ourselves in a shallow valley that bordered it. Slaný, however, refused to be ignored altogether, its western outskirts engulfing us. The world looked peaceful, the war far away, as the sound of tinkling harness came over the still air. It was late afternoon with men and women wending their way homeward after a hard day's work in the fields. I felt like one of them – only we had no home to go to.

A shout had us instantly on our guard. Unsure if it was directed at us, and wary of its reason, we ignored the summons. The shout was repeated and we recognised the word Anglicky (English). Hesitatingly we turned to behold a middle-aged bespectacled man who had emerged from the gate of a house and was beckoning to us. Obeying the summons in the hope that his broadcasting of our nationality would cease, we approached. "You are English soldiers", he said in poor German, grinning hugely, and I wasn't sure if it was a question or a statement. The chap wore a sober dark suit and a countenance that put me in mind of a characterisation of a bank manager. We were given to understand that we were invited into his home for refreshment.

Surprised at the lack of caution displayed, we complied and were treated to glasses of milk and a plate of mutton and potatoes. During the meal in a homely kitchen-living room we were joined by the man's wife, a small woman with kind eyes who spoke no German. We attempted to explain our situation but on the subject of enlisting in the partisans the man looked doubtful. But so far as our immediate well-being was concerned he came up trumps with the suggestion of a nearby hiding place in which we could lay up indefinitely, provisions being brought to us at regular intervals. We were immensely encouraged by this offer, having no desire to compromise the couple by remaining in their house longer than necessary. With the coming of dusk we were led away to a quarry within which, neatly tucked away, were a trio of shallow cavities. Leaving us to select a suitable one in which to take up residence the man later returned with an armful of old blankets.

Under the fading daylight Gordon and I set to work spreading them inside the mouth of the largest cavity which was big enough to hold the two of us inside its lip. When lying flat we were not easy to spot from outside, particularly since the quarry itself was hidden by a fold of land.

Settling down amongst the blankets we basked in this sudden upturn in our fortunes. Given the reliability of the promises we saw no reason for not remaining in and around our bolt-hole until eventual contact with the partisans or arrival of a liberating army could be achieved. Highly satisfied with the new situation we slept easier that night in spite of the cold hard ground.

Broad daylight opened my eyes to look upon the girl standing hesitatingly before the cave-mouth. She must have seen me stir but made no move away. She had a bicycle with her, a wicker basket clamped to its handlebars; I noticed – for no good reason – that one of the hand grips was pressing against her body, crinkling the dress she wore into shadow. She was dark, and her eyes, big and bright and blue, did not move either.

"Hello. I'm English." I said fatuously.

It was all I could think of to say. A combination of extreme fatigue and awareness of vulnerability eclipsed a more original remark by way of explanation of how two very dirty British soldiers came to be sleeping in a quarry in daylight. Beside me Gordon began the process of awakening.

The girl did not speak and I was struck in an extraordinary way by her silence and her motionlessness. There was nothing passive about it. Her stance was strong and definite and I knew that she was not afraid.

"Will you please not tell anyone that you have seen us," I went on, wondering if she would understand.

"Of course." She spoke in English with a calmness that surprised me. It was as if stray British prisoners deep in enemy territory were part of the landscape. "You have a good place to hide. Stay there and we'll do what we can to help."

She momentarily transferred her steady gaze to Gordon as he struggled upright, surprised as I was by the apparition. Then she delved into her basket and brought out some bread and meat wrapped in a cloth together with a flask which she passed to us. As she came close I caught the whiff of scent and saw in her face a perplexity of pleasure and shyness. I became abruptly aware of her youthful beauty.

She spoke again. "You are English, I know. Father has told me about you both. He likes to think you are his secret." The girl laughed quietly, her lips slightly parted in a kind of challenge. Only then did I realise that she was the daughter of our new benefactor.

Both Gordon and I emerged from cover and rose to our feet. Her eyes did not waver. I half expected Gordon to jump to the defence of his Scottish ancestry as was his wont but he remained, for once, mute.

"You are very kind," I replied, "but please be careful. What you are doing is dangerous." I approved of her use of my language, particularly the mid-European accent that invariably makes it sound more attractive. I wanted to hear it again. "What do you do?" I asked.

I was referring to her profession but she misunderstood. "I've been delivering cakes to the prisoners this last day or two. There are so many of them and the poor things are so hungry." As she spoke I noted afresh the slightly parted lips. Her eyes were fastened upon mine.

My mind was jolted back to practicalities. "What prisoners?" I asked sharply, suddenly aware that there might be other evaders in the vicinity.

The girl stared in surprise. "The roads are full of them. The Germans are making them march towards the west. Sometimes they allow us to give them a little food."

How out of touch we were becoming. Aeons ago we too had been among the herds of captives being evacuated away from the Russian front in the east. The columns must still be going through. "Of course. I was forgetting," I finished lamely.

"How old are you?" came Gordon's foray into the conversation with a soldier's directness.

"I'm eighteen." She switched her gaze back to him and I resented it.

I spoke again. "Do you work in Slaný?"

It seemed the only relevant question left I could put. I desperately wanted her to stay.

"I'm at college there but sometimes we have time off."

"You speak very good English. How do you manage that?"

"Thank you", came the reply. "I learn only from books as the Germans don't encourage it to be taught in the schools. So much I would like to visit England to improve my pronunciation. Perhaps one day it will be possible."

"Please come," I exclaimed with a fervour that surprised me. "You'd be very welcome."

"I should like that," came the quiet reply. She smiled and changed the subject. "My mother and father want both of you to come and have supper with us. Please come to the house as soon as it's dark. You know where it is."

"Will you be there?"

"Of course."

My mind was in a turmoil of emotions. Pleasure at the prospect of seeing her again, anguish for the danger the whole family would be incurring, incredulity that she should want to continue this fragile acquaintanceship. A strange excitement coursed through me.

"Have you any sisters?" broke in the irrepressible Gordon.

The girl smiled anew. "Two," she told him and began explaining why they were both away from home.

I watched every movement of her lips, every change of expression on her face as if mesmerised. She appeared younger than eighteen but self-assured with it and she held herself erect like a soldier; a real soldier not a prisoner. She bent over to adjust the position of her bicycle pedal and I noticed her legs were strong and smooth. Her neck had a contrasting fairness below the fall of her dark hair.

"I must go now. People occasionally come this way," she said and I detected a note of reluctance in her voice. "But we'll meet this evening."

In silence we watched her go. The loneliness I had felt earlier returned but this time it hurt.

The hours were leaden as we waited for the dusk. Most of the time we remained partly hidden in the quarry afraid to jeopardise our position. Only when the daylight melted into shadow did we breach cover and make our way towards the town.

The house seemed larger than it had the first time we had seen it. I half-hoped it would be the girl who would greet us but it was her father, obviously on the look-out, who opened the door. In the kitchen all was activity; the girl and her mother busy with the preparation of the meal.

We dined lavishly – or at least as lavishly as the strict rationing in a Nazi-occupied country would allow – and for a blissful couple of hours the war and its consequences were forgotten. Every now and then I looked across the table at the girl – again I knew better than to ask her name – who acted as interpreter for us and her parents. I watched her brows knit in perplexity as she wrestled with a strange language and saw her eyes full of a sort of indecisive wonder. Amidst interruptions from Gordon I tried to tell her and her parents about my home, family and myself. My monologue made up, in part, for what I knew would be a deficiency of what they dared tell us about themselves in return. Supported by Gordon, I attempted to express our gratitude for their help and kindness, but all the time, whenever I was speaking, I felt the undercurrents and noticed everyone around me listening, as it were, for a sound from outside; the knock at the door.

The meal over, I asked the girl if we would see her again at the quarry. She made a tiny gesture of dismay. "I have to go back to college tomorrow," she explained and I felt the bottom fall out of my world. I touched her hair briefly and, with Gordon following, slipped out into the night.

Our outlaw existence continued but, for me, a new and vital element was missing. The girl's father, and sometimes mother, brought the provisions daily but it wasn't the same. We had told them of our wish to join the partisans but nothing came of it so, more to counter our boredom and frustration, decided to undertake a little resistance work ourselves. We had found a railway line on our sorties from the quarry which would make a suitable target for our attentions.

Perhaps fortunately for all concerned the tools we had 'borrowed' from a barn nearby failed to fit the bolt heads of the rail shoes so we turned to the telephone wires that accompanied the track. The pliers did a better job and by shinning up a pole we brought the whole lot down. Heaven knows what else we would have got up to had we remained at large for longer than a week, our petty acts of sabotage merely putting at risk and inconvenience the local populace rather then the enemy.

It could well have been those trailing telephone lines that finally terminated our aimless existence. The fact remains that, one morning, we were visited by two apologetic members of the local constabulary. We had no chance to take evasive action for we were still beneath our blankets when the two policemen appeared at the cavity mouth.

A small assembly of locals watched in silence, some making surreptitious movements of encouragements with their hands, as we were escorted to the police vehicle on the road nearest to the quarry. The notion came to me that our presence among our nearest neighbours had been well-known; that the two

'*Anglicky*' in their cave had become an accepted part of the community. Maybe it had even been one of them who had decided we had been around long enough.

Our brief incarceration in Slaný's jail was not a great ordeal. We shared a cell with a sorry specimen of Russian soldiery afflicted by lice, to whom we donated most of our prison fodder; his need being greater than ours.

A few days later we were taken to the main square of the town. Again people stared at us with more sympathy than curiosity. We stood there, by the side of the road, our police guard shuffling his feet with embarrassment, until a ragged column of khaki-clad figures we recognised as yet another prison column came into view. At its head strode a German army officer and our escort sprang to attention. The officer pointed a finger towards the shuffling ranks and, aided by a push, we found ourselves back with the nomads of the road to nowhere.

It was as if the last two weeks had never happened.

Our new compatriots were from camps in eastern Bohemia and Moravia that had only recently been evacuated. They had avoided the worst atrocities of the '*Death March*' and were reasonably fresh and well organised. With them we began a new trek westwards.

But as we marched I had a new experience to ponder. There was something about the girl from Slaný that was intensely disturbing. Repeatedly I chided myself for being an impressionable and sentimental fool but her image would not go away – nor did I want it to. Was it or was it not my imagination or wishful thinking that she had given the impression of wanting to know me better? I probed my innermost thoughts, frantically attempting to separate cold reason from warm fantasy. Deep down in my soul I knew I could not leave matters like this. I knew I had to see the girl again if only to appease my torment. In the meantime, with a heavy heart, I lamented the fact that, though every step we were taking was one nearer the Allied armies it also was one further away from the object of my infatuation.

The current march came to an end in Bavaria, at the small town of Plattling where we were put to work in a glue factory. It was an odious place of work, the chief ingredient of glue being bone; and in the Greater Germany of 1945 this commodity was in plentiful supply.

From glue manufacture we were switched to track maintenance in Plattling's significant railway junction just in time for it, as well as the town, to be laid waste by a tight formation of some 400 USAF bombers. I had been busy leaning on my shovel in the very heart of the target area when the bombers struck, my life assuredly being saved by the proximity of a heavy-duty locomotive under which I, together with the young and terrified German light flak crew, took refuge.

Thereafter, all work on the railway ceased and, within hours, rescue parties and demolition squads were formed from the camp inmates together with political prisoners – tottering skeletons in threadbare striped suits – from a nearby concentration camp and put to work among the still-burning ruins. A train containing a consignment of Red Cross food parcels lying amongst the wreckage of the railway yards became the centre of attraction for soldiers, prisoners and *civilians alike. Even when SS guards were placed around it and would-be looters threatened with instant execution, the efforts of hungry people to collect the scattered goodies continue unabated. For five days we worked unceasingly in the gutted town unearthing buried victims alive and dead from collapsed buildings which included an air-raid bunker that had received a direct hit. I was given the task, in company with a couple of partly-alive Ukrainians, of removing the dead. Some hundreds of men, women and children had been jammed together in the shelter when the blow had struck; the heat had seared the closely-packed bodies, peeling off clothing and turning their skin black. Where the bomb had penetrated the concrete chamber nothing recognisable as human remained except for the odd limb amongst a dark syrupy substance. We laid the more complete corpses out in rows before, thankfully, being directed to less sickening tasks.*

Though a second raid seemed unlikely the sound of an aeroplane was enough to send much of the surviving population streaming into the open fields and even our own guards sometimes melted away for a while on the assumption that discretion was wiser than valour. The SS guards on the parcel train stood their ground however so the pilfering of the odd scattered chocolate bar or tin of spam became a dangerous game.

The granting of permission by the German camp commandant for his prisoners to remove some of the parcels was more a method of overcoming his not inconsiderable provisioning problem than an act of generosity but there was another purpose behind it too which was to meet with a howl of protest. One day the second week in April we were informed that, because of the threat imposed by the advancing American Third Army plus the fact of our now being well-victualled, we were to continue the march – eastwards, and away from the Americans.

Food having been for so long the pivot of our existence, the biggest problem that arose was that of the means of transporting our precious parcels. Handcarts, trolleys and a host of miscellaneous vehicles materialised as we bartered and stole while on our last work shift in the town. Gordon and I, however, were singularly unlucky in these endeavours, having to make do with a sickly wheelbarrow.

The first mile proved its uselessness, the solitary wheel emitting constant oil-demanding squeaks as we alternated in turn to lift, heave and push the thing along.

Five, six, eight and more kilometres we struggled, being overtaken all the time by compatriots with more efficient devices. Jettisoning some or all the cargo offered the only solution but gluttony can be a powerful persuasive when the memory of starvation is recent. Gordon must have been of the same sentiment for he took the words right out of my mouth when he said, "Let's get the hell out of this!" Thus our final escape was born of both gluttony and futility. And in its execution we were aided by the hand of providence.

The guards were more tolerant in their duties than had been the case earlier. The war in Europe was plainly drawing to a close and it wasn't their side who were going to win it. But that was not to say they'd let us simply walk away; there was still the odd firebrand who, given the opportunity, would shoot to kill.

It was soon after we had struggled through the township of Leyling that our chance came. A corner momentarily shielding the nearest guard and an overgrown ditch shielded by the bulk of a concrete water tower provided circumstances we'd never find again in a million years. "Now!" I hissed at Gordon and, together, we threw our barrow and ourselves into the bramble-choked trough the further side of the tower. Laying face downwards where we fell, the barrow up-ended, we waited, unmoving.

The nearest guard passed within a foot or two but, his view blocked by the tower, failed to spot us. We remained motionless while the column tramped by and even longer in case of stragglers.

It was already dusk when we ventured out with the object of locating less conspicuous shelter. We were back in hostile territory so could expect no assistance from the local populace though, at this stage of the war, saw no great danger from it either.

Lugging the uncooperative barrow, we moved away from the road and, on the verge of darkness, found a hiding place in the thick bushes encircling an isolated pond. Into one prickly sanctuary from another we settled down for the night. But sleep was hard to come by; the cold saw to that, and when finally successful we were awoken soon after dawn by a horde of curious children out on a pre-breakfast fishing excursion. Attempting to bribe them away with offers of Red Cross chocolate was not a good idea; admittedly they departed but soon returned with unbelieving mothers, stolid Herrenvolk who hadn't seen chocolate for years. Hastily we evacuated our refuge which bordered another village we hadn't seen in the darkness.

But the place produced for us one bonus. Since everyone seemed aware of our presence we walked straight through it and in the further outskirts came across a smart streamlined perambulator standing unattended outside a house, the owner having seemingly popped back into it for a moment since the door was open. It was an opportunity too good to miss. In a flash we had unloaded the boxes, gently transferred the sleeping infant together with its bedding to the barrow and threw the boxes into the pram. Then we were off at speed. My pang of guilt was momentary but I did wonder what the good hausfrau thought when she discovered her nice chromium-plated baby-carriage had turned into a broken-down wheelbarrow.

We left the road at the first opportunity on a track leading north. I was a little doubtful as to the ability of the fragile-looking wheels of our new acquisition to stand up to the unaccustomed weight and the rough country over which we would, in all probability, be moving. The drone of aero engines had become an incessant background to life and we were now seeing low-flying aircraft, easily distinguishable as American.

With halts for snacks we continued on our north-westerly axis, convinced it would lead eventually to the American lines. It was but a hunch though confirmed in a surprising manner late that afternoon when, atop a hill, we walked straight into a German soldier. Too late to avoid him we could only brazen things out. But the chap was most obliging.

That we were British was painfully obvious but he seemed not the slightest put out. He spoke good English and made the most of it with a monologue upon the unjustness of the Hitler regime and the futility of the war. We enquired politely of the whereabouts of the Americans and received a full situation report. He and his unit had the task of delaying their advance, he himself being part of a spotter team for an artillery battery hidden in a nearby wood. Not that they intended much resistance, we were assured, for what was the use? The other side had so much more artillery, he went on, can't you hear it? And then for the first time we realised the sullen roar that we had dismissed as the sound of aircraft was, in fact, that of the guns of the American Third Army. Our military friend then advised us on our best move. "The area will be overrun in the next day or two," he said, "so why not hide up and await your liberators?" Why not indeed.

We thanked our benefactor and moved off intent upon locating convenient refuge that, hopefully, would not be shared by any last-ditch defenders. The Bavarian scenery, bathed in sunshine, was idyllic; even tranquil but for the distant thunder of those guns. In the hedgerows the birds chirped and spring buds were beginning to open in total disregard of the folly of mankind. The well-wooded terrain offered plenty of potential hiding places in which to await our own personal salvation.

Intent upon moving nearer the German front line – if indeed a front line as such existed – we pushed on covering a respectable distance by late afternoon. American fighters, flying low, increased in numbers and we waved ineffectively at their pilots. The appearance of German soldiers in full battle kit and military vehicles of assorted type, caused us concern; not all enemy troops were likely to be so well disposed to marauding Britishers as was our friend on the hill, but before we could go to ground a most disturbing incident occurred.

Gordon was reloading the boxes into the pram following negotiation of a fence when out of the clear sky death hurtled down upon us in the form of an American Thunderbolt fighter-bomber. We had noticed it circling the valley through which we were passing but were too engrossed in what we were doing to hear the change in engine note as it dived towards us. My yell to Gordon was purely incidental, he having already spread-eagled himself close up against the fence where I joined him. The swathe of machine-gun bullets kicked up the turf around us, smashing into the abruptly-abandoned pram. Venturing to turn my face from the dirt I watched our erstwhile attacker bank steeply away and disappear westwards.

The pram was done for, its left-hand rear wheel demolished by a half-inch calibre shell. With Gordon muttering something about 'military targets' we considered our next move. With our food supply already depleted it was no great feat to carry everything to a small wood some 200 yards away. The undergrowth was thick, thick enough in fact to screen us from sight from even close at hand. There and then we put down roots and awaited developments.

Locating a leafy spot near the edge of the tree-line so that we could scan the terrain in one direction, we began the construction of a rough shelter. I even found a small brook that would suffice as a water supply.

Our Robinson Crusoe existence – the wood became our island – was to last for several days. We had food – even if some of the items had to be consumed in an uncooked state – and, using empty tins as cooking pots, we even felt bold enough to light a small fire on which to boil the near-stagnant water and make tea. It rained for a while as if to prove the shelter was not waterproof but lying on the cardboard boxes of our dwindling provisions we were spared the dampness of the ground. We ate frugally, not knowing how long the food would have to last.

In this manner we waited for the war to roll over us. And we didn't have to wait long. The growl of gunfire drew closer. Aircraft roared overhead, and on the third day came the indistinct rattle of machine-guns blending with the thud of tank and anti-tank fire. Excitement and a degree of apprehension gripped us. The waiting became intolerable.

Our first visitation was from a couple of displaced Poles. They almost walked into the shelter before seeing us, getting the shock of their lives as we cautiously emerged. A packet of Red Cross 'Lucky Strikes' calmed them and, in return, they recommended a nearby herd of cows as a source of fresh milk. Next morning Gordon tried his hand at milking using a milk powder tin as a bucket but did no more than annoy the beast.

Things really began to liven up on the fourth day as we perceived convoys of German transport pouring eastwards along a distant road we never knew was there. Nearer, groups of infantry could be seen crossing the ridges. And, as if to help them on their way, salvoes of shells began bursting in their wake.

A loud double crash, followed by the whine of shell-splinters, sent us grovelling on the ground. Two shells had actually fallen on the edge of our wood; things were becoming distinctly unhealthy. In the lull that followed we moved forward to find out the reason for this unsociable attention and got a nasty surprise when, looking out from the further edge of the wood, perceived German infantry retreating in droves; grey-clad figures moving across the open ground, some very close. Even as we watched, three mud-splashed soldiers entered the forward end of the wood bearing between them a heavy spandau mounted on a tripod. In considerable alarm we observed them place the gun in position, its barrel nosing out from behind a tree trunk. Vivid memories of last stands by SS suicide squads in Normandy and the holocaust of fire they drew, filled my mind. The additional danger of being discovered by them was not lost upon us either, and who could blame them for our speedy despatch in the circumstances?

But there appeared to be something wrong with the gun. One of the men hurriedly began stripping the breech mechanism, loudly cursing the world in general. Shattering explosions in rapid succession chased each other across our immediate front, the last burst again close to our sanctuary – and even closer to the do-or-die trio. The distinctive 'plop' of mortar fire could also be heard.

All this must have been too much for the spandau crew. Concluding there was more to life than doing and dying they picked up their immobilised weapon, together with its ammunition clips and bits and pieces and retired in some disorder along the border of the copse nearest to our position. We lay low as they scurried by.

Late in the afternoon a deathly hush fell, uncanny in its intensity. The view from the wood showed no movement. A hundred yards away our herd of cows was being milked by a solitary individual who not only knew how to do it but was plainly not going to let a small matter like a world war interfere with the routine. We walked over, whereupon the elderly cowherd gesticulated wildly in a westerly direction. A stream of words in a Bavarian dialect gave us to understand that American tanks had halted less than a kilometre distant, hidden from sight only by the ridge before us. Incredulous but unwilling to disbelieve this revelation we dashed off, forgetting even to sample the white nectar frothing in the man's bucket. With hearts pumping with the effort and excited anticipation we attained the top of the crest to behold the wonderful sight of six Sherman tanks stationary on the flanks of the subsequent rise. On their sides was emblazoned the white star of the Allied Expeditionary Force.

But our beholding was short-lived as a burst of machine-gun fire again had us burying our heads in the dirt. In the pause that followed we shouted our credentials across the lethal void of a momentary no-man's-land but it seemed that the GIs had heard similar stories before to their cost. There followed a ludicrous exchange in which our potential rescuers questioned us on the subject of baseball and football teams then in vogue. But it was our very lack of knowledge on these subjects that decided things for the Americans who concluded that, so ignorant were we, we must be limeys.

With our hands high in the air we were allowed to walk slowly forward into a multitude of levelled hardware. We were prisoners no more.

Savouring to the full the delights of liberation took many days, each adding its quota of new-found joys. Though the war in Europe was still only in its final stages this could not dampen the euphoria.

At a military headquarters we poured out every scrap of information we could about enemy movements in the locality to help ease the onward advance of the unit and even persuaded the local commander to allow us the privilege of joining his outfit until the end of hostilities instead of being sent to rear echelons to await repatriation. So, soldiers once again but wearing another nation's uniform, we became auxiliary gunners of a half-track vehicle belonging to a mechanised infantry division of the United States Third Army under General Patton. Living conditions might have been primitive by American army standards but it was fine by us and the food, if only the despised K rations, was supreme luxury. A medical officer checked our physical condition and though my weight was no more than six stone, he reluctantly allowed us to remain with the unit.

Those last weeks of warfare were very different from the savage fighting I remembered in Normandy. Rolling ponderously forward with much noise and

*clatter under an umbrella of supporting aircraft we advanced in the general
direction of the Czech frontier with a pre-arranged objective of the southern
Bohemian town of Ceske Budejovice, famed for its beer. Except for periodic
halts while aircraft and artillery dealt with pockets of fanatical Wehrmacht
rearguards there were no pitched battles or heroics on the part of the Americans;
the heroics were exclusively reserved for the enemy. And with each strongpoint
eliminated by a storm of shells and rockets, the unit ground relentlessly on over
the cratered ground, ruined farmsteads and the broken dolls of dead defenders.
I felt no compassion for the 16-year-old boys of the Hitler Youth suicide groups
since Nazism had turned these children into no more than killing machines, but
those defenders of the older generation, the elderly warriors of the Volksturm
(Home Guard reservists) were a different matter. Though they despised their
Nazi overlords they fought and died for their country with extreme courage.*

*Now and again our supporting Shermans would run up against a determined
pocket of anti-tank gunners and, for an hour or so, a duel would ensue, the
handsome landscape echoing to the rapid thumps of the German 88-millimetres
and the crack of the American 75s. My particular detachment were seldom
involved in these exchanges, my colleagues determined not to become casualties
at the very end of the war. I hardly fired a shot with the Browning 50-calibre
machine-gun in my charge.*

*And then came the cease-fire when we were within 10km of the Czech border.
The unit was disengaged and ordered back for rest and refit. In a way I was
sorry; fanciful visions of liberating Slaný had persisted though that town was
a long way off our present axis of advance. I suppose I saw myself, pistol in
hand, festooned with grenades, returning to free the captive princess, the lady
of my secret dreams.*

*Instead I accompanied my colleagues to a base near the Danube town of
Straubing where Gordon and I left them with many expressions of goodwill.
They had been a cheerful and generous bunch of men.*

*To make our way to the city of Regensburg, the airfield of which was reputed
to be preparing for the evacuation by air of freed prisoners of war, became our
next objective. We obtained a lift part of the way in a military police jeep and
then in an abandoned lorry we coaxed into life, picking up a group of Hungarian
refugees en route. In the outskirts of the picturesque but battered city the steering
shaft broke and we ended up nose-down in a bomb crater. Directed to the well-
plastered Messerschmidt experimental works airfield we found the place a
seething mass of released captives awaiting transport home and, since the first
aircraft were not expected for some days, Gordon and I drifted into town intent
upon occupying a more congenial billet.*

*Selecting a house virtually at random we rapped on the door and so made
the acquaintance of the family Schottenhammer. Initially Gordon played the
bombastic conqueror, demanding to be housed, and fed but I'd seen enough
misery over the last five months to last me a lifetime. They were a pleasant
family who put us up willingly, even insisting upon us occupying the best bedroom.
The two bovine daughters were particularly welcoming, attending to our every*

need to such an extent we began to suspect an ulterior motive. For German womanhood in those days a British husband was the ultimate prize.

Food in the shops was non-existent so, daily, Gordon and I went foraging, catching the odd chicken and digging up potatoes from allotments. These trophies the Schottenhammers cooked, everyone eating together like one big happy family.

The middle of May we boarded a Lancaster bomber stripped of its offensive equipment and, from the disarmed mid-gun turret I looked upon my own country through, I have to admit it, a sheen of tears. Though no longer a captive, and in spite of the not inconsiderable occurrences since we had met, I still carried with me the image of a Czech girl who had captured my heart.

We landed at a Buckinghamshire airfield from where, following processing by medical, intelligence and military authorities, I set out on the final leg of the journey. And because of petrol rationing in Britain I had to walk the last four miles to my home.

We left Prešov, Paul and I, following breakfast, wallowing in the knowledge that another hotel sojourn awaited us less than a couple of hours easy cycling hence. Luxury accommodation for two consecutive nights; we were in danger of getting soft. Leaving the town Paul had his first spill of the journey when his front wheel became trapped in a railway line at a crossing, pitching him onto the road though, except for a grazed knee, no damage was done. There was a choice of two roads to Košice; the new motorway and the original road that gambolled happily and traffic-free through a series of townships. The gambolling was not to last, alas, the smaller artery joining the motorway some 8km short of Košice. But some of its carriageways were being resurfaced so we utilised the empty lanes for a further few kilometres with no objections from the workforce. The long freewheel down the hill into the city we made in company with the densest traffic I have seen in eastern Europe, everything pelting to office and work site in an effort to beat the clock.

Attaining the centre of Košice on a bike in the rush hour is not to be recommended. Being hooted at, chivvied by fast-changing traffic lights, and pushed into the walls of underpasses had me on the verge of paranoia by the time we gained the Slovan Hotel in the heart of the city.

A tall ugly block was the Slovan, and its reception area put me in mind of New York's Grand Central Station on a Fourth of July holiday but without the grandiose architecture to match. Hardly had we arrived when we were involved in a hassle regarding storage of our bikes which had to be wheeled through a maze of tunnels, kitchens and store rooms in the bowels of the hotel to an underground garage. By the time we had found our way to the surface and obtained receipts in duplicate it was midday. As in Prešov, we had reached the hotel earlier than expected and though there were plenty of empty rooms this unscheduled arrival threw the gears of Cedok's tortuous workings which meant further delay. Things finally sorted out we emerged, somewhat punch-drunk, into the city.

Košice we found to be a reflection of its Slovan Hotel, a big, brash, bustling, sprawling metropolis. A diverse mix of Germans, Hungarians and Gypsies together with its Slovak population adds spice to the cultural scene while the

Gothic cathedral of St Elizabeth and the neighbouring old cremation tower are the high spots of the city's architectural glories. The Miklusova prison in a remnant of the old walls and its torture chamber are genuine pieces of pure medieval horror to be ogled at if you like that sort of thing.

Slovakia's second city has been inhabited since the Palaeolithic Age to grow into an important Hungarian trading centre in the mid-fifteenth century. With the Turkish occupation of the Hungarian homeland in the sixteenth and seventeenth centuries the town became a safe haven for the Hungarian nobility. Early in the present century Košice was knocked around like a ping-pong ball between Hungary and Czechoslovakia, the place changing nationalities four times before the onset of World War Two. Since then the Slovaks have made great efforts to eliminate the Hungarian influence in the city which, notwithstanding the current Hungarian minority's unrest, has been largely successful, though the present Hungarian border is but 21km down the road.

While exploring the central streets we stocked up on provisions and filled ourselves with dumplings, cream cakes and equally fattening goodies in the expectation of such items being more expensive in Hungary. A further incentive for this burst of extravagance was the necessity of spending our non-exchangeable Slovak crowns before leaving the country and this we did so successfully that I then had to change a further couple of dollars – with all the exchanging paperwork involved – so as to pay car-garaging rates for our bikes the next morning.

Delaying our departure only until the worst excesses of the morning rush hour had subsided we cycled off, suffering, not surprisingly, from indigestion brought about by a gargantuan breakfast on top of yesterday's substantial intake. We also lost ourselves, attempting to shake off Košice's industrial suburbs that extend for miles. Signs indicating Miskolc in totally opposite directions hardly helped matters, this Hungarian city lying on the route we initially wanted to take.

On the way at last the final 21km of Slovakia was a repeat of yesterday's minor road, devoid of traffic, bordered by orchards and unhindered by hills. The hint of the Carpathians we had observed four days earlier had entirely evaporated.

In spite of the political antagonism between Slovakia and Hungary the border crossing formalities were minimal though, on the Hungarian side, our passports were carefully checked against a list of, presumably, undesirables. Purchasing a fistful of forints from a laid-back official of the National Bank reclining in a deck chair beneath a warm sun we entered our sixth country.

Thereafter the day developed into, perhaps, the most idyllic of the whole journey with a well-paved, little-used road bordering a handsome range of volcanic hills called Zempleni Hegyseg. This remote district of north-eastern Hungary is known as the Myirseg. It is hemmed in on all sides by Slovakia, the Ukraine and Romania, and by the distant horseshoe of the Carpathians which have a habit of fading and appearing all over the place in this part of the world. Here, though, is a region of loess hills built of pale sand blown off the plains with the Tisza river and its tributaries wandering through the little valleys and damp hollows between the knolls.

The peasants of the Nyirseg are strong Calvinists, people with a tradition of independence that must have been encouraged by the knotted landscape where independence that must have been encouraged by the knotted landscape where there would always have been somewhere to hide. More was left of the past here than anywhere else I had seen in Hungary over the years. Many of the villages through which we gently pedalled had one or more Romanesque and Gothic churches, where medieval frescos had survived under the Calvinist whitewash.

Within a couple of kilometres of the Slovak border we had turned off the Miskolc road onto a by-road that daintily probed a way through the Zemplen Hills. Happily we followed it, enjoying the warm sunshine, gazing upon romantic hill-top castle ruins, listening to the purring of harvesters, and periodically stopping to pick plums and raspberries that profligated in the hedgerows.

Gradually the brilliant yellow fields of sunflowers gave way to sunlit slopes the topsoil of which nourishes the serried ranks of vines that march up the flanks of the hills. This is Tokajhegyalja, the mountain lee of Tokaj, 'Rich with the drink of the gods,' as one Hungarian poet described it. At the township of Abaujszanto we halted to photograph wine shelters tunnelled into the bank centuries ago and still very much in use today. The town's church bells were ringing lustily though it wasn't Sunday.

We camped, that first night of only two we were to spend in this seldom-visited corner of Hungary, close to a disused quarry, utilising a roofless concrete hut as shelter from prying eyes. All around were the tall rows of vines, haughty and aloof, whose guardians might not have approved of foreign campers setting up their tent in such close proximity.

On the southern flanks of the Zemplen Hills we descended by low, broken rocky stairs towards the lowlands. At their foot the Bodrog river twisted and turned to join the great Tisza at Tokaj. Above the town hangs the southernmost isolated member of the Zemplen chain, the Nagykopasz (Big Baldy), its cone, lined with frozen lava, rising in solitude at the edge of the Big Plain like an advance guard of the northern mountain region. The Tokajhegyalja, they say, is loveliest in the autumn when suffused, fading light veils the river, the humid sky is slate-grey and the silence of the last pre-vintage peace covers the vines. For us, in mid-summer, all we got was the slate-grey sky spitting rain.

I don't know quite what I expected of Tokaj town. I suppose I'd hoped for something along the lines of a French or Bavarian wine town or historic allure, flower-bedecked and containing a plethora of wine cellars loud with wine-swigging citizens. Instead we found a staid, undistinguished and rather shabby little town squeezed between the Nagykopasz heights and the Bodrog river. In point of fact some of Tokaj's smaller streets do climb the slopes of these heights where a labyrinthine network of cellars are to be found, all owing their existence to the 'royal wine' grown on the Nagykopasz. This golden nectar has brought both money and menace to Tokaj. Sometimes it was paid for with gold; at other times it was taken by force, the wine attracting thirsty robbers, looting mercenaries and tribute-levying armies.

Today its native and foreign visitors are accommodated in a sprawling camping ground amongst trees on the far side of the combined Tisza and Bodrog rivers which join in watery embrace above the town. We pedalled by this ants' nest of caravan and tent-residing humanity, thankful for our penchant for solitary camping.

We had acquired further provisions at Tokaj's seemingly only supermarket to find costs in rural Hungary to be only fractionally higher than those in Slovakia, but the new lingo had me in knots. Poland had produced a goodly selection of unpronouncable place-names but Hungary came up with some real tongue-twisters. Paul's Russian fell on deaf ears and, whilst Romanian was to proffer slight French overtones with even Czech and Slovak occasionally understood, here everything foundered in incomprehension.

The name of the sizeable town for which we were making was Nyiregyhaza and it lay at the hub of nine long straight main roads. Ours was Highway 38 and, clogged with heavy traffic, strictly no fun at all. The countryside abruptly fell flat on its back to become dull and characterless. However our subsequent gruellingly fast 40km of pedalling produced an appetite which we enthusiastically assuaged in Nyiregyhaza. We had ordered goulash which we thought was a Hungarian word and finally got it but not without the greatest linguistic complications. With the prospect of semi-starvation looming in Romania we promptly ordered a second helping by pointing to our empty plates and stomachs.

The long straight road out of the town towards Vasarosnameny was not only narrow and afflicted with speeding lorries but also graded as an expressway with, at intervals, notices displaying the device of a crossed-out bicycle. This we took to mean cyclists were forbidden to use it. But there was no other road in evidence so we pressed on. Only one lorry driver hooted at us – and I think that was no more than a gesture of friendliness – and we even passed through a police checkpoint with no comment being made. Heavily-populated storks' nests containing up to four of the big birds with standing room only was a feature of the Nyirseg, this easternmost region of the Hungarian Great Plain once part of the autonomous principality of Transylvania.

The name refers to the birch trees that grew up in the valleys between the low sandhills, and which were often half-sunk in stagnant water. Modern drainage has not only rescued the area for agriculture, but created a small paradise of orchards and groves, in which the silver poplar has tended to supplant the birches. Not entirely so however, and the impression one still receives as one pedals along tree-lined roads is of a constantly wavering silver and green light, a softness in outlines and colour that is a recurrent feature of the Hungarian landscape. It gave a surreal beauty to this otherwise bland countryside.

The Nyirseg escaped the ravages of the Turks largely because it was well protected by the impenetrable marshes caused by the Tisza's overspill. The result is that the concentration of population is much greater than on the plain proper. As if to illustrate this point we found ourselves riding through one small village after another, each of medieval aspect.

In one we halted to look inside a church. Outside it a man in baggy blue trousers scythed the verge. The door was open but we hesitated to enter, mainly on account of our naked knees. A tiny woman broke across the shaft of light at the doorway. She was dressed in black, with printed apron and kerchief. She smiled and beckoned us inside there to offer a commentary we could not understand. She touched a particular pew, pointed out an arch and nodded towards the carvings that graced the supports of the gallery. All of these small but exquisite details we would have missed had we been alone so her efforts were not in vain. We put a coin in the offertory box and thanked our voluntary guide profusely for which we each received a pat on the head.

It was only when we came off the expressway 18km short of Vasarosnaneny that we chanced upon these villages. Had we kept going we would have ended up in the Ukraine within a couple of hours but our next objective was Satu Mare, the first Romanian town and close to where the three borders meet.

Larger townships on the new route included Mateszalka and Csenger and it was west of the latter that we eventually found a site on which to raise the tent for our last night on Hungarian territory. With less than 18km to go to the Romanian border and well over 100 km behind us we were ready to call it a day, but finding a spot among the huge flat and impersonal fields containing not a vestige of hedgerow, bush or tree was a frustrating business. Having been turned away earlier from a rare knot of trees we headed in desperation up a dried mud track to raise the tent amongst the reeds bordering an overgrown river along the other side of which ran a railway line. Though tractors were still at work in the distance they were too far away for us to be seen – or so we thought. Then just as we were climbing into our bivi-bags a man appeared as if from nowhere to stand over our bivouac. He was a pleasant enough chap who. learning of our harmless intentions, wished us a good night and departed; seemingly he had spotted us even from so great a distance. They have sharp eyes in these parts.

The border itself was a few kilometres east of Csenger and just beyond the sleepy village of Nagygec into which we rode to purchase the inevitable provisions, still uncertain of conditions likely to be met in Romania. Though both of us had, at different times, visited the country during the communist era we remained apprehensive. Even following the death of Ceausescu the country was said to have the most repressive government in eastern Europe. It was a well-known fact too that, economically, Romania was in a bad way, lacking both food and the means of its distribution. And its secret police, though officially disbanded, was reputed to have maintained a subtle control.

Though our current spell on Hungarian soil had been brief we had heard stories of the shortages; probably exaggerated since there is no love lost between the two nations. But we could not ignore the vehemence with which Hungarians spoke about the poverty of the country, now bankrupt despite its abundance of natural resources in oil, minerals and land. "The people are starving," "They will steal from you," "The police are brutes," "Don't imagine your British passport will protect you," were some of the comments that stuck in my mind. Outside Nagygec village and barely a hundred yards from the first border post a line of ramshackle hutments had been raised by enterprising Hungarian traders selling quantities of foodstuffs to recently-arrived Romanian visitors buying everything in sight. Many of the Romanians had, it transpired, crossed the frontier for the sole purpose of purchasing items unobtainable in their own shops.

But what sent a cold shiver down my spine as we rode through man-made embankments topped by steel posts that plainly once supported barbed-wire coils was the revelation that here was the remnants of a one-time set of frontier barriers raised by one former people's republic to ensure minimum contact between its peoples and those of another. A stagnant canal also ran along this border line which seemed to have no purpose other than that of a prepared killing ground. This particular barrier had been Hungarian but assuredly a similar construction had lain on the Romanian side and, if a distant but distinct cable-mesh fence tailing off into the fields was anything to go by, maybe theirs was still part-operative. With Hungary for long having a higher standard of living than Romania as well as sharing a common border with the West the trend would be for illegal immigration from Romania. Those hateful days of border shootings in Europe were, thankfully, over but, for me, the memory of them was painfully vivid. My mind flew back to the 1950s when, the hot war at an end, the cold war was at its height.

Chapter 6
Romania: Northern Transylvania

The wire parted with a twang and I froze in terror. I was lying on my back beneath the triple electrified fence inexpertly wielding a pair of rubber-handled wire-cutters by the dazzling light of a row of arc lamps.

The year was 1951 when the hand of Stalin lay across the lands of eastern Europe and the Iron Curtain divided East from West. Here on the Bavarian-Czechoslovak border my mission that late summer night was to effect a tryst with the girl in the East and, all conventional means of achieving this end exhausted, the wire-cutters were my last resort.

With the parting of the first strand I knew that, in the nearest watch-tower, a red light would be flashing to alert the Czech guardians of the border, and my calculations, based upon months of research, gave me a maximum six minutes to effect my breakthrough without interruption.

If I lived to tell the tale those would probably be the most frightening minutes of my life.

My military service had ended in the British Army of the Rhine amidst the squalor of a shattered Germany. Back in Britain and demobilised, a dull, ordered existence as a businessman went some way to wipe away the reminders of the ugliness of war. Not that it could ever be a complete erasure. Those recollections of the uglier episodes would always remain in the background, like a wild monster in a forest waiting to emerge. Periodically something would prod them out; small things, ridiculous things. I hoped they would fade and go but they never entirely vanished. But in the immediate post-war years I had the antidote of a happier recollection – the vision of a nameless Czech girl that similarly refused to be erased.

It took, literally, years to locate and contact Anna – for that was her name – and consolidate our mutual affection for one another. A war-devastated Europe lay between us, a Europe devoid of postal and telephonic communication, a Europe where millions of broken families were struggling to be reunited in an environment that was a no-go void of despair. Thereafter, postal contact sporadically restored, our letters could but gradually express the sentiments and desires of a man and a woman inexplicably in love.

Came February 1948 and politics – the savage politics of communism – entangled the country of Czechoslovakia in a new nightmare as it slid, in company with Poland, Hungary and all eastern Europe into the harsh grip of a regime as ruthless as the one from which it had been so recently delivered.

But if this event had been engineered for the sole purpose of terminating my infatuation it would have failed dismally. That a purely physical barrier was being erected between us meant little; the dream could only wither in the knowledge that my feelings for Anna were not reciprocated. But this was not the case. The vow I made the last year of the war to see her again still stood. For her to come to me was an impossibility. For me to go to her in the face of repeatedly refused entry visas and an edict from the communist regime expressly forbidding liaisons with foreign nationals would require a miracle. I determined that it would have to be the miracle.

It was well into the summer of 1951 before I was ready to initiate the course of action that could perhaps achieve that miracle. For months I had painstakingly delved into the secrets of the Czechoslovak border defence system; its make-up, technicalities, weaknesses and the movements of its guardians. I had probed the intricacies of the ever-diminishing traffic across it by road and rail, and investigated the means of illegally entering – and leaving – a totalitarian state fanatically opposed to violations of its heavily-guarded frontiers. My enquiries took me the length and breadth of a fast-recovering Western Europe to cross-examine refugees and escapees from the captive lands, as well as West German border authorities, railway staff and intelligence services. Gradually, relentlessly, I amassed a storehouse of data to support the project I had set myself, a project I had to keep secret even from my parents who would have unequivocally opposed it.

An initial, unauthorised run across the guarded border openly but visa-less by train – a truncated portion of the Orient Express – I undertook more as a reconnaissance than as a means of seriously breaching it. As expected, I was removed from the Prague-bound train and held until I could be put aboard the next west-bound service. It was not a wasted exercise; I even learnt more details of the border installations from the guards themselves. And back on West German territory I simply turned straight round to approach on foot the brilliantly illuminated triple fence through which the train had passed. Delaying only until the very early hours of the morning when vigilance would be at its weakest and the passing of a Czech patrol I chose a point midway between two watch-towers and, crawling forward utilising the shade offered by the sawn-off tree trunks that stood on the western side of the fence, reached the base of the obscene structure. Then, spread-eagled on my back, I removed the wire-cutters from my small rucksack and, firmly gripping their insulated handles, attacked the lowest cable of the inital fence.

The glare of the lights half-blinded me so that I had difficulty in locating the further four strands directly above my head. And not knowing whether or not these particular ones carried an electric charge I could only feel for them with the insulated cutters. No sparks flew but I was taking no chances. As I struggled with the clumsy tool using both hands to manipulate it the dew-laden grass soaked through my clothes to mingle with the sweat of terror. I lost count of the vital minutes available to effect an uninterrupted breakthrough and cursed every lost second as I fumbled under the white glare.

Five severed strands made adequate clearance beneath which to squirm safely and, turning on my stomach, I crawled to the base of the second fence, sliced through the lowest cable, then, again on my back, repeated the manoeuvre. Time was the essence; I seemed to have been engaged thus for hours though I guessed it to be very few minutes. It was no use pausing to listen for approaching danger; already I had reached the point of no return and was ripe for a border guard's bullet.

Clear of the second fence I turned about once more and wriggled across the furrow of the ploughed strip leaving no distinguishable imprint beyond an untidy morass of disturbed sand. Next came the deadly swathe of ground alleged to contain Teller mines laid in this sector of the border. Here I did hesitate for an instant, my ears alert for the sound of imminent discovery but all remained silent. Taking a deep breath, I inched forward again and, like a swimmer on dry land, swept the grass with out-stretched hands feeling for the protruding detonators. Adrenaline coursed through my body and my mind visualised the bloody results of impact, the explosive tearing out my stomach or, at best, blowing off my legs or arms. Slowly, slowly I gained the third fence, there to breach it with an ease bred from familiarity, each snip of my cutters a drumbeat of triumph. I could see no insulators atop this last barrier so presumed it to be non-electrified but, again, played safe, cutting through it in the prescribed manner.

Rising to my feet on the further side I sped away out of the treacherous illumination into the protection of the woods ahead.

I ran, and kept running, the foliage of the pine trees whipping me in the face; the uneven ground tripping me as I floundered on through an abruptly intense darkness. Twice I sprawled headlong before my yearning to get away from the evil fence abated. Thereafter I slowed to a steady lope until forced to a brief halt to draw air into labouring lungs.

I could barely believe what I had accomplished though my triumph was tempered with caution. Danger remained acute. I was still deep within a border zone and patrols could be numerous as they maintained a look-out for West-bound escapers. They'd be looking the other way, of course. Moving eastwards I'd be catching them on the hop.

I buried the incriminating cutters, heaping turf and leaf-mould over them; it would never do to be caught with such a tool in my possession. My watch told me it was a quarter to two; in another couple of hours it would be getting light. Navigating by compass, I struggled on as quietly as the carpet of twigs would allow. Speed was essential if I was to be clear of the restricted border zone by day-break.

A track materialised leading in the direction I wanted to go but I sensed treachery so shied away. Tracks could be watched. The woods unexpectedly faded and I found myself walking over corn stubble, my shoes making a swishing sound in the heavy silence. A train whistle indicated that I was paralleling the railway line as intended.

My plan was to by-pass the town of Cheb, leaving it on my left which meant I would hit the line again as it curved south-eastwards towards Plzeň. At a station somewhere along it maybe I could catch a local train to Plzeň and, from there, to Prague.

Two hours of solid progress went by. My eyes had long since accustomed to the darkness and the walking was easy across the unfenced, unhedged pastureland. The first discoloration of the sky heralded the impending dawn. The rough grass had been scorched by the summer sun to a colour of dirty straw and, beyond, the slope of the land was stepped in a series of folds. On the lowest of these folds were white strips of cornland bare of crops harvested earlier in the year. It didn't look like border country any more.

It was my impetuousness that gave me away. The ambush occurred at a bridge spanning a small river I could have easily forded. Bridges of any description in or near border areas in such countries as this should have set alarm bells ringing in my head and, indeed, I stopped and watched this one closely for any signs of movement of a guard. But I gave way to the temptation of a dry crossing.

On the further bank a soldier stepped from behind the parapet. His order, "Stuj!" (Halt) struck me like a whiplash. I took a step towards him but four colleagues abruptly appeared from the shadow, their automatic weapons aligned on my navel. Hastily discarding the notion of heroics I came to heel and raised my hands.

I was taken to a series of local military and police headquarters, each one a step up in the hierarchy. At each I was subjected to a barrage of questions put to me in differing fashions, from the beguilingly friendly to screamed ferocious.

At one stark building I made the acquaintance of the STB (Statni Bezpecnost, the State Security Service). The resulting interrogation took place in a room devoid of decoration but for the statutory framed photographs of Joseph Stalin and Clement Gottwald (the then Czech president). Incongruously there was a bed. I sat down on it and was immediately told to stand up by a rotund officer who entered the moment I did so. He asked a single question and, not receiving the desired reply, laid into me with the butt of his pistol. The first blow was aimed at my face but, seeing it coming, I drew back my head quickly and all but concussed myself against the wall. In a daze I sat down again, only to be pistol-whipped up. All the time a sulky smile played about the man's fact but, unable to extract any satisfactory admission of guilt, he finally withdrew, leaving me a form to complete. That was the only time during my apprehension on Czech soil I was to meet with violence.

The form included a box which I was supposed to sign to the effect that I had been well treated. I left this blank, only completing the portions appertaining to my name, age, religion, nationality and address. My rucksack was emptied and an inventory compiled of the contents.

For another interview I was taken by police jeep to a small border township; I think it was As, where a suave but gentler male personage made me repeat everything I deemed necessary to tell authority at dictation speed so that a typist could record my statement for posterity.

Only towards evening did it become likely I would soon be learning my fate. I would be going to Cheb, I was told, and was optimistic enough to imagine prompt release. A two-coach diesel train took us; myself and two policemen who spoke not a word.

The town of Cheb is a district centre and, as such, possesses a sizeable police headquarters – and, as I was soon to learn, a prison. The latter was run by the STB and was, in fact, a transit barracks for political detainees destined for the nearby Jáchymov uranium mines. My escorted walk from Cheb station was the last I would experience for many weeks. But climbing the steps of the main entrance I still held hopes of catching the night train back to Nuremberg.

Yet another interrogation occupied the whole evening. Everything I had already told everybody had to be told again; the slightest discrepancy cause for more questions. My eyes kept closing with fatigue. After a while I staged a strike, refusing to answer another question until they fed me, an action that produced a stale bread roll and slice of sausage. Outside it grew dark and I didn't think I'd make the night train after all.

Finally it was all over and I was led up three flights of stone stairs to find sleep at last in a concrete-walled cell, too tired even to acknowledge the greetings offered by the other inmates.

In the morning I was to discover my new world. It measured fourteen by nine feet by about twelve high. My companions were, initially, two Czechs and a Slovak; all exceedingly friendly, especially Bohuslav, a middle-aged Czech with a sense of humour. The cell furnishings comprised two treble-tier bunks, a wooden table with three hard chairs, and a bucket for use as a toilet. A grilled window was set high in the outside wall, the only other source of light being a single electric bulb suspended from the ceiling. The bunks held straw mattresses, one threadbare blanket and a bolster. The only reading matter was the remains of a copy of the writings of Goethe in old-fashioned German print though its intended use was for more utilitarian purposes.

Morning also introduced me to the routine of confinement. The electric light had burnt all night but I had slept too well to notice; indeed I needed waking to participate in the stipulated chores. Blankets had to be folded and the floor swept with an old broom. The iron door contained a peephole through which the occasional official eye would peer.

For a time I continued to imagine that, at any moment, I would be released but as each new day came and went hope died and living became a basic existence. My sanity was saved by the good Bohuslav who invariably would raise my spirits when they had sunk to rock bottom. A schoolmaster, he was 'inside' for a 25-year stretch for the 'crime' of teaching history as it happened, not as communism decreed.

Meals were the only bright spots of the day though these were meagre enough. Breakfast was a bowl of luke-warm liquid they called 'coffee' accompanied by a small hunk of bread. The cell had been bequeathed a paper draughts set that was in constant use though we all came to hate the game. The bucket was to be used for its purpose prior to breakfast since it was permitted to be emptied just once a day with the arrival of the coffee. Anyone having to use it at other times went to the bottom of the cell popularity scale. The cell was permanently warm and this had a most unpleasing affect should the bucket have to be used at 'unscheduled' hours.

From midday onwards – and a clock in the town announced each plodding hour – we could start looking forward to lunch. It invariably arrived late and was heralded by a rattle of keys and the opening of the door – an event in itself. Potato soup was a permanent fixture of the menu. The soup was cold and congealed, having been deposited outside the door to await the pleasure of the duty warder who often made no effort to hurry the process.

Afternoons were given over to a pretence of sleep but mostly we were listening to the sounds of normality outside. The striking of the church clock, the hoot of a train, the revving of a vehicle, the shout of a child. Until one has been denied contact with their source, no one can know the extent of the longing that is generated. Bohuslav, I know, was thinking of the family he might never see again; the others too were, in their wakeful dreams, with their loved ones. My thoughts were mostly for Anna. I tortured myself with speculation on what might have been had I succeeded in reaching her home.

At dusk the light was switched on and a new mood settled upon us. The next opening of the door would herald the last meal of the day and blessed evening when the benefits or terrors of a removal from the cell could be erased from minds always taut with anticipation. Supper was more 'coffee' and a strange sweet-tasting macaroni; its consumption occupying another treasured five minutes.

Evening was always best. One more empty day ended and the next held hope as well as despair. Inert on our bunks we chatted at length, Bohuslav ensuring I was never left out of the conversation because of my ignorance of the language. We turned in early, blankets pulled over our heads to hide the glare from the electric light.

Such was the vacuum of the passing days which turned into weeks and then months. Once, my constant demand for an interview with a senior official was answered but all it produced was a brusque lieutenant of police who came to the cell. Bohuslav acted as interpreter as I demanded to be put in immediate touch with my embassy in Prague as was my right. The reply was evasive in the extreme so, over the days that followed, I wrote a statement disclosing my whereabouts and requesting consular help. I made two copies on the last blank portions of the pages of Goethe, one of which I dropped from the cell window to coincide with the daily arrival of civilian-delivered provisions. The other I surreptitiously passed to the barber who came to shave my hair. But one or both missives fell into alien hands for, a while later, the cell was invaded by a squad of irate soldiery who carried out a search during which I lost my precious pencil. But the episode indicated that my incarceration had not been, and was unlikely to be, reported to the British authorities, a disclosure that but increased my despondency.

The loss of the pencil was a grievous matter too, my scribblings in the borders of the diminishing Goethe tome the one activity left me. However I rectified the matter during one of the two further interrogations I was to undergo in the weeks that followed. Even the walk to the administration block was a pleasure. That first interrogation was, initially, a polite affair with a civilian clerk. Later a hard-faced STB officer took over and, true to form, the questioning became more ominous with much reference to the subject of espionage. In time-honoured fashion he saw to it that the glare from the powerful table-lamp was in my eyes as he listed the consequences of my alleged indiscretions and demanded that I confess my real intentions for illegally entering the country. And it was while he was yelling at me that I managed to nick the man's pencil as it lay on the table right under his nose. A search of the cell ensued soon after my return but only half the pencil was recovered as I had intended it to be.

Bohuslav too was to undergo a visit to the administration block and my heart remained in my mouth until he was returned. The other Czech – a heavy bespectacled man called Jan – and the Slovak were also removed one day but failed to come back. Thus for a week Bohuslav and I had the cell to ourselves before an excitable Hungarian named Kux and an East German joined us. Our fluctuating numbers sometimes confused the cooks and we were able to manipulate an increase in rations. This ruse became a sort of Russian roulette as the food orderly demanded our numbers through the closed door and received a reply in excess of our entitlement. Occasionally we were rumbled, so received no meal at all.

One November day all the guards were changed because, it was said, the original set were becoming too matey with their charges. Certainly most of them had been well-disposed towards me for I was a rare specimen – an Englishman – amongst the flock. Another influx of prisoners increased the cell occupancy to the maximum of six, one of them a badly beaten Czech who had been caught attempting to flee to the West. His face was a mask of congealed blood resulting from blows from rifle butts but for days he received no medical attention whatsoever, nor facilities for washing beyond that which we ourselves were permitted – access to a running cold water tap in the corridor that we seldom *reached because of the numbers trying to use it in the brief time allowed.*

The second interrogation commenced with a meeting with a customs officer who officially relieved me of my watch, money and the few valuables that had already been taken from me by the prison authorities. Since one of my 'crimes' was that of 'smuggling' – I'd not declared anything at the border – the state was exercising its right to appropriate them. The STB then took over and the familiar line of questioning resumed with espionage again high on the agenda. This, I was told with relish, would be proved at my trial.

My court appearance and the ensuing 'trial', which took place about a month later, was a complete farce. To reach the People's Courthouse involved a short walk in the open air – the first time I had been outside for a quarter of a year. The courtroom in a severe-fronted building contained few trial participants; most were uniformed border guards and police. But the judge, president of the court or whoever it was that placed himself, confronting me, in a high-backed seat beneath the national emblem, wore civilian attire.

An air of unreality pervaded everything that followed. One of the few other civilians present turned out to be a lawyer acting on my behalf, his table-top awash with documents. He occasionally rose to speak between lengthy pronouncements from the judge and though I had been assigned an interpreter, his English was virtually non-existent so, as a result, I understood nothing of what was going on. With my stubby beard and matted hair I must have looked something of a rogue deserving of punishment.

Once or twice I had to reply to innocuous questions concerning my life and occupation utilising my best German – which is saying little. Thereafter I lost the thread of the proceedings mainly on account of a generous slice of home-made cake my military escort was surreptitiously attempting to pass me below the lip of the dock in which I stood.

I was brought back to reality for a moment to plead 'not guilty' to whatever it was for which I was being charged, and for the final judgement I was pleased to note the judge at least didn't don a black cap. His summing up speech went on for an eternity and I was hardly surprised to learn I had been found guilty of all my crimes. Each one was listed – espionage, smuggling, illegal border-crossing, even insulting the People's Army since I had been rather rude to the sergeant who had painfully prodded my buttocks with his gun when I had first been arrested – and the penalties resulting therefrom. These all added up to a total jail sentence of 104 years. And since my prison was the last staging post before the uranium mines my future looked bleak.

But the judge was continuing. It appeared that the British government had finally learnt of my apprehension and had reacted strenuously mainly on account of the Czech regime's failure to report the fact. So now, as an act of socialist clemency, I was to be removed from Czech territory; expelled as an enemy of the

---

2. Some years later I was to learn from my wife that Boluslov died in captivity.

people, never to be allowed to return. My relief was overwhelming but sadness too clouded the disclosure. How was I now to make my vowed tryst with Anna?

I was welcomed back to my cell with a barrage of questions from my fellow occupants and the news of my impending release became cause for celebration. I could detect the strain in Bohuslav's voice at the prospect of my leaving but it was typical of this courageous man that he refused to let it interfere with the joy he felt for me.[2] Even the guards outside in the corridor joined in our hideous rendering of 'Rule Britannia'. Through the window I noticed it was snowing.

But another week was to pass before one of the heart-stopping door-openings became the one that was to close behind me forever. I was shaved and cleaned up, then driven to the border where, at an unofficial crossing point, my escorting soldiers pointed westwards saying "Nemecko" (Germany). I walked on alone.

Snow lay thick on the ground, scintillating in the weak sunshine and a while later, would you believe it, I was arrested by the Bavarian Frontier Police for illegally entering the Federal Republic of Germany!

Back in Britain I had more music to face. The annoyance and concern of my parents, the wrath of the Foreign Office for causing a rupture of diplomatic relations, and an edict from the Czech authorities confirming my rating of persona non grata in the country.

It was this last decree that worried me the most. My quest was getting me nowhere; worse, I had proceeded from square one into square zero. My mission to reach Anna was in greater ruin than ever before. But my private war declared against the communist regime of Czechoslovakia was not at an end. Indeed it had only begun. I vowed to return, by fair means or foul, via, if necessary, other people's republics bordering the Czechoslovak state, extending that challenge, if it came to it, to the whole Cominform of Eastern Europe. And that's exactly what transpired.

Paul and I felt like animals in a zoo at the Romanian frontier post. British visitors in this region were thin on the ground and being Brits *with bicycles* turned us into a rare species. The post was not open for business when we reached it at about 8.00 a.m. and a number of cars were lined up on the Hungarian side. At the opposite post a crowd of locals were awaiting the opening of the gates; mostly workers whose jobs took them daily into Hungary.

With nothing better to do the officials started to process us in advance of opening time, a process that took over an hour with an assortment of uniformed minions taking turns to examine us and our bikes. In Romania, more than anywhere else, a bicycle is considered the lowest form of transportation; about on a par with an ox-cart. Thus I could read their minds struggling to assess how a denizen of the affluent West could sink so low as to be seen with such a humble vehicle.

"Where are you going?" asked one official.

"Constanta," we told him.

"But that's a thousand kilometres."

"Yes."

There was a long pause as this revelation was digested and concluded to be the act of the mad, if harmless, English. Other customs officials, informed of our eccentricity, now left their processing of other less-entertaining travellers to come and admire our bikes, count the gears or laugh at our aspirations, each according to his wont. I was glad they spoke a little French, while even Romanian sounded easy after Hungarian; it was unmistakably a Latin language despite odd word-endings and Slavonic borrowings. Against a tide of west-bound Romanian workers we pedalled on to the road system of Transylvania

But surely this diabolical defile of holed gravel strung together by flakes of tarmac could hardly be termed a road. And since this rutted highway led directly into or out of the country wherein a degree of national pride was usually the norm could this be a *better* example than others within Romania? As we grimly bumped our way over the ten bottom-blistering kilometres to Satu Mare came the recollection of what Berkeley's guide to Eastern Europe had to say about venturing into the country by bicycle. 'Navigating Romania by bicycle is not recommended' it advises. 'If you persist you need to bring your own equipment including heavy duty tyres, many tubes and every conceivable spare part. A mask is also handy to keep out the omnipresent fumes while other drawbacks to biking include a general lack of understanding and compassion on the part of the natives. As you enter the country border officials will think you're crazy . . . and if you're attempting a bike odyssey in Romania, you probably are.' already parts of this gloomy forecast had proved all too accurate. If the highways hereabouts were a let-down the town of Satu Mare offered a degree of superficial optimism. Its three conspicuous but unmemorable basilicas – Orthodox, Roman Catholic and Calvinist – gave a dignity to the place, the parks a certain picturesqueness and , best of all architecturally speaking, was the allure of the beautifully-restored former Shoemaker's Guild building – now the Dacia Hotel, a sensational blue and green edifice of miniature spires and gables. Hoping to be able to reveal a hotel of striking quality upon my return home I went inside to enquire of rates at the reception desk. The girl behind it was knitting – and went on knitting even when I coughed and made impatient noises. Finally acknowledging my presence I was told that no tariff or prospectus was available and that the manager was too busy to see me. By pushing hard and displaying my travel writing credentials I was fobbed off with an under-manager who made it abundantly clear that he was not in the slightest interested in the prospects of guests with hard currency to spend. At first glance, the shops looked reasonably stocked but, on closer investigation, I was to find most of the stock consisted of what was displayed in the windows. The shops themselves were three-quaters empty and when I asked, in one, for a bar of soap the assistant as well as those customers within earshot simply laughed – either derisively or sympathetically. The supermarkets had shelves lined with bottles of plums and tins of vegetables but not much else. Bread was more available than we were to find elsewhere in the country though there were queues for it. Loaves were of standard size, a mottled shade of grey in colour and, as we soon discovered, of doughy unappetising texture and flavour. Bookshops held more promise though shelves recently emptied of the spurious works of Nicolae Ceausescu had not yet been topped up with many Western tomes except for a few French grammars and

German engineering textbooks.

Our lunch was, by contrast, relatively passable, the luke-warm soup, meat and veg plus a beer (all for about £1.20) quite the best restaurant meal we were to come across on our own in Romania. This gastronomic extravaganza emanated from a help-yourself bar-restaurant where the two dishes were the sole ones available.

The main road to Baia Mare, the subsequent and larger town on our projected route, was Highway 19 and, at least in Satu Mare's outskirts, was of no better condition than that of the border road. But our map showed us a lesser artery of probably even less quality that reduced the distance by a good 20km and more by luck than judgement we found it.

Indistinct hills showed on all sides though the terrain across which we now rode was reasonably flat. This far northern region of Transylvania is Maramures, remote and enchanting according to my guidebook giving away not much else as if to emphasise the point. But I was aware of Maramures and its people who have always remained stoutly independent, keeping out Romans, Huns, Avars, Bulgars, Cumans, Tartars and just about everyone else who came their way. They proudly claim to be pure Dacian and thus free of all Latin unreliability, were never reduced to serfdom or, in more modern times, to collectivisation.

Those distant hills hid villages containing the distinctive wooden churches dating from the last Tartar incursion of 1717; some even older, which have given the Maramures region its singular character. I had marked two such villages – Plopis and Surdesti – east of Baia Mare on my map with the idea of making a further detour to them but was told the arduous pedal to reach them was not worth the effort. The roads there are terrible, our informant told us. We could well believe it.

But our present detour was to show us one such hamlet blessed with a wooden church and we halted to examine its intricately carved wooden gates and neighbouring decorated houses, thankful that such communities had survived Ceausescu's infamous 'systemisation' policy which proposed hundreds of 'agro-industrial towns'. However if these tough little Maramures people could resist the repeated attempts at conquest with such success so they could devise ways of retaining their identity in the face of the mad-cap plans of their erstwhile leader.

Our small road out of Satu Mare was composed of concrete slabs, jarring but devoid of pot-holes, and carrying virtually no traffic. Things were too good to last – and they didn't. Switching to cobbles the road had us wobbling about on its sandy verges before conditions deteriorated further to reduce us to a crawl on the most rural of dirt tracks; stones and rocks playfully deflecting our wheels. Just right for mountain bikes, pointed out Paul, who revelled in biking across ploughed fields, but I was for more sedate pedalling.

In the village of Odoreu the inhabitants appeared sullen and blank. Collectively they had an ashen look that goes with hunger and poverty, a look common enough in the third world but rare in the faces of Europeans. Yet in the next village, that of Apa, we beheld a totally different picture. Partaking of an ersatz lemonade in a ragged bar we were joined by a lively throng of villagers, young and old, their fresh or gnarled faces alive with appreciation for our descent into their uneventful lives. Our bikes came in for universal appraisal and, upon our departure amid much jollity, a score of arms pointed the way to Baia Mare along the only road in existence.

We rejoined Highway 19 30km short of the city. And, being capital of the Maramures, I suppose it ranks as a city. Compared to the cobbles and the gravel, the distorted tarmac of the main highway took on the quality of an American Interstate and our progress was rapid.

Originally a Roman mining settlement there is, today, little left to show of Baia Mare's ancient past. A few old fortifications have survived including a trio of towers and a picturesque old inn much frequented by eighteenth- and nineteenth-century commuters but the whole city has since been inundated by a grotesque agglomeration of pollution-wreathed high-risery – courtesy of Mr Ceausescu – on the banks of the poisoned river Sasar.

It was along the banks of the river that we entered this unsavoury industrial centre which seemed to be entirely composed of suburbs. Snatching a hot snack meal at an outdoor brassiere of hardly Parisian ambience our next obsession became how to get out of the town by the fastest and most direct route possible.

Having accomplished 90km including a border crossing and two sizeable urban centres we were ready for a night's sleep and a well-sheltered camping site deep in a pine forest east of the village of Laposel was deemed adequate. We were now on the main Baia Mare-Dej-Cluj road upon which, near the village, we witnessed a man knocked off his bike by a car. However, generally speaking, we were warming to the opinion that Romanian drivers seemed to be more considerate of cyclists than those elsewhere – especially Poland. Maybe this was because motor vehicles had to contend with oxcarts, herds of animals, buffalo-drawn haystacks and other hazards around every corner which does tend to keep drivers on their toes.

The night's sleep, alas, was rudely broken for me by a violent bout of diarrhoea and vomiting before which, while struggling out of the tent, I had passed out cold to lie spread-eagled in the dew-laden undergrowth. This boded ill for the next day's progress but, by morning, I was fully recovered. The symptoms were of food-poisoning but Paul had consumed the same food as I without any ill effects at all.

Whatever the traffic density might have been later on the main road – now designated as Highway 1c – our early morning departure saw to it that few vehicles were in evidence for the first hour or so. And at the village of Somcuta Mare we turned off it onto a dirt road that made no pretences to be otherwise. But having received our baptism of fire on such excruciating arteries we were prepared for the worst; even ready to enjoy the challenge. The map showed the route to be an alternative one to Cluj using roads not all as bad as this, of no more mileage and certainly of more potential interest.

Ever since our last day in Hungary the weather had been glorious, becoming warmer by the day. It was now teetering on the hot with a furnace of a sun entrenched in a cloudless sky. Somcute Mare was like most other communities situated astride main roads, its impersonal co-operative farmyards containing ranks of trucks, tractors and combines – half of them rusting and stripped of tyres. But the roadside houses were often brightly painted, had neat gardens and luxurious vines giving an impression of prosperity that was not reflected in the less visible houses and the remoter communities together with their ragged cottages and dusty or muddy surroundings. In all villages were platoons of geese, startling white, strutting insolently about the roads hissing at passers-by. To generalise on Transylvanian village charms we found impossible, the poorest of them sometimes producing hidden appeal.

A case in point arose when we were some 10km into the latest dirt road, crunching gingerly along, often on the wrong side if the surface there was fractionally better. A car approached from behind, passed us and stopped. A man and a youth emerged and invited us to breakfast at their home 2km off our route. We were led to the hidden village of Ladara, not even marked on the map, a hamlet sharing its single dirt road with a stream there to be introduced to a family who lived in a group of houses bordering our host's smallholding. A tour of their vegetable plantation was the first item on the agenda.

The breakfast was more a brunch; thick slices of *slanina* (smoked pork fat) with bread, cheeses, tomatoes, plums, apples and tart, all home-made or grown, together with home-made wine, coffee and *tuica* brandy. Relaxing in the sun on the balcony of the man's house in company with his immediate family attempting to pronounce upon life in general made for the happiest of mornings. We were not allowed to leave without a food parcel containing a bottle of wine, a generous hunk of *slanina*, a loaf of bread and sundry tomatoes, peppers, and apples thrust into our panniers and when at last we were set to go half the village population waved us on our way. Such spontaneous acts of generosity with complete strangers opening their hearts and homes to us were to become a feature of Transylvania and a lesson not to judge communities by outward appearances.

Back on our route the way led over a grassy plateau, its minuscule uplands rolling into the infinity of a heat haze whichever direction one looked. Then, for no reason I could fathom, the gravel of the road turned to spick and span concrete at the approaches to a village and stayed that way until, again inexplicably, becoming tarmac. To cross the river Somes we utilised the railway box girder bridge, the ferry being for vehicles only.

The Somes Valley was radiant with wooded slopes and a scattering of villages of simple, single-storey cottages painted in faded lavender, delphinium blues or rosy pink. In the gardens were hollyhocks and bright yellow daises, while vines trailed along fences and formed arbours under which seats had been placed alongside the road. Elderly folk sat, relaxed but watchful, on these benches outside their homes greeting anyone who came by. On one such bench we rested ourselves and while so doing the old woman who lived nearby came out to regale us with a bowl of pears.

At Jibou we halted at an open-air bar for a soft drink only to become the centre of attraction when Paul offered rides on his bike to a horde of children whose eyes were only for our machines. Adults crowded round asking the inevitable questions: from where had we come and to where were we going, plying us with fruit juice so that we wouldn't go away.

Though the woods and forests provided camp sites galore inevitably there was somebody around everytime we pin-pointed the perfect spot on which to place the tent. Managing to reach, unobserved, the edge of a wood we concealed ourselves behind a bank to await the departure of the bevy of haymaking labourers and children together with their buffalo-drawn carts at the end of the working day – and this wasn't until long after dusk. But lying there munching our supper and listening to the gurgling of buffalo in the dying light was no hardship.

The cavalcade was back even before we ourselves had risen next morning. How hard these good farm people work over such long hours and for so little reward. We crept away to progress slowly towards Cluj, only 69km distant intent upon an easy day's pedalling and holing up again for the night this side of the city. The road changed gear again into a 'route principale' though not in the express or motorway category. Much of it was lined with tall thin birch trees in the French style providing blessed shade from the hot sun.

Romania is another of those countries where shops close at the stroke of midday on Saturday. And today *was* Saturday so we stopped in vain at village after village intent upon stocking up before the fatal hour. When at last we ran to earth a supermarket it was to find the shelves to contain no more than tins of sardines. But, big deal, there was a choice: tomato-flavoured or natural; so we purchased three tins of each. Bread was the next vital necessity but the shelves carried no such commodity. A French-speaking lady observed our dismay and asked if she could help.

"Ou est le pain?" I asked in my best French.

It's behind the counter, we were told, and lo and behold, a loaf was conjured from its hidden recesses. Hard as nails, at least two days old and for a price over the odds; it was an example of private enterprise for the 'benefit' of the likes of us caught without the staff of life on a Saturday. But, together with two flavours of sardines and a pocketful of juicy plums collected from under the trees in the graveyard of a church, our lunch was assured. We consumed it, with a beer, at one of a new breed of 'privat bufet' that are springing up all over eastern Europe dispensing, at a price, Western goodies like Mars and Snicker bars. Even the beer was imported German and expensive though there's nothing at all wrong with the Romanian stuff.

By mid-afternoon we were within 12km of Cluj so turned off onto another dirt road intent upon finding secluded ground where we could lie undisturbed prior to raising the tent at dusk. The landscape had abruptly shed itself of trees, providing little hope of a concealed site. Bumping through the village of Miru and out the other side we could find nothing suitable so returned, stopping for a beer at a roadside bar en route. A quartet of scythe-carrying farm workers, waiting for a bus home, asked us to take their photograph for which service we were rewarded with another beer. As we were knocking this down a man in, I suppose, his late twenties, appeared before us.

"Good heavens, you must be English!" he exclaimed, his pronunciation near-perfect. At first I thought he *was* English but Andras turned out to be exuberantly Hungarian. And from that moment onwards, for the next three days, he took over the running of our lives.

Though he held down a mundane job in a Cluj factory Andras's talents lay in his fulsome knowledge of the English language. To raise a little extra income he gave regular tuition to various aspiring young damsels who all happened to reside in Miru, and Saturday was the one day he could carry out his part-time vocation. So when manna fell from heaven in the guise of two real Englanders on his very doorstep his enthusiasm knew no bounds. "You come with me as my guest," he ordained and, since we had no trains to catch, we obliged.

There followed, in swift succession, visits to the households of the ladies receiving the undoubted benefits of his teachings, his ability to present each demurely admiring maiden to a brace of Brits in person being an enormous feather in the Andras cap. As we were prodded into pronouncing upon their progress in English grammar the doting parents at each house insisted upon receiving us like royalty; their rarely-used front rooms being the venue where we were topped up with coffee, *tuica*, home-made wine and finger cakes brought out in our honour. Each of these parlour-cum-guestrooms bore striking similarities; the tall tiled stove in one corner, a heavy cabinet of old cut glass and 'best china' in another and a handsome dining table – plainly an heirloom – covered by a table-cloth or tapestry of ancient splendour. One of the rooms held a settee piled high with ornately embroidered cushions purely as a display; everything pungently reeking of mothballs and must, putting me in mind of a badly maintained museum. I would have been much happier had these courtesies been offered in the cramped, ill-lit but cosy kitchens in which everybody lived most of the time since our semi-naked and none-too-clean persons were out of place in such exclusive salons. In another house our *tuica* was served from an enormous decanter surrounded by a brood of delicate liqueur glasses, the amber liquid obviously a cut above the average since it had, we were informed with pride, been treble-distilled to a point of absolute perfection. I fear it tasted to me like the firewater it was, but then I am no connoisseur of alcohol at the best of times.

One of the simpler households of our royal walkabout was that of a multitudious gypsy family and here we *were* received in the kitchen for it was the only room in the house. These gypsies were quite different from those we had seen strutting among the sombre peasants in loud, fiery-coloured bands though they too wore multi-coloured costumes; the national dress of their kind. Not by any means are all gypsies poor; many are hard-working and prosperous. But the ones who entertained Paul and I in Miru had poverty etched in their faces and reflected in the simplicity of the rude furnishings though the children looked well-nourished and cared for. Virtually everyone in the village was of Hungarian stock; a real stronghold of Magyarn nationalism was Miru.

The sequence of receptions at an end, Andras invited us to attend the village 'ball' that evening scheduled to follow a wedding ceremony which involved the newly-weds being officially received into the community. Night had fallen by this time but the main street was aflicker with flaming torches as the bride and groom processed from the church in company with most of the local populace to be ceremoniously passed through a ribbon stretched across the road. There was much merriment and confusion; with a backcloth of house façades and the church tower illuminated by the flames, here was a scene straight out of the Middle Ages.

The 'ball' turned out to be a village hop which took place in a stark community hall, the band pumping out 1960s pop tunes with gusto. I paid the small entry fee and distributed beers to all and sundry, while Paul pranced around the floor like a young bull, much to the amusement and admiration of the onlookers.

It was after midnight by the time we returned to the farm in which we had stored our bikes there to be served an ample supper of which *slanina* again formed the chief ingredient. Our bed for what remained of the night was the hay in a barn, there being no beds to spare in the house. This suited us well, the experience forcibly reminding me of similar accommodation circa 1945, 49 years earlier. I would have slept like the proverbial log had not a vicious attack of cramp sent me thrashing about in agony; this affliction, alas, was to be a re-occurring event of the journey.

Andras suggested $10 would not be an unwelcome contribution for the services offered by our host prior to leaving the village and, equipped with an ill-drawn sketch-map, we were instructed to report at the Andras residence, a flat in Cluj, later that morning, he catching a bus to the city. This new initiative of his involved using his flat as a base for a night or two which would enable us to acquaint ourselves with the city and locate a couple of contacts whose addresses I held. The arrangement suited us well enough but I wondered, rather unkindly, what was in it for Andras. I was becoming a mite disenchanted with the chap, in spite of his seemingly generous attentions.

Bumping down the rutted dirt road we gained the highway of yesterday and reached Cluj within half an hour though the hunting down of Andras's flat took considerably longer with frequent resort to enquiries of passing citizens. One advantage of searching for an address in a strange city is that the exercise, exasperating though it may be, offers the best method of becoming familiar with that city's layout. By the time we had come upon the object of our quest the streets of Cluj were becoming exceedingly familiar.

German Klausenburg, Hungarian Kiloszvar, Romanian Cluj to which the title Napoca is appended in honour of the Dacian town which once stood on the site – thus calling attention to the Romanian right to the territory – is the historic capital of Transylvania and the centre of Hungarian culture there. It is an important university centre and had a ruler of which the city is justly proud: Matthias Corvinus, King of Hungary, who was born locally. His father, Iancu Hunedoara, was of Romanian stock but this notwithstanding King Matthias was indisputably the greatest Hungarian of his day, being illustrious as a soldier, statesman, orator, legislator and administrator. Born in 1443, he was for a while King of Bohemia, establishing his capital, after defeating the Austrian Emperor Frederick III, in Vienna

We had entered the city through a labyrinth of streets torn by heavy vehicles, over muddy tracks where the road dissolved at the approaches to a part-built bridge and past a Ceausescu-land of concentrated phalanxes of high-rise apartments. And it was on the fifth floor of one such concrete dormitory that we were reunited with Andras. His block – one of serried and sordid ranks of them – was at the further and crime-ridden end of town, a district in which I would not care to be at large at night. Though such premises offered little encouragement to be of a house-proud disposition, Andras's flat was, to put it bluntly, a mess: untidy and filthy, while the bathroom ceiling had partly collapsed, water from the flat above seeping through it. But the premises were put entirely at our disposal – well-plastered bath and all – so I am being churlish by finding fault.

Andras had his own affairs to attend to for the rest of the day leaving us free to roam the city and make our initial contacts before meeting up with him again that evening. I have to admit again to finding our new friend to be something of a pain though I don't quite know why. Both Paul and I evoked the feeling that Andras was obtaining as much benefit from us as we were from him; nothing wrong with that. But additionally it was increasingly hard to accept his constant cynical criticism of my own mannerisms and habits (imperfect as they are) bearing in mind that I was old enough to be his father. He also possessed an unfortunate mannerism of his own, that of fondling me at every opportunity. This provoked my gravest suspicions and Paul was quick to notice the growing friction between us. But I surmised we might survive a couple of days on amiable terms without open warfare breaking out.

We ran our first contact to earth at the second attempt. This was Doctor Andras Bodor who lived in a more exclusive set of apartments near the centre. A former headmaster of the city's famous Unitarian High School (Unitarianism was invented in Transylvania, mainly in Cluj) we found him surrounded by his books, daughter and grandson in his snug study. We took tea and accepted an invitation to lunch the following day at Cluj University's Faculty Restaurant on condition that we be allowed to entertain all of them in return at the same location in the evening.

Our next contact was one Professor Romeo Ghircoisiu, a Romanian composer-conductor, whose home was more difficult to find; in fact it was only because a complete stranger to whom we made directional enquiries took the trouble to get out his car from his garage and personally drop us outside the door that we found it at all. A wonderful old man, totally sunk in Romanian and classical music, Romeo with his enchanting wife entertained us to coffee and a cut-glass dish of wild cherries garnished with an exquisite syrup. Their living room, full of lovely old furniture, pictures, music scores and tapestries imbued with the professor's life-work, held an ambience light-years away from a country currently beset with problems of a more utilitarian nature. Before we left we accepted an invitation to meet him outside the cathedral at mid-morning the following day for a walking tour of his beloved city.

Andras too wanted to show us the high spots of Cluj and he was to do so following our return to his flat. The heat of the day had faded and walking the streets was pleasanter than it had been earlier

Actually St Michael's Church in the very heart of Cluj is not a cathedral, though you would be forgiven for thinking it was for it is one of the largest Gothic churches in Romania. The evening sun came slanting through a glorious stained-glass window of almost Chartres quality while we gazed upon it, tinting the Baroque carved wood of the interior in a scarlet hue. Outside the church – with his back to it – King Matthias Corvinus sits on his charger, clad in full armour while his warrior henchmen below his plinth trample the Ottoman's crescent banner. To its citizens Cluj is still Koloszvar, with its dignified public buildings and rambling university and the white-and-ochre opera house with bronze chariots rearing from twin towers. Fragments of the old walls appear now and again, some still adorned with bastions, and I was intrigued to be shown a smaller copy of the famous Prague statue of St George and the dragon I had often looked in upon the Czech capital. There was also a Romulus and Remus statue, seemingly a favourite adornment in east European towns. Cluj's cathedral – and there is one – stands domed, aloof and Orthodox in a lesser square.

We entertained Andras to dinner at an ill-attended open-air restaurant in the old part of town before strolling home to the bed – actually Andras's bed – I shared with Paul, the rightful incumbent fortuitously having arranged accommodation with neighbours.

Since Andras had to leave early for work he insisted that we meet him for a late breakfast at his factory canteen thus gaining another aspect of Cluj. Foolishly Paul and I walked it; all of 10km of industrial suburb through another of Andras's ill-drawn maps that intimated a lesser distance. The food in the spacious, efficiently run canteen was plentiful and good, though I would have preferred more breakfastly items than soup, meat and two veg plus a half litre of beer. A tram carried us back to the railway station from whence we walked to St Margaret's, there to find Romeo Ghircoisiu awaiting to escort us around his city.

The day was hot and sultry and, speaking for myself, I was none too keen on tramping anew the hard broken pavements but we could not disappoint the old chap. As we strolled he pronounced upon Transylvania in general rather than Cluj in particular and my fatigue lightened as I listened to his words.

Transylvania can be seen as a symbol of Hungary's defeats, a fact that still irks those of Hungarian blood. The province had been part of the medieval Hungarian kingdom but remained autonomous when the rest of the country fell under Ottoman and Hapsburg rule, to be reunited with Hungary in 1848. After World War One, when the Hapsburg Empire was parcelled out, Transylvania was awarded to Romania. During World War Two most of the territory was again held by Hungary but once more returned to Romania at its close. This is seen by Hungarians as a penalty exacted for the Horthy regime's support of the Nazis though, in 1940, Romania likewise had become allies of Germany, only a timely coup at the tail end of hostilities allowing that country to ally itself with the victors.

Thus Hungarians see Transylvania as the lost mountainous soul of their land. They say – not without reason – that the purest Hungarian qualities were preserved there through the years of foreign domination, that even today the Transylvanian Szeklers – descendants of the Avars and Attila's Huns and looked upon as pure Magyars who were sent in the early Middle Ages to defend the east Carpathian frontier (the name 'Szekler' means, literally, 'Frontier Guard') – speak the purest form of the Hungarian language. Although the two million Hungarians of Transylvania are now out-numbered by Romanians, many Hungarians believe the land is theirs by ancient right; their historians have argued that the region was practically uninhabited during the early migrations and was settled gradually from the ninth century onwards by Hungarian tribes. The Romanians argue that they were there first and that the Romanian peasants are descended from the ancient Dacians who lived there originally.

Romeo, of course, was Romanian himself though this is not to say he was unsympathetic to the Hungarian claims. And he showed contempt of immediate past as well as present Romanian governmental unspoken policy of systematically diluting Hungarian culture in Transylvania in spite of minority rights being, in theory, assured. He mentioned cases of the 'Romanianisation' of Hungarian schools and the placing of Romanians rather than Hungarians in positions of power at all levels. He told us how, in the spring of 1988, news broke of a projected agrarian reform by the Ceausescu government which would entail the 'systemisation' – effectively, the demolition and resettlement – of 7,000 villages. Details were vague; no-one made clear *which* villages and when. But the Hungarians knew it would be the Hungarian villages that would fall to the bulldozer. He concluded on a startling note. "Do you know, had it not been for the USSR, Romania and Hungary could have been at war. Now, with the USSR no more, this could still occur. Feelings between the two countries run very high."

These last words were spoken as we sat sipping a sand-heated coffee in a cafe our host particularly favoured. Long after we tendered our farewells I pondered upon this Hungarian-Romanian question which appears to be as insoluble as is our own Irish problem.

Lunch with Doctor Bodor and his grandson was, fortunately, late and the helpings at the university restaurant frugal. I drank mineral water, my stomach audibly objecting to the day's abruptly larger intake.

And then, blow me, if the good doctor didn't take it into his head to likewise give us a tour of the city, our third within 24 hours. We finished atop Cetatuia Hill containing a plush hotel and the scant ruins of a fort where we sat on a wall and gazed over the city. Frenetic industrialisation may have transformed Cluj since 1970 but, from our viewpoint, its ancient heart displayed a compact oasis of faded beauty. According to rumour, local Hungarian and Romanian Party officials united to defend the centre of Cluj from 'systematisation'. To the Hungarians, who still form about two-fifths of the population, Kolozsvar is their beloved capital, symbolising a millennia of achievement, in which for the past three humiliating decades they have been made to feel like second-class citizens. Yet there is the other side of the coin. In painful and dangerous contrast, the Romanians think of Cluj as the city from which their ancestors were for centuries physically excluded as mere serfs, despised 'Vlachs' – a term of contempt equivalent to 'nigger' and still, tragically, in use. Among the Hungarians, old attitudes do die very hard indeed.

On leaden feet I limped, with the others, back to the Bodor home, hoping my stomach would hold out. And at the college restaurant again, joined by the Bodor daughter, we partook of our third meal of the day. At least Paul did justice to it.

A tram lurched Paul and I back to the vicinity of Andras's unappetising abode where, in the dark and among groups of unsavoury characters idling on the concrete walkways between the tower blocks, we searched for our valhalla no different from a thousand others. Bed, even this one, was bliss.

Next morning we arose once more with the dawn, retrieved our bikes and retasted the freedom of the road. I still was unable to make out my antagonism against Andras; except for a couple of meals and a few beers at our expense which I was pleased to offer him he had made no demands upon us. I think it was no more than his manner that was the source of the irritation.

Pushing our bikes we began struggling up the long hill out of Cluj, the historic city of conflicting loyalties, fading into the morning mist behind us.

Chapter 7
Romania: Central Transylvania

One of our new friends had mentioned in passing that we should meet 'a bit of a hill' on our way out of Cluj, omitting the fact that it was 8km long and, with a bike, entailed plodding all the way; a frustrating hike that lasted well over an hour with each attained ridge only revealing another. So the Carpathians *were* in evidence if not in the Swiss Alpine sense expected.

Though the compensation was some freewheeling down the other side this in no way measured up to the climb, which indicated that we were crossing a plateau and the cooler temperatures supported the belief. But the road – the E60 and the nearest Romania can rise to an international highway – was reasonable.

The 31 kilometre mark found us in Turda, a town we had been warned about as the penultimate in industrial despoilation. Instead we found a not unattractive urban centre, its hub an expansive market square where we purchased our provisions for the day. I had evinced a craving for jam to make the bread more palatable so bought a jar in a supermarket. There was no question of what *sort* of jam for there was only one available. It was simply jam – *jem* as they call it – or nothing and we were lucky to find even that.

Of Roman origin, Turda is another Magyar stronghold, its fifteenth-century residence of the Bathony family and former seat of the Transylvanian Diet now a historical museum. A few kilometres away is to be found the Turda Gorge buried deep within near-perpendicular walls 300meters high and honeycombed by prehistoric caves. But we were not to escape the industry that virtually rings the town and on our way out had to pass huge plants, their towering red and white-striped chimneys belching vaporous smoke, black and evil yellow, into a hazy sky that had us coughing and spluttering; everything in the vicinity covered in thick grey dust.

The industry had engulfed village after village through which the road led, and heavily laden trucks driven by uncaring drivers forced us into the pot-holed verges. But we were fortunate in not having our bikes flattened as happened to one unfortunate cyclist wheeling his machine by a factory entrance out of which a lorry was inexcusably backing.

Beyond Turda and its phalanx of polluted villages our route was joined by the combined rivers Aries and Mures. With them we entered Cimpia Turzii and Ludus, the latter another handsome township, this one overlooked by a ridge at the summit of which we lay down to rest beneath a tree. Many a Romanian driver is to be found similarly stretched out during the hottest hours of the day so when in Rome. . . . The view over Ludus was splendid, the enlarged Mures river curving serpent-like below, putting me in mind, strangely, of Symond's Yat in Herefordshire. My tummy remained unsettled and following a squat behind a bush my precious toilet roll, brought all the way from England, took off down the slope and was lost forever. Heaven knows if I'd ever be able to obtain another. Continuing, we descended to the river. Its waters were low, threading mildly among occasional rocks while on the flanks of the valley eccentric hills began their approach to unseen higher ranges. Each was scattered with woods and pastures, cut up by rectangles of maize and stubble; the jagged points of trees ruffling the tops and their slopes rippled by the outlines of abandoned terracing.

Outside a village women were washing clothes in the broad river. The rhythmic smack as they beat them against flat rocks carried up to the road. To me it sounded of India; if I closed my eyes I could picture the long coloured lengths of saris spread out to dry on ghats and riverbanks. The village was long and sprawling and possessed a fourteenth-century church, its cemetery crowded with wooden crosses and the haphazard hummocks of graves.

Beyond the village we recommenced the eternal quest for a campsite for the night since we were within easy striking distance of Tirgu Mures, the next sizeable town on our agenda. Again all sheltering woods abruptly evaporated or scampered to far horizons just when needed so we took to a farm track leading into the open hedgeless fields. Groups of gypsies gleaning corn paused to watch us pass, their stares hard and penetrating. We raised a hand in greeting but received no response. Though we had taken with a pinch of salt the dire warnings from well-wishers of the danger of gypsies and their alleged hostility we played safe and moved on deep into the outback until well beyond possible observation, a patch of shrubbery becoming our eventual resting place. Having had no hot meal that day we made ourselves mugs of soup to help wash down the none-too-fresh and suppurating *slanina* we still held, and finished with a jar of plums together with bread and *jem*. To complement the meal Paul took a hefty swig of what was presumed to be home-made wine from our friends from Ladara and turned purple. "I think this wine's gone off," he remarked upon recovering his breath. I took a cautious sip to discover the liquid to be a particularly potent *tuica*.

Humidity made sleep difficult particularly with the tent's mosquito-net fully closed. But leaving it open was to invite hordes of insects inside so we sweated it out until after midnight when temperatures cooled. And in consequence of our early morning striking of camp we were in the suburbs of Tirgu Mures before many of its citizens had risen from their own beds.

The E60 into town deteriorated sharply at the approaches, its deformities transferring us onto the pavement which was but a degree better. We planned to make four contacts in Tirgu Mures, so selected the first name on my list, a Doctor Zoltan Brassai, who was reputed to reside in Strada Ghiocelului, translated as Snowdrop Street. While in the suburbs we questioned taxi-drivers as to the street's whereabouts but though they, in turn, asked other taxi-drivers the general consensus of opinion became that no such street existed. So we switched enquiries to Pasajul Violetelor, Violet Passage, and the Virag family whose daughter, Andrea, had recently been in Britain. Violets are obviously a more potent symbol than snowdrops in Tirgu Mures for, after a few mis-directions, we came upon a very unviolet-like but not unagreeable estate of high-rise apartments. On the seventh floor we came face to face with the Virag parents.

We appeared to be expected; a bedroom lay ready for us and, in no time at all, we found ourselves part of the family. Having hauled our bikes up seven floors (the lift was too small for bicycles but managed the baggage though refusing to stop at the seventh floor) we collapsed on the living-room sofa exhausted before being pressed to a mouth-watering meal in the tiny kitchen.

Both Gyorgy Virag and his wife spoke a little English but relied heavily on the expertise of Andrea whose command of the language was near-perfect. But a lack of English subtracted nothing from the warmth of the parental welcome which was of a quality I have rarely experienced. Gyorgy held an administrative job on the town council while his wife worked part-time in a shop. Though Tirgu Mures was rapidly losing its ethnic Hungarian identity it has long been considered one of the main spiritual and cultural centres of Magyar Transylvania so that its administration had not yet been entirely taken over by Romanians. The family, of course, were staunchly Hungarian with Andrea studying in Szeged University in Hungary since the universities within Romania were being ruthlessly 'Romanianised'.

Gyorgy was middle-aged, balding and blessed with a smile that could befriend a worst enemy. Furthermore it was genuine. His slightly younger dark-haired wife was a handsome, capable and warm-hearted woman of equal sincerity and openess who was not the slightest put out by our unannounced arrival. The daughter, Andrea, was an attractive girl of about 20 blessed likewise with the easy Virag smile and currently being courted, so we were led to believe – by a Scotsman. There was also a son undergoing national service in the Romanian army and stationed in the town but not allowed home from one year to another by the most restrictive of military rules. Perhaps it was as well the younger members of the family lived mostly elsewhere since the Virag apartment was minuscule though undeniably cosy; no more than a living room, kitchenette, a small room currently occupied by Andrea, and the main bedroom into which Paul and I had been installed. Where Gyorgy and his wife slept I never learnt but felt unhappy about having even temporarily usurped them.

We were to stay with the family for a whole three days and nights, our programme of activities mapped out for us but in a far less mandatory fashion than had been the case with Andras in Cluj. Would we like to see the town's museums? Would we like to go swimming in the river with Andrea and her friends? Would we prefer to go camping with some of Andrea's young friends or go on a day's family outing to Sovata and its salt lake? I simply dared not make any alternative suggestions of my own for fear these wonderfully generous folk would initiate arrangements irrespective of the expense and inconvenience to themselves. The one suggestion I did put forward was that we give them a respite for the rest of the day while we searched out our other contacts in the town which would, as in Cluj, provide an excuse to obtain an idea of its layout.

And indeed Tirgu Mures is a town worthy of study. It holds a wealth of Baroque architecture typical but more pronounced than that of other Transylvanian centres. One end of the Piata Trandafirilor is dominated by the huge Roman Catholic church built for the Jesuits in 1750 while the magnificent Palace of Culture, crenellated and turreted, forms part of the comely town centre ensemble. The town has had the same sort of tormented history as most of Transylvania even including, in recent times, a number of people killed in the 1989-90 revolution who are commemorated by a stark cross in the high street. There is little remaining of what is really old of the castle, the not-so-ancient walls enclosing a park and sundry edifices including a church, the whole set on a mound bulwarked by trees.

Our subsequent contact address proved to be barren. Shuttered and lifeless, the home of Robert Houlihan, conductor of the Tirgu Mures Symphony Orchestra, was occupied only by an elderly caretaker who gave us to understand the master to be in Paris. A shame this, for he sounded an amusing chap from what I had learnt of him. My colleague in England, who knows the fellow, told me of how he once congratulated the maestro on loosing off Beethoven's Third Symphony in the rapid and stormy manner that was obviously intended by the composer but never obeyed nowadays in the West. Robert Houlihan was delighted with the compliment but replied that some of the members of the orchestra objected, complaining they couldn't play all the notes accurately at that speed. So he quoted Beethoven at them – "bugger the notes, play the music. That's all that matters." Seemingly music critics have forgotten that sentence written into one of Beethoven's scores.

Another absentee was Doctor Janos Jung, Vice-Chairman, or something equally prominent, of the Hungarian Democratic Front in Romania. I would have much enjoyed hearing his views on the Hungarian minority question. There remains a misconception in high places both in Britain and Hungary – a misconception triumphantly quoted by Romanian politicians – that the Transylvanian Hungarians want rebellion in Romania so that they can rejoin Hungary. But nothing is further from the truth. Transylvanian Hungarians and native Hungarians are not that much enamoured with each other, though Transylvanians have been forced to emigrate to Hungary in large numbers, or to go to Hungarian universities, like Andrea Virag, in order to preserve their Hungarian culture currently being destroyed by the Romanian politicians.

An English-speaking lady who *was* at home and delighted to meet us was Zsuzsa Kiss (pronounced Keesh) who had spent three months carrying out medical (I think) research at Oxford. Together with her mother we were entertained to a tasty snack lunch ending with delicious home-made cake into which Paul was making serious inroads until I kicked him under the table. Zsuzsa's mother was a doctor and she kindly played the part by treating my still painful elbow and wrist, applying various ointments. We spent an educational hour answering their numerous questions on matters British before we moved on to locate the elusive Snowdrop Street, which we were assured *did* exist. We were to meet up with

Zsuzsa again next morning for a visit to a couple of the town's celebrated museums.

Doctor Zoltan Brassai, his wife Erzsebet, and their daughter, also Erzsebet, were likewise at home when we finally ran them to earth to be straightway invited into their elegant and superbly furnished drawing room. The Brassai family were Romanian and prosperous with it, their ownership of two cars putting them in the millionaire bracket. The good doctor held the title of assistant professor at the Faculty of Medicine in Tirgu Mures. His two sons were away, one in Germany holding down a job as a top designer for Ford – which perhaps explains the two-car acquisition. Everybody spoke good English, which made life easier for Paul and me, though I was to learn they preferred French if it couldn't be Romanian. Why hadn't we come to them for accommodation in the first place, they demanded to know. Why indeed. But of course things don't happen like that; we were not even expecting to stay with anybody. Instead they insisted we stay to dinner; and a real dinner it turned out to be, superbly cooked and served on a table laid with heavy silver cutlery and exquisite cut glass. The home-cooked salami and tomatoes followed by macaroni with a delectable mushroom sauce and then fresh peaches with Tokaj wine and, finally, a very special *tuica* was a feast we were to look back upon wistfully as we were hacking at our stale *slanina* with a Swiss army knife. Though we had changed out of our filthy shorts and wore reasonably clean if creased trousers and shirt I was acutely aware that our attire hardly did justice to the occasion, though nobody minded. Upon return to the Virags our fodder intake for the day was not over, they producing a mouth-watering *gomoc*, or apricot dumplings and blackcurrant compot washed down with English tea, our one contribution to the Virag larder.

Our walking tour of the town next day with Andrea and Zsuzsa took us initially to the Palace of Culture and its museum remarkable for a row of stained glass windows depicting episodes of early Transylvanian history, the region forming part of the Roman province of Dacia from AD 103. Incorporated into Hungary at the beginning of the eleventh century before being virtually independent for over one and a half centuries, it was then swept into the maw of the Austro-Hungarian Empire from which the present, as yet peaceful, conflict stems.

Probably the most significant of Tirgu Mures's fine buildings is that which houses the Teleki Reference Library dating from 1804 and chock-a-block with early books produced by famous early printers whose names are household ones to modern printers and publishers; these include several very early English works.

We were also shown around the modern and impressive National Theatre, backstage and all, before walking up the hill behind the town to the former hunting lodge of Ceausescu, once heavily guarded and unapproachable by his doting subjects. I was told that Ceausescu allowed no one else to hunt bear, wolves, deer or wild pig *anywhere* in Romania, which resulted in immense damage to crops. The black joke was that he seldom shot even a rabbit himself – he simply wanted to protect a macho image of himself as The Great Hunter. The building is now a hostel, seedy and run-down; not the sort of place in which I would have thought a megalomaniac like Ceausescu would care to reside even for the occasional weekend. But maybe it has seen better days.

The sun had blazed down all day and climbing the hill was an effort; descending it was nicer, and, following a late lunch back in town, Andrea together with a couple of agreeable girl students took us bathing in the Mures river. Immersed in the cool water this was nicer still. The following morning Andrea showed us the gypsy quarter of Tirgu Mures. With its rough unpaved alleys, mean tin-roofed dwellings surrounded by amassed junk and an invisible boundary separating two cultures the neighbourhood put me in mind of a wartime Jewish ghetto. It was not quite a no-go area but Andrea was visibly ill at ease as we strolled through it, attracting a retinue of ragged and raucous urchins as well as a mixture of hostile and friendly stares from adults.

The considerable gypsy population of Romania no longer carry the term 'tenters' by which they were once known. Though, always coming and going, the days when gypsies roamed the country at will are over; after World War Two they were compelled by law to settle. Their repression continues to be virulent and the attitude to them makes British racialism seem almost benign. Frequently I heard gypsies denounced as racketeers, robbers and work-shirkers, though I sometimes gained the impression that these remarks stemmed from unconscious envy of gypsy vigour, initiative and sheer impudence in the face of rules and regulations. In spite of repression and large-scale annihilation under the Nazis they have escaped being terrorised and standardised, though admittedly many gypsies are now insolent and aggressive; a natural response to being despised. Quite a number have made themselves rich, possibly in ways not greatly approved by the authorities. But at least they stick together and display an undoubted pride in their appearance. Their costumes are worn with a certain dignity and self-respect.

Our cheerful retinue of none-too-clean children followed us back to the town centre, Paul and I exchanging playful insults with them in our respective tongues. In the centre I had noticed the multitude of free-enterprise boutiques, small shops and kiosks that had sprung into being here as elsewhere. We partook of a coffee and an ice-cream in one such establishment, being served with a smile at small tables tastefully covered by gingham cloths and laid with real napkins in place of the tiny squares of flimsy tissue provided in many Romanian 'bufets'. A far cry this from the drab state-run emporia in lifeless streets I remembered so well in east European countries – including this one – during the communist era. And it was all the more startling here where the trappings of capitalism are still very much in their infancy.

In the afternoon Gyorgy Virag took the three of us to the spa town of Sovata, 60km away, in his lively little Lada saloon. Another cross the long-suffering Romanians have to bear is that of the acquisition of petrol. We had noticed the long queues of cars tailing back from every filling station holding supplies of the commodity (those with no queues were barren) and I remonstrated with Gyorgy beseeching him not to waste his precious ration on giving Paul and me a joy-ride. But he would have none of it. "That's what the stuff's for!" he laughed and that was that. However I had to admit to great satisfaction in being able to visit Sovata since our continuing route eastwards bifurcated 20 kilometres outside Tirgu Mures to take in either Sovata *or* Sighisoara; yet both places we had been implored to see. The chief attraction of Sovata lies in its celebrated salt lake, so saline, they say, that by diving in you can do yourself an injury. Bathing is forbidden during the middle of the day so as to restrict the stirring of the health-giving muddy sediment which bathers enjoy plastering all over themselves. The town itself holds little visible charm but a plethora of lakeside hotels are of a higher standard than most. The director of one of them, upon learning my profession of travel writing, took us for tea and cake to his home where he extracted a promise from me to do what I could to bring him British guests. We also met the mayor of Sovata who was eager for his resort to be promoted. It was refreshing to discover that some Romanians could still display a sense of enthusiasm for their product after the lack of incentive given them over four decades.

While Gyorgy called on associates of his in the town, Andrea, Paul and I swam and lazed in and by the lake, plastering ourselves in the blue-tinged mud as was the custom. Though the water was reputed to be more saline than any other, it held none of the unpleasant sting or smell so prevalent in Israel's Dead Sea. One section of the lakeside is taken up with bathing platforms, changing rooms, tatty kiosks and a cafe but the further end remains in its pristine state, beautiful against a background of forested hills veined by way-marked footpaths. We returned to Tirgu Mures by a different road, smaller but more picturesque and following a narrow-gauge railway line linking the two towns. There was just one train a day, we were informed, taking 4½ hours to cover the 60km. But what potential there is hereabouts for the entrepreneur with money and, hopefully, good taste. Not that the government would be much interested in any promotion of a Hungarian area, was one bitter remark made to me.

In conversation with all English-speakers we had met, the subject of the Transylvanian problem invariably arose. I was occasionally asked my opinion by both Hungarians and Romanians and my response had to be in neutral vein since there would seem to be equal right on both sides though surely it is the people currently living in the disputed territory who should have the final say in such disputes. Periodically I aired an opinion of my own that human beings should stop looking back into history and digging up ancient grudges as if they still held relevance today. Why can't the nations of the world clear the clutter from their desks and lay out the problem on a clean sheet of paper?

From force of habit our hosts spoke little of life in Romania; their life in particular. On several occasions, as our acquaintanceship deepened, I had gently attempted to elicit a few facts about their work, activities and views but, though some exchanges foundered in incomprehension, I formed the idea that this line of conversation was a source of embarrassment. I noticed too that, beyond the most superficial of polite enquiry, we were likewise never asked about our respective lives.

I was well aware of the reason for this reticence which, even in the new era of freedom the country was experiencing, had indelibly installed itself into people's minds so that caution remained an ever-present element. As with all the one-time people's democracies their hapless citizens had for decades looked for the meaning behind every such question. Informers had been created within the very fabric of the family structure so that even one's own mother, father, wife, husband or child could, intentionally or unknowingly, release some scrap of information to the omnipresent secret police and their network of agents. Thus I had come to realise that it was bad form to ask too much; polite query about matters that we take for granted had long been taboo here.

But this reticence appeared to hold no sway when it came to less personal matters and I was gradually able to build a picture of some of the more unpleasant occurrences of the Ceausescu regime though this all too often reflected the same unpleasantness I knew about only too well and, indeed, had experienced in other parts of the old communist empire. "Had Ceausescu been alive today, it would not have been possible for you to stay with us," was a reoccurring comment and no surprise to me. "Even talking to foreigners, let alone inviting them into our homes, was strictly forbidden. The *Securitate* were everywhere. If caught you would be taken away for questioning, probably beaten and heavily fined or jailed. People sometimes simply disappeared altogether. We never knew who to trust." It was all horribly familiar.

I had suggested that, hopefully, things had improved since the revolution.

"Not really," had been the stock reply. "A lot of things are worse and finding food is a big problem. The queues are longer now than they were then, only now we can complain about it."

Thus it remains a fact that the Romanian people are, at least, freer to vent their feelings and opinions and to speak to foreigners without the constant fear of one citizen betraying another by informing the omnipresent *Securitate*. "As soon as someone had fallen target to the *Securitate*, they would be followed wherever they went and would frequently be forced to leave their jobs or home; even lose their right to live in a particular town. Their friends would be harassed, followed and questioned to an unbelievable degree," my informants continued with the catalogue of evil practices, revelling in the new ability to speak their minds though still plainly uneasy about doing so.

Little faith is vested in the current President Ion Iliescu and his post-communist government of seasoned time-servers. The people of all descents are united in the knowledge that, beneath the new veneer of democracy, Romania's ills and sadnesses are the same ones they encountered, in their different ways, under the Ceausescu regime.

It is not only upon economic issues that the Romanians are struggling to come to terms with their 'liberation'. Their unease is also partly due to the fact that the *Securitate* have remained almost as rife as ever though operating under a new name, in a less visibly repressive manner, and with the blessing of communists remaining in power at the top. Freedom continues to be an elusive commodity in the country in spite of the manifestation of capitalistic enterprise. "We are like China," someone suggested to me. "Free enterprise blossoms, prices go up, but where is the freedom?"

The *Securitate* in Romania, the KGB in Russia, the STB in Czechoslovakia. All have been consigned to the dustbin of history. Gone? Who knows. But certainly not forgotten.

In the land behind the wire they came for Anna, one early summer morning. It was barely three months after our engagement and she was in the orchard of her Slaný home, picking cherries. A man and a woman, sternfaced, appeared at the foot of her ladder. She looked down at the couple and smiled.

"You want some cherries?"

There was no return smile. "We don't want cherries. We want you," replied the man. "We're from the STB."

Anna climbed slowly to the ground. "You want me now," she asked.

"Now."

"May I go and get my coat?"

"Yes but don't tell anyone who we are, you understand? Say we're from the employment office if you have to explain anything." The man was emphatic. It was as if he was ashamed of his profession.

Anna ran into the house. Her mother was in the kitchen preparing lunch. "Afraid I'll be a bit late," she told the slight grey-haired lady fussing over the stove. "The STB are here. They want me to go with them." She wasn't going to tell fibs for them.

"Where are they taking you?" her mother asked anxiously.

Anna shrugged. "Their office I presume. Don't suppose it'll be for long." She spoke unconcernedly, trying to hide her own alarm.

Donning her coat she returned to the couple in the orchard and, with them, went out through the garden. At the gate they were met by Miluška, Anna's eldest sister, coming back from a morning's shopping.

"Where are you going?" she enquired gaily.

"I don't know," was the reply as they hurried along the street leaving Miluška, perplexed, staring after them.

The woman spoke for the first time. "Why didn't you do as you were told?" she demanded in a hard voice.

Anna remained silent.

The man was short and bulky, dressed in a belted raincoat and squashed black hat. The woman's jacket and skirt were as severe as her tight hairstyle. She was young but no joy showed in her youthfulness.

A black Tatra saloon waited around the corner. A second man sat, relaxed, behind the wheel. Anna was bade sit between her escort on the back seat.

Slaný STB headquarters was on the other side of town, a discreet concrete building in the outer suburbs. It took only ten minutes to drive there and would have been less had they chosen to ignore the traffic lights near the square.

Anna was taken to an office on the ground floor. Its four dirty walls were stained with what might have been blood but was probably damp and the only decoration was a framed portrait of the country's new president, Antonín Zápotocký, which went well with the stains. The door was closed behind her.

Captain Josef Koudelka,[3] district head of the STB, sat behind a plain deal table bare except for two telephones. He had a bald head and a pink face and his prominent eyes sparkled but not with mirth. Tyrannies everywhere – if they

_____
3. Not his real name.

have a hope of establishing themselves – must be able to draw on a steady supply of such men. On orders from above, he would carry out any duty required of him without permitting considerations of personal taste to interfere with the strict and loyal discharge of his obligations. When ordered, he could even be polite; sometimes almost gentle.

Like his minions, Captain Koudelka wore plain clothes. Oddly, it made him the more sinister, for the ordinariness of the attire was in disquieting contrast with the far from ordinary appearance of the room; the stained wall, the high, small, barred window, and the over-strengthened door.

Today Koudelka had a pleasurable task; a simple interview with, and preliminary investigation of, a pretty girl. It would not be so onerous a task to show his gentle side. He looked over at Anna seated opposite him and smirked.

"Miss Krupičková, we are sorry to have inconvenienced you like this. It won't take long but we must have some answers to a few questions. It's a matter of state security, you know. Would you please tell us about your contacts with your friends."

Anna showed bewilderment. "I'm not sure what you mean," she said.

"Just tell me about your friends."

"What do you want to know about them?"

"Who are they?"

Shrugging her shoulders, Anna replied that she had many friends; schoolfriends, colleagues in the Prague office where she had worked as a secretary and translator, neighbours, friends of her parents. . . .

"Have you friends abroad?" he cut in.

Making no immediate reply, Anna considered the implication of the question. Then she said, "As perhaps you know, I was at school with Vlasta Pučkova before she, er, left for Australia." She referred to a school-friend who had succeeded in leaving the country illegally two years previously.

The captain smiled, softly, depreciatingly.

"No, I don't mean her."

There was a long silence in the room.

"Why did you visit the British Embassy in Prague the other day?" The question came like a shot from a gun and the smile faded.

"They asked to see me."

"Why?"

"Because of another friend of mine, an Englishman."

"Have you many friends in West Europe?"

"Not many."

"How many?"

"I once used to know a Dutchman who studied in Prague. He returned to Holland and for a time we kept in touch. Is there anything wrong with that?"

The captain evaded the question but asked another.

"Are you still in contact?"

"No."

"But you are with the Englishman?"

Anna saw no point in denying the fact.

"You have applied to marry this Englishman, I think, in spite of our governmental restriction of foreign marriages?"

"Yes."

"Why?"

"Because I'm fond of him." She soft-pedalled the degree of affection, conscious of the fact they were discussing personal relationships, a subject she thought was no business of his.

Koudelka returned to the subject of the embassy visit.

"What did they have to say?"

"Not much. They just wanted to know the situation and, like you, whether I really wanted to marry a British national."

"And do you?"

"Yes."

"Isn't it more the glamour of living abroad?"

Anna shook her head.

"Was the embassy helpful?"

She allowed a melancholy smile to flit across her face. They had not been at all helpful. Instead they had displayed outright suspicion, even antagonism, for reasons she was unable to fathom.

"Not very."

"So you are setting your cap at this Englishman when you've got the chance of marrying one of the most prosperous and eligible bachelors in Prague. Any other girl of your age would jump at the chance you're getting. Why, he even owns a house in the capital."

Anna was nonplussed. So they knew about Martin, who had been after her for years. But she didn't love Martin, or even like him much.

"I suppose it's for the love of this Englishman that you've given up your job?" he continued, once more startling Anna with his knowledge of her affairs. His tone turned 'love' and 'Englishman' into dirty words.

"My parents are old and I have to help them at home," she explained defensively, knowing that he was aware of the real reasons; that to be unemployed by the state gave her more chance of being allowed to leave it.

"Quite so," Koudelka brought the tip of his thick fingers together, leaned back until the chair squeaked a mournful protest. *"Quite so,"* he repeated.

Smiling again, with a sort of gentle reproachfulness he went on, *"It may well be true that you've done nothing against the New Czechoslovakia, Comrade, but,"* and the eyes were mildly rebuking, *"neither are you doing anything for it."* He signalled an end to the interview with the words, *"I advise you to be careful, young woman, very careful, And say nothing, nothing, about this talk of ours to anyone, do you understand?"* The prominent eyes turned to steel gimlets.

After the sinister and depressing room the fresh air was nectar, and Anna was glad they made her walk home. Maybe next time, or the time after, she was summoned to the STB they would not be letting her go home at all.

My months of imprisonment had played havoc with our communications, her letters to me being, by force of circumstances, unanswered. And with the imposition of Czech censorship together with letters, inexplicably, being 'lost in transit', it could only be a matter of time before our fragile correspondence could be severed.

I therefore considered it vital we meet, albeit briefly, so decided to follow a well-trodden path. Hadn't I already managed to cross the West German-Czech border using the Prague-bound portion of the Orient Express the previous year? Unless my earlier unbidden arrival at the border station of Cheb, some 15km inside Czech territory, had altered the pattern of control on both sides of the border, the way still lay open. Anyway, there was only one means of finding out.

I chose the Easter weekend 1952 for the repeat attempt. With a four-day holiday and my still-apprehensive parents under the impression I was visiting friends in Buckinghamshire, I left for Nuremberg. In earlier letters to Anna I had indicated a necessity for her to be at Cheb railway station on the Easter Saturday.

Everything went, almost clinically, according to plan. Though I was politely requested for my own good to leave the train by the Bavarian frontier authorities at the West German border station of Schirnding on account of not possessing a Czech entry visa, I had slunk back onto the coach when they weren't looking. An hour later, the almost empty train delayed by Czech border guards for the customary search for 'spies' (this to maintain the pretence that the fences were there to act as a barrier against 'Western Imperialism', rather than curbing illegal emigration by their own people), we drew into Cheb station.

My mind was a whirlwind of expectations and emotions as I scanned the platforms. All at once I caught sight of her, a lone figure I knew to be Anna. She stood beneath an iron foot-bridge and I wondered, for an instant, if she'd experienced difficulties reaching a platform serving a train from the West. Even while it drew to a halt our eyes met and I had the coach door open. Seconds later we stood on the platform together.

"Hello," I said, idiotically, "Glad you were able to meet me." Suddenly all the phrases and words I had planned for this, our first intimate conversation, fled from my mind. I looked at her in wonder. She was wearing a dark coat but all I could take in was the pale shape of her face upturned towards my own.

"Was it difficult – the journey?" she asked concernedly and the sound of her voice transported me back over seven years to that day in 1945. All I had seen of her since then had been photographs but now a warm, live Anna stood before me and I was lost in disbelief.

"No, it was quite easy," I found myself starting to explain the unimportant details and lapsed into silence. "But us, what about us?" I burst out. "We've got to find ways of seeing more of each other."

I leaned towards her, one arm around her waist, and I felt her smooth cheek against my own. There were so many things I wanted to talk to her about but this was not the place. Instead I desired no more than to effect a transition from the practicalities of regaining contact to a demonstration of tenderness that before could only be expressed in the written word.

I held her there for some moments feeling glad all the time because she was young and warm and because, though Czech, she was close to my own world: the world of being young and on the edge of danger. As I held her I looked across at the station building half expecting the intrusion of officialdom but pleased it was being so slow about it. I thought of the pleasant English countryside now scented with spring blossom and how, one way or another, I would make Anna part of it, with the Cold War and all this surreptitious border-crossing business a far-off, unreal, laughable memory. It seemed unreal even now, holding her to me, her face cool against my own weariness. Then the unreality became real as I turned my head and placed my lips against her throat and kissed her. It became real because the stupidity of one thing was sharpened by the naturalness of the other, and suddenly it was all I wanted; to hold her there on the platform, under the iron bridge and not care about time.

"You're tired," she said.

She lifted her face. Her voice was very tender.

"A little," I admitted, angry with myself for letting it show but grateful to her for what I took to be an invitation to display a more fervent demonstration of affection.

I waited a few moments and kissed her full on the mouth. Her lips were warm and soft and she reinforced the intimacy of the past minutes in the way she let the kiss go on, unprotesting and unevasive.

She broke away only of breathlessness and I laughed self-consciously, abruptly aware of the fact that we were no longer alone. Down the steps of the bridge clattered half a dozen minions of the expected interference.

"The vultures are descending," I observed quietly and unwound myself from Anna.

An officer of the border guard was the first to reach us. He seemed nonplussed.

"You're supposed to remain on the train," he said in German. He turned to Anna and a fierce exchange of Czech ensued. She interrupted the flow to explain.

"He says I'm not supposed to be on this platform or talking to you."

With no other passengers to 'process', the group of officials went through my bag and visaless passport like a dose of salts. We were led to the same immigration office to which I'd been taken the previous year and given a dressing down for carrying out such an illegal tryst with a citizen of the Czechoslovak Socialist Republic. Our individual statements were laboriously typed and signed, and then Anna was removed from the room.

The formalities completed I managed to persuade the officer to give me a few more minutes with Anna. At first he refused point-blank but gradually weakened. At heart he was a reasonable man.

"You can have the few minutes before her train leaves for Prague," he conceded, and led me out of the office.

The Orient Express still waited. It had moved to another platform and eight more coaches added to it. These were filling up with citizens en route to the Czech capital or towns along the route.

Ignoring my escort I walked briskly along the train staring in at the windows. Most of the second-class coaches were full and there was an overflow of passengers in the corridors.

She was in the fifth coach. A soldier stood ostentatiously outside her window. Ignoring him too I rapped on the glass and swiftly Anna left her seat to emerge on the platform smiling happily.

"I've come to say goodbye, but on stolen time," I explained.

Her smile faded slightly. "A long way to come for so short a time together," she said. There was a note of great pathos in her voice.

As I stood there on the platform, holding her close again, I knew that leaving her would be the hardest thing I had ever known. I kissed her again and again, my sense of frustration and anger growing as the agony for her grew, until I knew that she, too, could feel it and bear it no longer.

And then all the sweet nothings that are everything to a girl and a boy in love came in a flush of words. All the plans, hopes and intentions we had written about, and which we knew in our hearts might never be, we shared between us in those few minutes of ecstasy on Platform 1. And the good people in the corridor, who had learnt of the renegade Englishman in their midst, crowded about in friendly encouragement and sympathy.

Stolidly ignoring everyone, Anna and I spoke our last few words together.

"You'll wait for me, Anna darling?" I pleaded in a choking voice.

She saw my misery and whispered, "Perhaps one day. . . ." Her words tailed away as she buried her face in my coat.

A whistle blew. To the delight of the crowd I took Anna in my arms and kissed her passionately. The officer and the soldier shuffled their feet.

The whistle was for another train, but the time of departure for the express was due. Again Anna buried her face in my shoulder to hide her tears and I felt both the trembling of her body and a sickness in my throat. Stroking her hair I murmured, "I'll come back, darling, whatever they do."

Her voice, muffled, was almost inaudible.

"Yes, dearest one, come back. Please come back."

Another whistle shrilled and there was a banging of doors. Anna slipped back into the train. I watched it slide out of the station through the fog of my own tears.

For the rest of the day and through the night I was held in detention before being put aboard the next westbound Orient Express to be returned whence I had come.

A total of fourteen minutes together with one's girlfriend might seem poor return for a journey well in excess of a thousand miles but, to me, it was well worth the effort and the risks involved. A romance on paper is doomed to eventual extinction without an occasional physical encounter, however brief and unsatisfactory the circumstances.

Though the subject of our becoming husband and wife featured in our exchanges, I was aware that I had not actually put the question to Anna. But it *came to me that the munitions of our battle to be together might be enhanced if we were officially engaged to be married; 'girlfriend' has a far less permanent sound to it than 'fiancee'. Yet simply to write the question and obtain a written reply would have made little impact. No, the occasion should be marked, in the time-honoured fashion, as is the right of lovers everywhere.*

It was now 1953 and another Easter weekend had come round. Equipped with a toothbrush and an engagement ring I set out once more upon a familiar train ride.

For my friendly but inconvenient antagonists at Schirnding I had evolved a new tactic. By locking myself in the through-coach toilet of the Orient Express and placing a 'Kaput' (Out of Order) notice on the door I was able to evade their attentions.

At the physical border of the so-called Czechoslovak Socialist Republic nothing had changed. The repressive apparatus of the multiple fences stood stark and terrible in the early afternoon sunshine, the ploughed strip and mined zone of death running like a poisonous snake through wood and field killing all that lay athwart its path. White insulators, like obscene growths, mottled the posts that carried the barbed wire curtain. I shivered as I looked upon it and wondered how I had managed to pluck up the courage to cut my way through it those two years before. Again, I appeared to be the only passenger in the lone coach of the train and I maintained a low profile, pretending to doze, in case my all-too-familiar features should be recognised.

Approaching Cheb it was as if I were watching a film for the umpteenth time. Hanging out of the window I frantically scoured the platforms for the girl I had come to ask to be my wife. But the concourses were empty; not a soul in evidence except for a soldier by the water tower and a group of railwaymen at the head of the furthest platform. My heart was pounding wildly and despair raged within me. So the latest message had failed to reach her. She had been prevented from keeping the appointment. I'd given her the wrong date. She'd not been able to understand my disguised instructions. A host of explanations surged into my mind as I leapt onto the platform, the momentum of the still-moving train carrying me towards the foot-bridge. From its shadows a figure detached itself and I was in the arms of Anna.

I held her close while a cascade of emotions swept through me: relief, joy, triumph and pride. Kissing her hard on the mouth I closed my eyes to record the moment for eternity.

Breathlessly I broke the embrace. "Any trouble getting here?" I asked anxiously, aware that we were about to go through the same exchanges as a year ago. Were we destined for a lifetime of clandestine meetings and enquiries as to how we had managed them?

The film flickered relentlessly on. "No, did you?" She looked at me with wide, worried eyes.

"None at all. Not yet, anyway," I replied glancing ominously towards the administrative buildings across the tracks. "But listen, darling, in a minute those vultures will be onto us but there's something I want to give you first. It's what

I've come for."

While I fumbled in my pocket my eyes rested lightly on the girl before me. She had changed since the last time. The dark hair cascaded down around her shoulders but the face was more aware, confident, adult. The eyes were rimmed by dark lines and I knew the reason. The bastards were already starting to get at her. I knew too that Anna, as never before, was for me.

"There's no time for pretty words – and anyway I'm not much good at that sort of thing – but you understand I love you and want you to be my wife and – well, I've brought our engagement ring, if you'll accept it." The words came tumbling out of me as my eyes tried to hold hers and watch for the approach of authority at one and the same time. Then, ignoring the threat, I looked her straight in the face and added, "You will marry me, won't you?"

The smile on Anna's lips deepened and her eyes were moist. She held up the third finger of her left hand and nodded her head, unable to trust herself to speak.

I flung myself into her arms again and kissed her long and forcefully. Still no official had put in an appearance. "Let's go," I said, leading her towards the exit.

I suppose it was a hopeless quest but the notion of leaving the station unobserved had lain at the back of my mind. And we nearly made it. The immigration people obviously thought they were dealing with the usual empty train and had not bothered to leave their offices following a cursory glance at the coach. I had tendered my ticket to the railway official at the barrier and we were on the verge of passing through when the policeman just inside of it laid a hand on my shoulder. Passengers flowed around us, thinned and dissolved. We stood alone, naked before authority.

Taken to the administrative building we found ourselves before the same officer that had been on duty the previous year. Recognition was instantaneous and mutual.

The film was running again; the same old bits were showing on the screen.

"You again!" he all but bellowed. "I presume you do have permission this time but you can't just wander out of the station." He held out his hand for my lame passport.

Its shortcomings again revealed, he was really quite nice about things. I told him I'd come to see my fiancée.

"How long have you been engaged?" he asked.

"About eight minutes," I said.

This time the officer allowed us to be alone together for another ten. He glanced at his watch. "She must return to Prague on the express. I'm sorry."

Once more under escort we walked back to the train but the soldier with us insisted upon Anna going aboard the coach. I stood by her window and through the glass I could see the reflection of her features, cloudy and unreal, beside my own. It was very white; I could hardly believe in the reality of it and simply stood there watching mindlessly as if she were a cloudy memory in the glass. Then she got the window open a little but it was too high and her breath was forming on the cold glass. I fancied I could hear her breathing very quickly, with small gasps of pain, as if she had been running to find me and was frightened, and I saw she was trying to talk to me at the same time.

A passenger helped her lower the window further and we were able to touch one another and whisper our last words so that nobody could hear.

"Now we're an engaged couple," I declared brightly, "they'll relent, just you see. Never fear. I won't give up now."

Anna, recognising the need for mutual support, attempted to drown her own misery in a welter of practicalities. "In spite of the ban I'll apply to be married and I'll go and see the authorities in Prague. And I'm leaving my job so that my usefulness to the state is no more, and. . . ."

The whistle of the train ended, for us, the torture of our feigned jubilation. At that moment I wanted more than anything in the world to put my arms around her for I saw she was crying and I could do nothing about it. In the long seconds before the train eased from the platform I perceived she was not crying just for herself, or because she was young, or for the sadness of the moment. She was crying for something that I would never have understood without her, and now did understand because of her. Deep within myself, all these factors became part of the same thing, and I knew that what she was really crying for was the agony of all that was happening in the world.

Our hands were dragged apart as the train slid away and I was left staring after a receding coach, a small arm forlornly waving from it

Locked in a small unlit room adjoining the police office to wait enforced home-going I was, with the spur of despair, already planning the next move. Through the barred window the empty platforms were dazzling in the late afternoon sun.

Chapter 8
Romania: Southern Transylvania

Leaving Tirgu Mures and the Virag family was, at least for me, quite an emotional affair. Seldom have I come to feel such an affection for a family in so short an acquaintanceship. With such as the Virags there is hope for the world.

Our road leading out of town in the general direction of Brasov remained the E60 and for the first 24km to the junction village of Balauseri was a retracing of the route covered by car the previous day. Two uphill slogs rewarded us with two lengthy freewheelings as we traversed a couple of minor passes and it was as we were contentedly gliding down the long descent into Balauseri that the second unpleasant incident of the journey occurred.

Very thoughtfully, Paul had elected to follow in my tracks throughout, adapting his speed to that of mine. Only on long downhill runs did he forge ahead to enjoy his ability to go faster than I. And it was while I was more ponderously descending this hill, with Paul far ahead of me and unaware of the situation, that the gypsy attack took place.

From the side of the road the three dark-skinned youths, armed with staves, ran at me, one hitting my already damaged arm, another trying to knock my camera bag from the handlebars. Forced to a standstill, I ran my bike at them though I could barely hold it for the pain. Unable to remove the bag – presumed, I suppose, to contain money – the attackers gave it another clubbing. A passing car momentarily discouraged further offensive action and I was able to jump on my bike and, steering with one hand, escape downhill. Paul, awaiting me in the village, was on the point of returning to investigate my non-appearance. He had seen the three gypsies but had taken little notice of them, or they of him. With an ugly black weal blossoming across my arm we took the road to Sighisoara, our views on gypsies undergoing radical reassessment.

Hardly out of Balauseri and we came under a second assault but this time no more than verbal as another group of gypsies, including a girl, yelled obscenities at us, and approached threateningly. The girl was screaming something; the fact we didn't understand sending her into paroxysms of rage, her face contorted into a mask of pure hatred.

In spite of these setbacks and the pain of my arm we covered the further

45km to Sighisoara by midday, there to relax under the warm sunshine in the town's central park. Here we were able to assess the damage to my cameras and partake of a picnic lunch, much of it provided by the good Virags.

If nothing else the one fact known about Transylvania by the English-speaking world is that it is the home of Dracula and the reputation – wholly undeserved – inflicted on the province by Bram Stoker's novel. Those visitors who come to Romania invariably have Bran Castle – which is everyone's idea of what a vampire's castle should look like – in their sights. Yet Dracula, or Vlad Tepes (Vlad the Impaler) to give him his full and proper name, seldom visited the establishment and certainly never lived there. But his birthplace is assuredly Sighisoara.

The town's most celebrated citizen was the son of Vlad II, or Vlad Dracul, as he is better known. Vlad Dracul, or Vlad the Devil or Dragon to complicate things further with translation, was so named not because of his devilish deeds but because he was a member of the Order of the Dragon with which he was invested in 1431. Son Dracul simply inherited the name of his father and was known as 'the son of the devil, or dragon'; indeed, in later years he signed himself 'Dracula' or 'Draculea' upon securing the throne of Wallachia in 1436, taking up residence in Tirgoviste. These were cruel days and the Turkish and Hungarian threat to his territory served only to fuel this cruelty with impalement upon sharpened stakes as the standard punishment for perceived or actual wrongdoers. Hence the 'Impaler' appendant to the younger Vlad's name though his barbarism was no more intense than that of other rulers, especially the Turkish sultans.

Sighisoara, the most perfectly preserved medieval town in Romania, is first mentioned by historians as far back as 1191 when it was already old. It is a German town with the German name of Schassburg, one of the original fortified towns established in Transylvania in the twelfth and thirteenth centuries by immigrants from Saxony. Its teutonic past is reflected strongly in the high, tightly clustered roofs resembling those of historic German cities such as Augsburg or Nuremberg. The citadel sits atop a hill, ringed by walls which climb steeply around it; their corners marked by a narrow turret with a triangular red roof. Within the outer walls rise the points of Gothic spires, the knotted tower of the main gate, and, on the very summit, the brooding bulk of the Bergkirche.

The old streets were bare and neglected, the cobbles worn and in need of replacement. The Pied Piper was once credited with bringing the Saxons to Transylvania and it is easy to picture the Piper jigging through these ancient streets. The story goes that the children of Hamelin whom he lured into the mountainside were conjured a thousand miles to the east by some subterranean channel and released in the Carpathian hills, possibly to this very spot.

Our frugal picnic might just as well have taken place on the stage of the London Palladium for the entertainment it gave to a pack of Sighisoarans who came and sat on adjoining park benches to watch the spectacle. I appeared to be the centre of attraction; my rust-coloured beard and a T-shirt proclaiming an incomprehensible message in Nepalese. Maybe they took me for a reincarnation of the gentleman from Hamelin.

Following an appraisal of the damage done in the gypsy offensive – my main camera beyond repair, the smaller one dented, my arm repairable – we took leave of our admirers and wended our way out of town. I had toyed with the idea of visiting a doctor but dreaded the findings might discourage progress by my having to ignore the prescript of resting the offending limb. I had heard that doctors were not highly regarded in Romania. They were paid less than workers who thought themselves superior as a result – until they were ill themselves when they would come to the surgery with flattery and a packet of American cigarettes.

Apple and cherry-plum trees lined the smaller road that branched eastwards off the E60 some 12km beyond Sighisoara. We gorged ourselves with windfalls when the realisation struck that it was a Saturday afternoon and therefore deficient of shopping opportunities. And it was a Saturday afternoon par excellence in the small town of Cristuru Secviesc of empty, lifeless streets; most of the population crammed into a grotty juke-box-blaring cafe which at least sold ice-cream cornets and the usual hair-oil-tasting lemonade.

The villages hereabouts contained houses solid and well-built, with windows like half-closed eyes in their tall red roofs, the curved and elongated dormer windows of Germanic central Europe. Some looked older than their Baroque fronts; irregular medieval buildings shrugged into symmetrical façades. Inside their massive carved doors and gateways lay vine-enshrouded courtyards about which could be glimpsed covered stairways and galleries. The acquisition of food might have been a problem but we would never go short of water; sturdy pumps stood on the street verges, their output cool, clear and free to all-comers.

Our campsite for the night was on a slope at the edge of a wood and in an arbour of thorn bushes reached by a punishing uphill push of our bikes and baggage; our supper a reserve packet of soup. Thunder rolled about the hills but no rain fell.

Even before Tirgu Mures the intensifying heat was encouraging us into making increasingly earlier post-dawn starts with correspondingly earlier camp halts, often with a couple of hours rest around midday. Thus we could reap the benefit of cool mornings for the first hours of cycling. And here at the approaches to the Harghita Mountains these early mornings were delicious with surrealistic views of far horizons above belts of low-hanging mists. We were not only up and about with the lark but also with herds of cows, buffalo, sheep and goats, their guardians taking advantage of the empty roads. Being nudged off a bike by an ambling buffalo or inquisitive goat was to become a regular morning occurrence.

In the one-time Szekler town of Odorheiul Secuiesc we went in search of another contact address; a passing cyclist out for a Sunday spin being good enough to lead us to it amongst the usual dragon's teeth of tower-blocks. But the address was wrong; Istvan and Agnes Balint lived elsewhere on the estate. However the young woman who answered the door that still early Sunday morning not only knew where the Balints lived but took us there clasping her sleeping baby in her arms. Alas, the Balints were elsewhere (in Tirgu Mures!) but we were generously entertained to a breakfast of tea and home-made cake by Istvan's mother.

Grappling with the language barrier – the lady spoke no English – we were apprised of the couple's devotion to old traditional Hungarian dancing. During the Ceausescu regime *tanchazak* became very popular, the Hungarians claiming that, being a 'cultural activity,' it was perfectly legal while in actual fact, of course, they were simply illegal gatherings of Hungarians cocking a snook at Ceausescu.

We left Odorheiul Secuiesc marvelling at the boundless kindness of Transylvanians – whether of Hungarian or Romanian origin – who would go to such trouble to help strange foreigners. I wondered if my own countrymen generally speaking would so universally go to these lengths were the boot to be on the other foot. I fear not and, in this judgement, include myself above all.

The onward road to Miercurea-Cuic was a pain; distorted and a morass of ruts and pot-holes that were in danger of shaking bikes, baggage and riders to pieces. The route lay over the Vlahita Pass incorporating some of the steepest climbs come across so far, all up, up, up, which, as we trudged interminably onwards, counting each kilometre stone, had us yearning for the long-anticipated downhill run that surely must follow. Our prodigious thirst prompted a topping up of water at every well in sight.

For the tongue-twisting pronunciation of the town names in these parts we had devised our own English equivalents. Thus Odorheiu-Securiesc had become 'Social Security' and we were not heading for Miercurea-Cuic which we re-christened 'Misery Quick' – though at our present tortuous rate of progress maybe 'Misery Slow' would have been the more appropriate.

The actual pass, when we reached it, turned out to be rather pleasant; a view obviously shared by the scores of campers and backpackers that congregated upon its summit. The little road had relentlessly climbed, twisting through narrow valleys between beech-scarved hills, their lower slopes pastureland. Only sheep bells and the rushing of a boulderous young river broke the stillness. Gradually the beech woods became mixed with tunnels of spruce firs to produce what to me was an enjoyable, if dingy and mysterious, melancholy. This was rudely shattered by the summit's 'leisure development' of refreshment bars and acres of litter proving, if nothing else, that Britons are not the only culprits when it comes to discarding rubbish. In Romania each county is responsible for its own road maintenance and on entering the Harghita region it was apparent that the authorities had neglected their duties. But following the municipal rubbish dump of the 'leisure development' the road surface improved as the way snaked through dark forest alternating with miles of bright hilly pastures, yellowed by cowslips and dotted with lone spruce saplings or pale larch groves.

And then, joy oh joy, came a near 10km non-stop freewheeling downward run on the best road surface we had yet experienced in the country. Road resurfacing operations had been in evidence prior to the lip of the descent so maybe my harsh words about Harghita county's neglect of its highways were premature. Alas, the long effortless glide was, for me, blighted somewhat by the difficulty of prolonged application of the brakes resulting from my injury.

At the bottom of the hill lay Miercurea-Cuic – Misery Quick – basking in the lower altitude midday heat. So as to make an extended study of the map we patronised an open-air bar in the town enjoying a couple of well-earned beers as we did so. Our subsequent destination was the town of Sfintu Gheorghe –

translated, correctly, as St George – about 70 km southwards by the direct route but more if we were to take a diversion to the spa resort of Covasna. Scanning the map my eyes fell on the place-name Iasy – known sometimes as Jassy – a town not a tremendous distance away near the Ukrainian border and I remembered it as the place through which I had passed on my first-ever visit to Romania.

It was 1970 and I had been on a rail journey across Siberia to the Pacific returning homeward by way of Uzbekistan and the Ukraine in the then Soviet Union. Though I was not indulging in any of my earlier clandestine indiscretions I nevertheless was deficient of the correct USSR visa, the one I possessed being valid for Moscow city only. This shortcoming miraculously went unnoticed when I was 5,000 miles off course but it *was* detected on the Ukrainian-Romanian border when only 2,000-odd miles from the Soviet capital. Things being what they were in those days I was straightway removed from the train to spend an uncomfortable 48 hours under arrest in a border guards' barracks while efforts were made to obtain instructions from Moscow regarding my disposal. What was worse, the authorities, while they waited, attempted to make me pay for my enforced board and lodging. This I flatly refused to do which threw everybody to the extent of them persuading a spotty-faced Intourist guide from Kishinev to come and pacify me. Telephonic communications in the USSR being no better than they are today in the Russian Federation no instructions were forthcoming and eventually I agreed a compromise with my compulsory hosts. They purchase my onward rail tickets to Bucharest and I would pay for my lodging such as it was. Glad to get rid of me and honour satisfied, we went our ways, mine being over the river Bug into Romania – and Iasi.

Lame or non-existent visas have become a fact of life for me but none more frustrating than those absentee mauve stamps in my passport of 1954.

It was my customary lack of proper documentation that caused the failure of an operation I instigated in the Soviet zone of the then three-power-divided Austria with the object of making another tryst with Anna. The venue this time was the Czech border township of Horní Dvořiště just across the frontier from the Austrian town of Summerau and the plan was to be of similar ilk to those tried and tested on the Czech-West German border. Being a 'softer' border than that of a direct East-West confrontation I foresaw few difficulties for her; the snag on my side being that I would have to cross Soviet-occupied ground between Linz and the border. I had come by car from the then-Yugoslavia, making my way to Vienna, from whence I had managed to drive to Linz avoiding, more by luck than judgement, the attentions of the Soviet checkpoint at Enns Bridge who inspected the required 'grey card' document in one vehicle out of three. Needless to say, I possessed no 'grey card'.

And in Linz that first night an extraordinary thing happened. I was walking back to my small hotel through the darkened back streets of the city when I became aware of a car following me. No headlight beams flooded over the cobbles and abruptly it struck home that the vehicle was not intending to pass. I glanced over my shoulder. A big saloon with no lights crawling slowly in my wake drew to a halt and the cold recollection of tri-power-controlled Vienna, city of intrigue, arose within me. I moved on, chiding myself for an over-vivid imagination, then stopped. The car, closer now, stopped too.

I spun round and realised that it was not imagination. At the same time the vehicle accelerated to draw level with me. About to make a run for it, I was checked by the voice emanating from the white blob of a face at the open rear window.

In broad American it said, "Are you Mister Portway?"

The brim of a Homburg hat crowned the face but it was the accent that prevented me from running; it wasn't the one I expected.

"Why?" I asked defensively.

The car door opened but the man in the back seat made no effort to get out. Instead he put his hand into his breast pocket and I backed away, still apprehensive.

He spoke again. "Take it easy. This is who we are," he said, handing me a white card.

I took it warily and strained to read the writing. With difficulty I made out the words 'United States Military Intelligence'.

Some of my fright evaporated but I remained suspicious. "What do you want?" I demanded.

Out of the corner of my eye I saw the driver flick on a lighter for his cheroot, the small flame illuminating a check shirt of lurid hue. The glimpse was gratifying. Surely no self-respecting Soviet agent would be seen dead in a thing like that.

"We want a few words with you, if you don't mind," came the answer. "Come and sit in the car; it's warmer."

Hesitatingly I climbed into the back seat. They could have got me in by force anyway. The man moved to make room for me and the driver swivelled to face us.

"We understand you're intending to take a train to Summerau tomorrow morning," announced the man beside me.

It wasn't their business, but I saw no reason to deny it. I nodded.

"You know it's in the Russki zone?" he went on.

"Yes."

The American continued undeterred. "We have no authority to stop you, but very strongly advise you not to go."

I decided to ignore the advice. "Much as I appreciate the concern of the United States," I replied primly, "I cannot – will not – cancel my arrangements."

I noted their looks of concern and wondered how it was that America should be involved in my problems even though Linz did lie in what was technically part of the American zone of Austria. To explain my uncooperative attitude I started to tell them the reasons for my proposed journey.

"We know." The driver spoke for the first time.

His remark confused me. I tried to work out from which of the various possible sources the information could have been gained. Additional to my last letter to Anna from England mentioning my intentions in cryptic fashion, there had been my postcard from Zagreb and, of course, the telegram from Vienna. In a place like that, one might as well broadcast it on Radio Free Europe.

I spent nearly an hour in the car, the conversation getting bogged down in a groove. The Americans worked every gambit to prevent my proposed excursion and, equally relentlessly, I declared my determination to go.

"Well, it's your funeral," was my companion's last word on the subject. "Like a lift back to your hotel?"

They even knew which hotel.

Li nz Central Station is a modern, airy building and I was there in good time for my train. I purchased a ticket for Summerau, not being able to obtain one through to Horní Dvořiště.

My train drew in on platform 4, a slow personenzug, scheduled to stop at most stations. By the central clock I checked my watch. Fourteen minutes to go.

Depositing myself in a second-class coach facing the engine, I waited. Since the border would be communist territory on both sides – Czech and Soviet – I envisaged little likelihood of heavy controls and vigilance. I looked at my watch. Eight minutes to go.

Four had gone when a trio of faces appeared at the window. Two of them I recognised. "Good morning, Chris," said the one who had sat next to me in the car the previous evening.

"Good morning to you," I replied brightly.

"Then you're going?"

"Yes."

"Well let me introduce Inspector Salzbach of the Austrian Border Police," he turned to the third member of the group. "We have news for you."

I nodded to the plain clothes policeman.

The American continued. "The inspector's district includes that of Summerau. His men there reported a couple of hours ago that two members of the Soviet Security Police are waiting at the station for the expected arrival of a British national. All right, it might be someone else but I don't know what Summerau's got to draw trainloads of Limeys there so early in the morning." He looked at me quizzically.

But I still refused to be deterred. It was wholly too incredible that the intelligence organisations of the two major world powers should be mobilised to catch one small insignificant Englishman going to visit his girl.

The American was continuing. "And what the Russkies know it can be assumed the Czechs know too. No doubt they've been alerted on their side of the border."

I felt a slither of ice in my bowels. Anna would be at Horní Dvořiště within the next hour or so – if she wasn't there already. Would anything happen to her?

"How do I know you're not making all this up?"

For an answer the inspector produced a cable reply form and showed it to me. The printing was in German but I understood most of the text and it looked authentic. I continued to hesitate.

The American noticed my hesitation. He shot another bolt.

"Last night you asked us how we knew about you and the girl," he spoke

quietly. "In Vienna you sent her a telegram, didn't you, and a postcard – a postcard – from Zagreb? You gave everybody plenty of warning."

A whistle blew; doors slammed. But I was off the train as if it were red hot, my worst fears confirmed.

That first broken tryst was a bitter disappointment. I thought dismally of Anna waiting on a strange hostile border station for a man who never came. And my anguish as I worried about her safety was such that it partly eclipsed the sting of defeat.

There came another defeat the following spring though on this occasion I possessed at least a Soviet-granted visa. Its acquisition was by no means easy since it was for the then Soviet-administered German Democratic Republic – East Germany – and it permitted me to attend the first Leipzig Industrial Fair to be held since before the Second World War. However, by using the notepaper of my family firm and presenting myself as a prominent businessman eager to sell products to the East Bloc I had pulled it off. Actually the visa was valid solely for the city of Leipzig and nowhere else in the GDR but I was banking on the expectation that no German police authority would understand the Russian hieroglyphics, whilst the purple blaze of CCCPs and impressive tax stamps across it might even encourage them to help me on my illegal way.

Anna and I had, in the meantime, evolved a secret code between us that we hoped would be more efficient than the cryptic hints and innuendoes that sprinkled my letters to her when I had something to say that I hoped would not be understood by others. We used it for the first time on this occasion, the arrangement being that, if there was no possibility of her being able to travel to Leipzig to meet me at the fair's main entrance, then I would come, again by train, to Bad Schandau, near the East German-Czech border, and attempt to link up with her at Děčín on the Czech side of it. Again it was a 'soft' border – or so I thought – since the GDR and the CSR were communist allies.

I thus spent four uninspiring days in Leipzig feigning an interest in Soviet tractors, East German turbines and Chinese carpets between visits to the main gate in the unlikely supposition that Anna might be there. During this period I also obtained a rail ticket to Bad Schandau in spite of the necessity of a police permit to visit a border area and an Auslander – foreigner's – travel permit, my Soviet visa working as a kind of magic wand. On the fifth day I left Leipzig on the Dresden-bound train from whence I transferred to the Berlin-Prague Express which carried me in style to Bad Schandau. Now would come the tricky bit.

Remaining on the train I awaited the batch of passport and emigration officials passing through the coaches. They were plainly impressed with my collection of hieroglyphics but they still failed to add up, in their Teutonic minds, to a Czech entry visa and I was politely ushered off the coach. Waiting demurely on the platform near the exit until half the train had been 'processed' I then began retracing my steps towards the processed portion only to be brought up short by a loitering police officer. The good fellow, catching a glimpse of my visa and feeling it his duty to undertake a good deed for the day, ushered me *back on the train. Unfortunately it was a first class compartment into which I had been ushered and hardly had I sank down into the luxurious upholstery when the ticket inspector hove into view. That worthy promptly directed me, with disdain, to the neighbouring coach where I ran straight into one of the immigration crowd who instantly recognised my Anglo-Saxon features.*

"What are you doing on this train again?" he demanded.

"One of your men put me on it," I explained fatuously, dismay precluding a more constructive reply.

Again I was removed from the train, but this time in a more heavy-handed manner and taken to the Soviet Kommandatura across a neighbouring street. Here a good-natured Soviet army captain took a peek at my visa; its deficiencies revealed at last.

"The Volkspolizei are anxious to hand you over to us," he told me, smiling, "but it was they who caught you so it's they who must deal with you." He gave me a wink as if he liked German authority as little as I did.

Under close arrest and with an escort of four heavily-armed 'vopos' – Volkspolizei or People's Police – I was taken aboard a one-coach diesel train. It didn't seem to be a service train at all, rather a police special, and it stood at a platform not used by the public. Once in the coach the quartet became exceedingly friendly, one even offering me a bottle of lager.

An hour later the train jerked into motion, moving out onto the main southbound line in the wake of the Prague Express. Alas, however, it was not going as far as Děčín, only to the physical border, a wayside halt used by GDR border guards and shadowed by the eastern wall of the Elbe valley. The river ran close by, wide and sluggish. On it a string of barges were moving downstream.

"Tschechoslowakei," announced one of my escorts, pointing to a pier that projected into the water less than 500 yards away.

My eyes fondled the rough wooden structure, my heart thumping against my ribs at the realisation that now only 8km lay between me and Anna, again awaiting me in vain.

Transferred from rail to water I was taken by open police launch diagonally across the river. My eyes continually turned towards Czech territory so tantalisingly close. Maybe if I made a dash for it, . . . but four men with machine carbines made the odds too high.

Disembarking at another jetty we walked about a kilometre along a path to an unkempt villa. The villa was one of several in a hamlet basking peacefully in the sunshine. But no life showed in the village; this one had paid the price of lying in a frontier zone, its former inhabitants removed.

In an almost bare room I was put through a mild form of interrogation.

My questioner was a small man, slight in build but with a large close-shaven head and enormous dark, luminous eyes. He was quite pleasant and seemed to be questioning me more out of personal curiosity than a sense of duty. I told him all I deemed it necessary that he should know and then asked him a few questions of my own appertaining to my immediate future.

"I don't think you'll be delayed long," he told me with a marked lack of conviction.

Then I had a brainwave. *"I have a friend at Děčín. Do you think I might telephone her at the station there?"* I asked innocently. At least it would be a method of assuring Anna I was close at hand.

The man wanted to know who she was.

"Oh, just a girlfriend," I said in a manner of the sailor who had a girl in every port.

"We'll see about it," came the rejoinder, but the tone implied he wouldn't.

My next interviewer was the jovial Russian. He too bombarded me with questions, these emphatically not inspired by line of duty. It appeared he was something to do with the military police, and his liaison duties frequently took him to border posts.

Again I was so bold as to put my request regarding Anna. *"We'll see about it,"* came the stock reply.

I remained in the post for two nights and the best part of two days, my bedroom being a dormitory containing rows of bunks. I was well treated and, under escort, allowed out to view the border defences that cut through the village. At the fence were a troop of East German armoured cars, their 20mm cannon aimed at Czechoslovakia. The fence was less daunting than those on the Western borders but nevertheless offered a strange adjunct between countries of a similar political hue. Honour among thieves, I thought.

The second day I was informed that I would be returned to Berlin sometime 'tomorrow' though I had not the slightest desire to be 'returned to Berlin' since not only had I not come from there in the first place but the city was not on my route home. However that was not the point. The longer I could remain close to the Czech border the better chance I stood of breaching it and reaching Anna – either at Děčín if she was still waiting or her home if not. I was determined not to let my close proximity to her country go without a single bid for success. My only hope now lay in escaping my present 'house arrest' or getting away from my escort en route back to Bad Schandau.

The following midday I found myself back in the company of the four troopers who had brought me to the post. They were now to return me across the river. My final opportunity to breach the lesser-guarded border had arrived and I simply had to take it.

We walked in single file along the same path. It was a fine day but not warm enough to have dried the muddy track. My eyes sought out the ridge of higher ground I had previously noted as well as, near the river, the belt of willows and thin undergrowth that lay to the rear of it. They offered momentary cover from the inevitable bullets – if I could reach it before my fleeing figure could draw fire.

I turned my attention to my companions. The non-commissioned officer walked ahead of me; he carried no more than a stick he had picked up with which he was idly flickering at tufts of grass. A pistol in a holster was at his belt. The man directly behind me posed the most serious threat for he cradled a machine carbine though not in a state of readiness. Unless there was a round in the chamber – which was unlikely – the gun was unloaded; no magazine was *clamped to the breech. Even as I watched he slung the weapon over his shoulder and, as we neared the river bank, joined his two other colleagues in throwing stones into the water.*

We drew level with the ridge. From the moment of take-off I estimated an eleven-second delay before things could get nasty; three seconds for the men to recover from their surprise, ten for the unslinging of their carbines, clipping on of magazines, cocking of the mechanism and opening fire, less two for luck (theirs not mine). I thought I could be over the ridge inside of eight. The NCO might react faster but I could but hope he was not a crack pistol shot.

One of the thrown stones 'plopped' into the river and bounced along the surface. The man behind me bent to pick up another. Taking a deep breath I hurled myself sideways. Precisely four steps I took before my feet slid from under me on the wet, greasy shoulder of the path. Winded, I lay on the ground staring fixedly at the nearest 'vopo', his gun aimed straight at me, loaded and cocked. It occurred to me my calculations were out by at least five seconds.

Thereafter the atmosphere amongst us became distinctly frosty. Miserably I looked back towards the Czech pier as we chugged back across the river.

They stopped the Prague-Berlin Express at the halt just for me. The silver locomotive screeched to a standstill; the driver's face an exclamation of surprise. Heads peered from windows. I was ushered into a first-class coach but only one 'vopo' came with me.

We spoke little on the ride to Berlin's Ostbahnhof. He tried to make me pay the fare but I refused, arguing that I never wanted to go to Berlin in the first place. I even got the chap to come with me to the ticket barrier to forestall any complications there before I released him.

It was my one small victory in the whole sorry episode.

My summons to Department M11 at the War Office was perfunctory and curt. An anonymous major wearing a Brigade of Guards tie brought out a folder marked 'Secret & Confidential'. He said he expected I knew why they had asked me to come. I replied that I hadn't the faintest idea.

"This is on you," he added, tapping the folder.

"All mine!" I exclaimed with perhaps a shade too much enthusiasm.

"It's a matter of concern," I was tartly informed. The major lacked a sense of humour.

The gist of the subsequent discourse was that, by my activities of late in Eastern Europe I was not only putting myself in grave danger but compromising the security of my own country by laying myself open to communist-inspired blackmail. Wasn't I a commissioned officer in Her Majesty's Territorial Army?

"I'll resign if that's any help," I vouchsafed. But he didn't want that. The TA were desperately short of officers.

The major then chronicled a run-down of my nefarious deeds in Yugoslavia, Austria and East Germany right down to the smallest detail. As the toneless voice flowed on, the hairs on the back of my neck rose in awe at the recital of disclosures.

Only later did I discover that Anna never received my telegram from Vienna though the Zagreb postcard got through as did my missives appertaining to East Germany. Thus she'd spent days hanging around the stations of Horní Dvořiště and Děčín waiting for every train that arrived from outside her own country. But at least she was, so far, safe though I was by now aware that everyone – Czech, Russian, American and British – was making damn sure I never reached her again.

Miercurea Cuic is a town with a troubled history, a former Szekler centre fought over by Tartars, Turks, Hungarians and Romanians as well as, later, Germans during their world War One offensive against Moldavia and Wallachia. A pleasant enough town, we discerned, even if we couldn't pronounce it. And the tortuous lingo had is cycling several kilometers in the wrong direction when we confused Gheorghe Gheorghiu-Dej with Sfintu Gehorghe (the former town has become a more pronounceable Onesti since the 1989-90 revolution; the signs in Miercurea Cuic were out of date).

Our camp site that night was on the bank of a fast-flowing river, amongst well-fruited rasberry bushes though the proximity of water also spawned an epidemic of mosquitoes. during the night a violent thunderstorm raged with lightening flickering incessantly, and if this wasn't enough to keep us awake, the quacking of ducks, frightened by the storm, made their contribution.

The storm brought an abrupt change in the weather, the morning being wet and heavily overcast, the rain accompanying us as we pedalled damply towards Sfintu Gheorghe, a town in which we held the name of our last contact. If we had been able to see it through the murk, the countryside was engaging, but low cloud hung over the land, sweeping down the sides of the distant hills that were not quite mountains. Flocks of crows pecked at flattened carcasses on the wet road and the verges were obstructed by broken-down Trabants and lorries fallen victim to the deluge of water. Our proposed diversion via Covasna was voted down two-nil.

Crossing the Defileul Tusnad – presumably the Tusnad Defile, or pass – again through the Harghitas the scenery would have been sensational had we once more been able to see it but our eyes were only for a source of food, particularly bread. Village after village through which the way led could raise none though at last, after repeated enquiries, we obtained a loaf from a factory that had nothing whatsoever to do with the manufacture of foodstuff. Our road, all along, performed somersaults involving much walking, a mode of locomotion we preferred anyway in the rain. Herds of cows being driven to pasture antagonised the few motorists who came this way; their impatient hooting and shouting doing nothing to aid progress. A convoy of gypsies we eyed with the deepest suspicion as we cycled by.

A car accident and its attendant bevy of police cars provided the last village before Sfintu Gheorghe with the event of the month, though our vocal efforts to acquire a bowl of soup in the local 'bufet' might have provided another. And then the rain stopped, the sun came out and we were on the threshold of our destination.

We could find nothing initially of which we much approved in Sfintu Gheorghe except for its people, the town itself holding little to impress the casual visitor. Ravenous, we went in search of a 'bufet' and came upon a vegetarian restaurant wherein one queued for a hot meal comprising beans or cheese-potato or macaroni or tomato soup, each serving having to be weighed and measured meticulously. But there was no 'or' about it for us; we ordered the lot which had to be weighed and served on four individual plates. The other clients gazed in awe as we swiftly polished off the feast, our flooded shoes leaking rivulets of water across the floor.

In a smoke-filled bar we concluded the meal with a beer and elicited help in locating the street in which Albert Levente and his girlfriend Emese Malnasi, a young journalist couple, were reputed to reside. But though the brigandish company lent over backwards to oblige, even leading us to the nearby police station, it became a hopeless quest – until we came upon Strada Infratirii entirely by accident. Alas, nobody answered the door of the flat and we were on the point of moving on when one of those incredible acts of spontaneous generosity so typical of Transylvania took place.

Opposite the apartment block was a school. Purely on the offchance that somebody there might know Albert Levente we made enquiries which brought into our presence the lady secretary who spoke a little English. Yes, she knew Albert and promptly phoned his father, appropriately a master in another of the town's schools. What was arranged I don't know but, without preamble, we were taken into the good woman's care, led to her apartment and pressed to soup, apple-cakes and China tea. This interlude concluded and our bikes hauled up flights of stairs to the safety of the tiny kitchen, we were whipped off in her car to a couple of villages outside the town in which lived various members of her family. In one resided her mother and father occupying a rambling old farmhouse into which we were ushered to be received as if we were long-lost relatives by the older couple. Coffee and a special *tuica* flavoured with caraway seeds was served in an airy, high-ceilinged and thick-walled living room, each time I drained my glass it being quietly replenished. Adjoining the house was an example of the region's ancient fortified churches – part church, part fortress, all turrets and battlements surrounding a devoutly pious core into which we were led on a tour of inspection. Then it was on to the next village to be introduced to the good lady's daughter and her husband – or maybe it was her son and his wife – for more coffee, more *tuica* and apples picked from the tree served in the garden under a red sunset. So finally back to Sfintu Gheorghe, collection of our bikes, and a fond farewell to a gracious lady whose name we never learnt.

The Levente flat was well and truly open when we returned there, a lively party in progress into which we were pitched. Albert was an engaging young man who spoke limited but understandable English as did his partner, Emese, a good-looking, rather reserved young lady. Who the others were I was never to know. The Hungarian wine flowed; we were pressed to an assortment of delicacies and, in the middle of proceedings, offered a hot bath presumably either as a simple courtesy or because we ponged so highly. This was taken in a neighbouring apartment block, the water in Albert's block having been turned off. Finally we got to bed, not unthankfully, upon a mattress on the floor for what remained of the night at the end of an eventful and somewhat bewildering day.

The young couple, whose home we had again usurped, slept elsewhere, not returning before midday thus giving plenty of time to wash our clothes in cold water ladled from a bath serving as a reservoir, a common practice in Romania where the water supply is erratic to say the least. When Albert did return to assuage both his and our hangovers with pungent black coffee he was to insist upon us staying a second night so giving him opportunity to show off his town.

The couple were members of an association of artists that had organised an exhibition of tapestry designs in the local museum so we dutifully did the rounds of these before moving onto the church which is probably the nicest and certainly the oldest edifice in Sfintu Gheorghe. Again of castle-like construction its ornate organ contrasted strongly with a plain interior. From the cemetery was a fine view of the town together with the encircling Baraoltului and Bodacului hills.

It had rained in the night but the sun blazed down as we tramped the streets finally to end up at the printing and composition rooms of the regional newspaper in which our host and hostess worked. Introduced to the staff, we learnt how happy everyone was to be able at last to undertake creative writing after decades of state censorship and inability to publish anything other than that acceptable to the regime. Even now, we were told, the situation was not as free as elsewhere mostly on account of editors not yet being able to shake off the over-cautious habits of a lifetime. The remainder of the afternoon and evening we were left to our own devices which suited us well. It began raining again which offered the perfect excuse to return to the flat and do absolutely nothing; something that circumstances rarely allow me to indulge in.

Rain fell in buckets overnight and we were relieved to be under a solid roof. It wasn't actually raining when we left but the low grey cloud gave warning of more to come. At a supermarket I attempted to top up our emergency rations but cardboard-like wafers were all that could be raised – and I even earned a telling-off for not collecting a plastic supermarket basket as I entered the premises.

On the Brasov road out of town we were overtaken by military trucks carrying soldiers back to their barracks. In all the Transylvanian towns in which we had strayed at night we had noticed the silent presence of armed troops patrolling the streets or hanging menacingly around intersections fingering their weapons. We had enquired as to the reason for their presence but had received only contemptuous shrugs. It's the government, we had finally been told, they still have the idea that Hungarians in Transylvania are poised to revolt.

We were still in a part of the country that had once been a stronghold of German immigration and influence, Brasov and Sibui to the west being the chief centres of their settlement, a settlement encouraged, during the twelfth century, by the Hungarian occupiers of this part of southern Transylvania. These Saxons established communities throughout the area often clustered around castles or fortified churches of the likes of those of Sighisoara, Sfintu Gheorghe and its attendant villages to which the population could retreat when attacked, as frequently happened, by the Turks of Tartars. But with the overthrow of Ceausescu, many of Romania's ethnic Germans had taken advantage of their right to re-emigrate back to Germany so denuding the region of its Saxon-descended populace.

Our route by-passed the city of Brasov, small roads leading us erratically towards the Buzaului mountain range through which, in company with the Buzau river, we would be making our exit from Transylvania. At the village of Ozum, 10km from Sfintu Gheorghe, it started to rain again and continued spasmodically for much of the day. Close to Telia a sign indicated a monastery as but 1½ kilometres along an uphill track so, not being pushed for time, we decided to investigate.

The track led sharply upwards to the Marcus Monastery, the chapel of which was in the process of being rebuilt in the original style with a wooden dome and cupolas. The famed monasteries of Romania are mostly to be found in Moldavia but there are a number in Transylvania though we had not come across any until now. A set of dormitories was also being built close by though whether these were for expected visitors or for the nuns themselves we were not then able to assess. The only other building in evidence was a tumble-down cottage outside of which stood a leaky military tent and some farm implements. Two women were working in an adjacent vegetable plot and upon observing our interest they hailed us and invited us into their simple abode.

Of course we had to stay for lunch: cheese, onions, tomatoes, *salina*, salami and bread together with delicious mint tea. From what we could understand the two elderly women and one younger one attired in black habits were part of a community of 14 nuns, the others being away while the new chapel was being constructed. The meal over, they showed us their temporary chapel, a kiosk of a shrine decorated by damp-stained religious prints, plastic flowers and a crucifix on the miniature altar. Barely was there room inside for the five of us. Their male administrator, who was alleged to speak English, was currently in the neighbouring township of Teliu but would be visiting the monastery within half an hour so could we remain a while to meet him, they implored. We hesitated, afraid of outstaying our welcome, but the eldest nun, with beseeching brown eyes, induced our acceptance. The half-hour expanded into one and a half during which we were bade stretch out upon the two gigantic beds that took up most of the space in what appeared to be the only liveable room in the house. Above our heads the twelve apostles stared reproachfully down from the table of their Last Supper.

The sound of an approaching car heralded the arrival of the administrator and over a glass of wine the man described plans to accommodate small parties of tourists at the site. So the dormitories were for *visitors*, not the community, though where all the nuns resided was not made clear. The administrator, middle-aged, well-dressed and fast-talking, spoke German, not English, which was disappointing. In spite of the low-lying cloud we could recognise the high degree of beauty of the countryside; the panorama from the monastery was breathtaking with real mountains rearing on the far horizon, altogether a sensational outlook for a morning-awakening visitor.

Barely had we left when down came the rain in a no-nonsense fashion that gave little hope of let-up. We took initial refuge in the woods part-surrounding the site but the dripping trees became as wetting as the downpour so we moved back to the embryo chapel. Here we waited miserably, shivering in the cold with water splashing down from roof joists that held no roof until dusk drove us back to the trees to raise the tent as best we could upon the sopping ground. Creeping into damp bivi-bags we settled down for what turned out to be a night of non-stop deluge. Had the good folk up at the monastery known of our plight I'm sure we would have been invited to share the communal beds!

Breakfastless and decidedly moist we moved off, glad to leave the treacherous shelter of still-dripping foliage to discover the rain had ceased and the clouds lifting. At a 'privat bufet' we even managed to obtain a hot light meal, the woman owner much intrigued to have clients so early of a morning, and British clients to boot. When she heard we had spent the night in the forest she became highly concerned for our welfare; not so much because of the rain but on account of the wildlife.

"There are wolves in those forests," she told us.

"Surely they don't come so close to roads and human habitation?" I countered.

"You don't know conditions in this wild and remote neighbourhood. Take my advise and stay in hotels," she went on, adding, "and there are bears too."

I knew bears to be shy creatures, having had some experience of them in Canada, but felt disinclined to argue. What with gypsies, wolves, bears and robbers, people would have us never venturing outside at all.

A bashful sun began to push through the scurrying clouds to cast pools of light upon this last stretch of the Transylvanian plateau. The topography reminded me a little of the Andean *puna* of Peru and Bolivia. One can cycle along ridge crests for several level kilometres, with wide shallow depressions stretching away on either side and, in the middle disance, fold after fold of mountains encircling the horizon. Everything was tinged the colour of rust and buffeted by a cold wind; dark clouds dashed across the peeping sun and from them fell further drops of rain that were instantly swept away. In the meadows the haymaking was almost over. We halted for a rest amidst a sea of maize; beyond the tossing stalks rose the Buzaului Mountains, sullen and blue. Across the road a trio of women worked with rakes, their black skirts and scarves billowing.

At Teliu the road started to climb; not dramatically but steadily and interspersed with occasional downhill sweeps. By degrees too the sun took over a sky which turned clear and blue as we struggled up incline after incline pleased at last to be among real mountains. From Teliu, the town of Buzau, clear of the mountains and on the great plain of Wallachia, was about 130km to the south.

Though the gradients were neither stiff nor prolonged the Buzau Valley narrowed into a defile that could almost rank as a gorge, the river winding evasively at its base, a swift unpolluted river, sparkling and noisy. Later the valley chilled, as the shadows lengthened, the hilltops blotting out the sun and the river growling with the sound of waterfalls leaping wildly down the high rock walls.

The descent was marred only by frost-fractured road surfaces and a horrible industrial town – Nehoiasu – in which a giant concrete hydro-electric dam complex was being raised to hold back and pollute the joyful waters of the Buzau. On both sides of the valley the mountains were perceptibly shrinking.

As they shrank and sunshine reappeared we found ourselves in a rich mid-summer light that set fire to the beechwoods and blond pasturelands that materialised with the lessening altitude. We skimmed on downwards, the wind singing in our ears.

At Nehoiasu and Patiragele we paused to locate a meal but the dowdy 'bufets' could produce only beer or 'coke'. Whenever we requested food a bottle of the ubiquitous coca-cola was produced with a flourish as if it was a status symbol and a cure for both hunger and thirst. The broken road had abruptly become soiled and dangerous with grinding convoys of concrete-mixing lorries; the magic of the Carpathians was fast dissolving into man-made dust and the heat of the plain.

We camped that night among a belt of silver birches alongside the river; one of our more successful sites with a warm sun to dry out the tent and bedding though our evening meal could be no more than biscuits and *jem*. Next morning, in the township of Cislau, we undertook a prolonged search for bread which ended in the local bakery where we spent an educational couple of hours watching the mixing and baking of the grey flyblown flour before being presented with the first two loaves out of the ovens. Outside, the bread queue of citizens offered a round of applause as we departed clutching our prize.

Our daily mileage had dropped considerably since Cluj and now averaged about 70 km. Another 60 would bring us to Buzau on flatter roads but we planned to hole up for one more night short of the town. At the 50km mark the hills had faded altogether; the sun beat down with a ferocity we had never known in the uplands. Trying to place the tent away from prying eyes that next late afternoon became a game of hide and seek with children, cow-herds and bevies of villagers popping up all over the landscape. Finally settled amongst a thicket of thorn bushes our efforts were rewarded with the first punctures of the journey.

It was Friday the 13th with a vengeance. And somewhere back along the road we had crossed an invisible provincial border so were no longer on the soil of Transylvania.

Chapter 9
Romania: Wallachia

It was a sad moment when the realisation struck that we were no longer in Transylvania. It was as if something had suddenly dropped out of our lives; and indeed it had. Of course it was people that had made Transylvania such a delight so far as we were concerned but, geographically too, that province held enormous attraction, perhaps appreciated the more as soon as we were out of it. Uplands are invariably more evocative than are bare plains while mountain people carry a special charisma and warmth of nature sometimes lacking elsewhere. Maybe it was because we could raise no more predesignated contacts, but during the time we took crossing the plain we met with no more than standard courtesy. And as we neared Constanta and the Black Sea resorts that courtesy became plainly inspired by a brash new commercialism.

Of course Wallachia is mountainous too in parts; not just the plainlands through which we were to pass. Tradition gives 1290 as the date of the founding of the Wallachian state by Radu Negro (Ralph the Black) but the southern movement at that period of Vlach peoples from the mountains to the Danubia plain can be affirmed with certainty. The new principality at first remained under the domination of Hungary, but the voivode (prince) Bassavab defeated the Hungarian King Charles Robert in 1330 and secured independence. The early days of the principality were conditioned by the struggle against Hungary, but with the reign of Mirca the Old a new period began, that of the struggle against the Turks. The continuance and extension of Turkish control became inevitable and Wallachia therefore became a line of communication for Turkish expeditions against Hungary and Transylvania. Not that the Turks had it all their own way. During the sixteenth century much of Wallachia was again under Hungarian domination though attacks and penetration by Moldavians, Poles, Greeks and others peppered the years. Michael the Brave is the leading Romanian hero, partly because it was he who made the last stand before the era of Turkish and Greek domination, but chiefly because for the first time since Dacian days he brought all the Romanians, scattered in three principalities, under one rule, thus weaving the stuff of the national dream which was not to become reality until 1918.

A history of subjugation therefore that made another nail, if only for me, in

Wallachia's coffin; an unfair supposition I know, for assuredly there were many brave deeds by Wallachian warriors. But the inspiration of Transylvania was still strong within me and I was all too ready to criticise everything Wallachian as Paul and I pedalled on, still downhill – though I could hardly find fault with that. And in Buzau, a supermarket actually raised meat roll, passable cheese, bread rolls, an unidentifiable spread and the nicest *jem* yet, together with a two-litre bottle of Romanian cola – which we purchased more for the bottle and its capacity to hold well water than for the bitter-sweet contents which tasted no worse than 'the real thing'. As I left the store I began to re-appraise Wallachia; maybe it held hidden depths – if but those that satisfy craving stomachs.

Buzau. The place, for us, had become a terminus at the bottom of the mountain road. It was quite a substantial place and, Ceausescu tower blocks notwithstanding, even handsome with its voluminous square fronted by civic buildings of pleasing design. In the open market we obtained some tomatoes, taking it in turns to guard the bikes, there being a lot of shifty-looking characters among the crowd.

While Paul mooched around the stalls a man approached to ask if we were English. He was thin and wan, giving the appearance of recovering from an illness. Obviously he must have been watching us for some time.

Our nationality affirmed he told me he had been trying to get to Britain for several years. A relative of his lived there who could probably get him a job in a canning factory but he had been unable to obtain a visa from the British consulate in Bucharest. "I first applied in early '89 during the Ceausescu regime which resulted in a lot of unpleasantness from the security police," he told me, adding with justifiable bitterness, "and now restrictions are lifted on our side you English raise restrictions there."

I asked if he had applied to take up employment in Britain or simply to visit the country for a short stay.

"It's no use me blowing all my savings to get to Sheffield just for a week or two," he replied. "I would want to stay at least a year or two and I have qualifications."

I sympathised with him and explained how our own unemployment situation restricted the issue of work permits for all foreigners, not just Romanians. But I was aware how prolonged and difficult it was for Romanians in particular to obtain even visitors' visas. The country was still looked upon with suspicion by British immigration authorities.

Visas. The damn things would forever haunt me. Now it seemed that Britain and the West – the Lands of the Free – were being the awkward squad. Again my mind flew back 40 years when it had been the East who raised the 'No Entry' sign.

My own efforts to extract an entry visa from the Czech Embassy in London continued unabated. But the response was always the same: no, ne, niet. In addition to the Czech Embassy I launched countless overtures to a wide range of organisations and individuals who held, or might have held, even the smallest key to the problem of my union with Anna. Since last seeing her she had had her marriage application turned down by the Prague authorities while her brushes with the STB – the secret police – were increasing.

As well as letters to, and meetings with, the Foreign Office, Home Secretary, Ministry of State for Foreign Affairs, a prominent socialist MP who specialised in reuniting families separated by politics, the Chairman of the Council of Ministers of the USSR and the Secretary of the Presidium of the Supreme Soviet on the occasion of a state visit they made to London, I had also applied for help to the Secretary General of the United Nations' Organisation together with the Director of the UN Division of Human Rights in New York who, indeed, did take up my case. But all it achieved was a sharp reprimand from the Czechoslovak government for meddling in its internal affairs.

Though I stirred the pot of trouble with a steam shovel, results were meagre. The Foreign Office was predictably aloof and coldly discouraging as were the other governmental departments. My own MP, Mr (later Lord) R. A. Butler, as Home Secretary, had – with respectful proddings from me – cautiously taken up the case as did Mr (later Lord) Fenner Brockway from the opposite benches, while even the Ministry of Defence suddenly became interested though not on my account. Having labelled me as a 'security risk' they now perceived distant possibilities of my becoming useful to them. Fenner Brockway obtained several interviews for me with the Czech ambassador, Dr Jiří Hájek, who, though I never knew it then, really did stick his neck out on my behalf.

Meanwhile I stubbornly refused to give up on the visa issue though taking a new tack. To the consulate in London I was a marked man so I turned by attention to others scattered about the European continent. Electing to visit a country lying north or south of Czechoslovakia could provide reason for the acquisition of a transit visa, which was easier to obtain since the validity was limited to 48 hours. The obvious consulates to approach for this exercise were those in the four Scandinavian capitals if my pretended destination lay southward in say, Vienna. Again wearing my businessman's hat and with a load of pamphlets lauding my firm's products to support it I sped northwards, initially to the furthest Scandinavian capital, Helsinki.

On the stroke of ten on a Monday morning I was on the mat before the Czech Consulate door. The consul himself deigned to see me but remained singularly unimpressed by my commercial credentials though he could offer no reason why a transit visa should not be granted to facilitate my journey to Austria.

"Come back in two weeks," he advised upon my completion of a bundle of forms.

I was taken aback. "But I want to go at once. My time is limited. Surely it doesn't take two weeks to stamp a passport."

The diplomat wore a face devoid of interest, humour or even pathos. I felt I was talking to a robot. He explained patiently that the application had to go to Prague. This I knew but remained hopeful that some bored clerk in the Czech capital would omit to delve too deeply into my records.

"Couldn't the application be telegraphed?" I suggested.

"If you're prepared to pay for the service, yes."

"I am prepared to pay for the service."

"In that case," he told me, "it will take only four days. Come back on Thursday."

So I spent four days kicking me heels in and around Helsinki, reporting back punctually on the designated day.

The consul offered me an icy smile as I sat before him in his office. He cleared his throat, glanced at a paper and intoned: "I have the honour to inform you that the government of the People's Socialist Republic has considered your request for a transit visa but regrets that it is unable to empower its representative to grant this facility."

"You mean no," I said wearily. It wasn't a shock or even a great disappointment. I hadn't expected anything else I suppose; it was simply a stone turned.

A day later I was in Stockholm and sitting before another consul who, at least, raised more enthusiasm for my alleged commercial undertakings than his dreary counterpart in Helsinki. He even offered me a glass of wine which I hurriedly drank before the grand disillusionment. Again I asked if my application could be telegraphed.

"We can do better than that," he purred. "My assistant is telephoning the department concerned in Prague this very moment." He smiled anew, refilling my glass.

And then it was all over with the assistant whispering in his superior's ear. The smile was replaced by a scowl. I left, wishing I'd drunk more of his damned wine.

I arrived in Oslo on a Sunday so had to wait until the following morning before repeating my act at the respective consulate in Norway. The embassy lay in Frederick Nansens Plass and once more it was the consul himself whom I enticed from his lair.

Again the interview got off with a swing. The man was older than the others and seemed less inclined to stick to the rules. He read the letters I had brought with me from the Prague import agencies with genuine interest, asked a few pertinent questions and, abracadabra, granted me, there and then, a transit visa without by-your-leave of his lords and masters in Prague. Unbelieving, I almost ran out of the office in case he found reason to change his mind.

The rest of the day was a pleasant marathon of obtaining tickets and a vain attempt to raise a transit visa for the German Democratic Republic since I would have to change aircraft at East Berlin's Schonfeld Airport. This request I made at the Soviet Embassy where I was tartly told that since the USSR were not in the business of interfering in the affairs of the GDR they could do nothing about it. And since East Germany was not represented or acknowledged as a legitimate state by Norway there was nothing I could do about it either. My flight was from Kastrup Airport, Copenhagen, so I caught the overnight express to the Danish capital after sending a coded telegram to Anna saying, in effect, miracles permitting, I'd be at Prague's Ruzyne Airport the following day.

And, by way of CSA's Flight OK 432 out of Kastrup I was, in spite of a hiatus at Schonfeld when my deficiency of an East German transit visa was revealed.

Much to my relief Anna was there to meet me. "Have a good flight?" she enquired, gazing at me with a tender eagerness.

My inability to rise to the occasion showed again. "I was sick," I responded.

Ruzyne is situated midway between Prague city and Slaný but first we had to go to the Czech capital, there to play the part for which I had attained my visa. At the airport immigration counter I had been instructed to stay overnight at the Alcron, a foreigners-only hotel but though we tried eight smaller and more discreet ones my nationality forbade us staying in any of them. So the Alcron it was and into which I smuggled Anna for our rapturous first night together.

Next day I presented myself at the offices of Motokov, the state import agency for mechanical appliances and actually managed to sell them a sample of my wares which would be dispatched upon my return home. And I played my part so well that I gained permission to remain in the country an extra 24 hours which compensated for the three I wasted obtaining it. Another two were spent in a police office having my visa endorsed but Anna was with me for this chore.

Late in the afternoon I broke the rules by leaving the environs of Prague to accompany Anna to her home though retaining the Alcron booking. We took a taxi the 35km to Slaný since the fewer people who saw us together the better. On the back seat of the Skoda saloon we held hands but spoke little, not wanting the driver to learn I was British. Only as we entered the small market town I had last seen in 1945 did my attention stray outside the vehicle. The square had barely altered, the town hall remained exactly as I remembered it. I pointed to a door at the side of the main entrance.

"That was the lock-up in my day," I whispered to Anna.

"It still is," came her laconic reply.

We came to a halt outside the substantial house surrounded by the overgrown garden and guarded by the line of poplars I remembered so vividly.

"It's all state property now. We're expected to live only on the ground floor; all six of us." I detected bitterness in her voice as she referred to its confiscation by the regime and the fact that her parents, two sisters plus the husband of one of them had but four rooms in which to reside.

I received a great welcome from the whole family, being hugged, kissed and bombarded with greetings in a melee of tongues. The meal Anna's mother had prepared for us was a milestone of memory and a celebration of Anna's and my commitment to one another as well as full acceptance by her family. That the parents were prepared to accept harsh treatment and likely further confiscation of goods in the furtherance of their daughter's happiness moved me intensely.

That evening, in the warm security of a 'safe house', Anna and I settled down to talk treason. With the attitude of her family made so abundantly clear I felt it time to reveal a long-dormant scheme for her extraction from Czech territory should all else fail. As I unfolded the plan I could not help reflecting upon the aura of unreality surrounding what was surely the most desperate venture on which a young engaged couple could embark.

A new country had entered the list of those featuring in my ongoing saga of evasion – Poland. For both of us the mountainous district of the sparsely-guarded Slovak-Polish border – the Carpathian Tatras – held a fragile key to one of the closed doors that surrounded us. Moreover Poland itself seethed with the ferment of a broken revolution that boded only good for our cause. If we could reach Polish territory another barrier would be breached.

But what then? Still a communist country separated from the West by the gulf of a fanatical regime in East Germany we would hardly be home and dry. My plan, however, embraced a method whereby Anna would be able to reach safety wearing male attire and in possession of my passport, suitably doctored and endorsed with a Polish visa much easier to acquire at that time. Meeting her on the Polish side of the Tatras, I would accompany her to Warsaw where, disguised as me, she would fly direct to London on a ticket and documentation obtained by myself. I had already approached a theatrical agency in London who were exceedingly cooperative and willing to advise on and supply the necessary items of facial and body disguise. What would happen to me with Anna safely on her way was less clear but an invented story of a robbery could hardly be disproved even if it meant a spell in detention while investigations were carried out.

I emphasised the fact that the 'Polish Plan' was a last resort but expressed the opinion that present circumstances offered no more than the prospect of us being condemned to the half-life we were now living. In this she agreed and we discussed details of the plan well into the night. Anna knew the Tatras better than I did but I intended making a reconnaissance of the Polish side of the alpine border myself – possibly even utilising it as another entry point for a further visitation to Anna – though I kept this idea to myself. Anna then told me she had re-applied for a permit to marry me and that, in view of a slight reduction in governmental control, this stood a better chance of being granted.

Putting further deliberations behind us we attempted to spend the next day more fittingly as a newly engaged couple. Arm in arm we strolled in the garden, sat together on the sofa, and discoursed upon plans for our life together in England. But, alas, fate was to intervene once more.

Came a telephone summons to Slaný police headquarters. So they had known of my illegal excursion from Prague. I suppose it was naive of me to imagine otherwise. Anna and I were to report there without delay.

At the police station we were taken before a uniformed lieutenant who passed us onto a nameless official in plain clothes. He inspected my passport with grave deliberation.

He turned to me and said in English, "You are presumably aware that you are outside the jurisdictional district of Prague to which the restrictive nature of your visa entitles you. What do you have to say about this infringement of the regulations? What is the object of your illegal visit to Slaný ?"

I answered the second question first.

"To see my fiancée and her family."

This was received with a sardonic smile.

"Was that the object of your business visit to the Czechoslovak Republic?" he enquired with heavy sarcasm.

I told him it wasn't but that, with my preliminary commercial undertakings in Prague carried out, I felt I could take the opportunity to enjoy a little pleasure. The fact that this took me a few kilometres outside the capital's statutory limits was surely – .

The man interrupted my excuses to say accusingly: "So you knew you were contravening the regulations."

I raised my hand in an expansive gesture. "Come on, it's only a few kilometres outside your precious limit. How am I to know exactly where the line runs? But I'm sorry if I've offended anyone; it wasn't intended. I'll go back to Prague tomorrow."

The civilian snapped back at me. "You'll go back today."

He then turned to Anna and spoke sharp words in rapid Czech to her. I saw suppressed anger suffuse her face.

And then it was all over; the interview at an end. I suppose I got off lightly.

Repacking our bags and bidding farewell to the family, we returned, by train, to Prague, my original 48 hours exhausted. The jaded offerings of the Alcron Hotel once again encompassed us and a nondescript little man in the foyer jumped perceptibly as we entered its doors.

The third and last morning was spent, not entirely fruitlessly, at the British Embassy. The consul knew about us and expressed his surprise at seeing me. He asked about Anna, prudently waiting outside, whom he had met, and I gave him a resume of the developments, such as they were, that had occurred in the meantime. He told me that our case remained 'on the file' and that, at suitable intervals, was brought out for an airing. The fact that a few 'big guns' – as he described Messrs Butler and Brockway – were being brought to bear on the Czech authorities was indeed good news, since at the very least it would keep Anna from being 'silenced'. The oak-panelling of the consul's office was dark and gloomy, doing nothing to raise my confidence in the embassy doing anything constructive to help. For the remainder of our time together, Anna and I wandered around the lovely Mala Strana – the Little Town, as the heart of Prague is called – strolling its narrow streets trying not to watch the hands of the clock inexorably creeping towards the hour of another parting. The lengthening shadows of St Nicholas Church fell across us as we reached the great square. I shivered in the cool of evening and felt a corresponding shiver in Anna. The striking of the church clock reverberated across the square then, one after another, from all the different churches around, the chimes rang out, echoing through the streets, and died away. It was time to go; time to tear ourselves apart. With the validity of my visa already expired we took reluctant steps towards the railway station. We had worn ourselves out walking aimlessly about the city and subjecting our hearts to as much torture as our feet. The man following us only had his feet to worry about.

Anna insisted upon seeing me off. I kissed her goodbye lightheartedly as if I were going away for the weekend. She held me tightly. "Next time, I'll be coming with you," she whispered.

The train moved away, crawling out of the station, dallying cruelly before entering the adjoining tunnel. I could still see her etched in its darkness.

At least I had won that round; my score was three out of five. I chided myself for making a game of it and cast my eyes northward once more, to the one Czechoslovak consulate in Scandinavia I had not yet put through the hoop, that of Copenhagen. It was no use repeating things at Oslo; a phone call I made met with a curt rejoinder and a loud click.

Within the year I was back in the Danish capital and, would you believe it, my reception there, following my disclosure of my commercial worth, was exalted. Plainly there was no cooperation between the consulates in Scandinavia. This time my overtures brought forth both the consul as well as the commercial attache, the former a florid individual with a few hairs on his head carefully trained to cover a premature baldness. His whole face shone with bonhomie as we discussed the Czechoslovak iron industry about which I knew next to nothing. Again there was no nonsense about a reference to Prague; simply the completion of a visa application form for an entry visa *no less. My passport removed, I was left alone for a few minutes to toy with a coffee. I did my best to hide my incredulity at the turn of events and then the consul was back with my passport in which reposed another mauve stamp that aroused in me as much pleasure as twins to a sterile wife. A double aquavit, a welter of good wishes, and I sallied forth into the clean sunshine to make a beeline for the airways terminal in the city centre.*

By midday I had acquired a seat on an old friend, Flight OK 432, departing that very afternoon for Berlin and Prague. The Czech consul had told me that the East German authorities were taking a more relaxed view of passengers in transit through Schonfeld Airport so I had little to worry about on that score. There had been no time to send Anna a cable so I basked in the delicious prospect of affecting a surprise arrival at her home.

Thereafter everything went according to plan as far as East Berlin. We rolled to a standstill on the grass runway of Schonfeld and, with the other passengers, I rose to leave the aircraft but was restrained by the hostess. From then onward things went not at all according to plan; not mine anyway.

Through the door of the now empty aeroplane came a East German police officer followed by two of his men. They made straight for me, the officer offering a perfunctory salute.

"You are Herr Portvy, I think?"

My heart sinking, I replied that I was, more or less.

"Then please I must ask you to come with me."

"May I ask why?" I enquired.

"A matter concerning your visa," he replied. "We won't keep you long, I assure you. Please be so kind." He turned on his heel in the knowledge I would follow him. His two henchmen took up positions behind me to ensure it.

As we crossed the flight apron I aired the opinion that a GDR transit visa for changing aircraft at Schonfeld was no longer a vital necessity.

"It's not that visa that is the cause of concern," was his mysterious comment.

In a neon-lit office I was introduced to a bad-tempered civilian who, it transpired, was second secretary of the Czechoslovak Embassy in East Berlin.

He came straight to the point.

"Mr. Portway, you not go to Prag. You go back. You understand, yes?"

"No," I said, understanding too well.

The sour-faced diplomat deigned to release an explanation. It appeared that the granting of my visa in Copenhagen had been an error which had been discovered too late for me to be stopped at Kastrup. A message had therefore been flashed to the Berlin Embassy which had resulted in a disgruntled second secretary being sent, on his afternoon off, to a draughty airfield to rectify a mistake that wasn't his. To emphasise his displeasure the man proceeded to stamp indelible cancellation marks across the offending visa in my passport as if swatting a particularly obnoxious brand of earwig.

With realisation and shock seeping into my brain I beheld the demise of my aspiration. As it disintegrated, cold anger filled my heart.

Still clinging to my well-tried businessman theme I launched into a torrent of invective aimed at the wretched little secretary. He stared at me owlishly through thick-lensed spectacles probably understanding little but assuredly aware of the murder in my eyes. His infuriating shrugs only served to prolong his punishment, and when he at last got in a word of his own it didn't help.

Departments, formalities, entry visas, transit visas, double transit visas, exit permits, marriage permits. Frustration at all the ridiculous machinery of delay welled up inside me and burst out.

"All you bloody government lackeys are the same," I roared to an astonished audience which included clerks behind a battery of typewriters. "All locked up in your stupid little departments not caring a brass farthing what happens so long as your fat arses are comfortably seated in your departmental chairs!" During the course of my recital the clatter of typewriters had ceased and the silence that followed was as positive as applause. I felt slightly better.

The upshot of all this was that I was held in detention with a German guard on the door for some five hours pending the next flight to Copenhagen. Because of my lack of a GDR transit visa I was not even permitted to cross the few kilometres of sacred East Berlin soil to the Western sector of the city which would have been my quickest and most direct route home. Instead I had to fly hundreds of miles in the wrong direction. It was no use arguing further; it was like talking to a brick wall. Anyway I was out of steam; all the stuffing knocked out of me.

At least Anna wasn't waiting for me in vain on this occasion, which offered some consolation. Metaphorically I chalked a long straight line through Scandinavia.

With the flattening out of the terrain Paul and I were back on 'overdrive', putting well over a hundred kilometres behind us each day with no great effort. Buzau to Slobozia was 90 km on a peach of a small, uncluttered, reasonably well-surfaced road with the wind mostly – but not quite always – in our favour.

By now we were permanently hungry but by no means starving. The trouble was that by burning up so many calories we needed a greater than usual input of food to compensate, Paul more than I for the young have demanding appetites – though, in my son's case, a reduction in his waistline could do no harm. Basically we had been living on a peasant's fare of bread (when we could get it), occasional salami or *slanina* or cheese, plums and peppers plus a daily intake of oily sardines which at least provided protein. The grey bread lay heavy on the stomach while the sawdust-tasting biscuits and bitter chocolate intermittently available held few vitamins. Our few restaurant meals were invariably no more than a fragment of fried meat and a handful of rice or chips – whatever was available and with no choice; the portions tiny, measured out in grams, and to feel satisfied at the end of the meal it was necessary to swallow a tasteless chunk of bread between each mouthful of meat. Even those meals provided by our kind and generous hosts could rarely assuage our hunger; the raw materials for them just not being obtainable and thus raising a compulsion to restrain consumption.

Our latest lunch meal partaken as we made our way towards Slobozia, was better than most thanks to the larger stock in the Buzau supermarket. The meat roll was worth its weight in gold but the spread, which we liberally smeared on stale slices of bread, tasted odd. Not until later did we discover the tin contained floor polish!

I had entertained the notion that Wallachia might be better endowed with the comforts of life than Transylvania since Bucharest lies in its territory and not that far distant from where we stood. But here in Pogoanele, which admittedly was somewhat remote from a main highway, things were little different. The clothes of the people in the street remained sombre; men in double-breasted jackets and women wearing styles that harked back to before World War Two. I had been told that Romanians are wont to follow Italian styles, like their temperament, but I saw little evidence of this here or elsewhere.

Outside the barren supermarket I was accosted by a citizen who displayed a touching anxiety to air his considerable knowledge of English. He was ardently Romanian and upon learning that we had recently been in Transylvania launched into a tirade against the Hungarian minority. I listened with interest, pleased to hear an opposite opinion.

The Romans called their land Dacia Felix and it was the only time in history that it was a happy country, he alleged. Since then it has known nothing but trouble and discontent. The man lectured me on the recalcitrant province, reversing all I had heard from Hungarians there. The truth was, he went on, the Hungarians had been there a thousand years – a mere snap of the fingers – and all through that time the Romanians, who were the majority and had existed there for aeons, were given no vote until the 1860s. "Do not believe what the Hungarians told you. They are cold and hate us Romanians. Yet we are a gentle, Latin people; our natural friends are in Western Europe, in France and in your Britain. The Romanians are cultural: see how easily they learn languages. Now look at the historic encroachments of greedy empires: Mongol, *Hungarian*, Turkish, *Habsburg* – also Hungarians of course, and Russian ever wanting to pounce on us".

Though I was sceptical of his reasoning I'm sure he was part-correct in essence but my old contention arose. What happened in history is no excuse for punishing later generations who have nothing whatsoever to do with the injustices of the past. But I could see that any support I gave to the Transylvanian Hungarians would cut no ice here so I switched the subject. I asked instead for *his* views, as a Romanian, on his country. He was quick to confirm that Romanian politics were a mess, more of a mess than in almost any other former East Bloc country, largely because of the success of Ceausescu and his *Securitate* in stamping out all opposition. Thus there had been no one of equivalent stature to Vaclav Havel or Lech Walesa to lead an alternative government when the time came, and the eventual revolution was hijacked by a new generation of communists under a new name. As a result there had been little structural reform, above all of the economy, although prices had risen and the populace was increasingly cynical and disillusioned. There were even those who now regretted the end of the Ceausescu era, saying that then there was government action and nobody starved, whereas today it's all talk and there's nothing to eat; they remember the better things and conveniently forget the bad.

What existed now was something of a looking-glass world, in which the only east European state to undergo violent revolution had changed the least, over 200 political parties existed but there was no real political structure, a parliament met every day but took no decisions, where previously people queued not knowing if there was anything at the other end but aware they could afford whatever there was; now they knew there were enough goods but also that they couldn't afford them.

I'm not sure if I could reconcile his last comment with my own impressions of the availability of goods. Having seen the empty shops, stores and supermarkets all over Eastern Europe, including Romania, under communism I could find little improvement in the country at the present time. Except, perhaps, in the larger towns and cities; where at least the window dressing had improved. But I accepted that Romanian citizens knew more than I did.

Our little road was quite the nicest on which we had ridden in Romania. And not only because it was flat. Most of the traffic was horse-drawn, open carts or covered wagons, while the few cars that passed were mainly those of Polish tourists. Occasionally the serenity was besmirched by an international truck taking a short cut between main thoroughfares. These would sweep by, driving the carts and us onto the verges. Here and there a wagon had halted; the drivers sprawled on the ground like corpses while the horses grazed contentedly. With the heat of the scorching sun increasing with each kilometre eastwards we more than ever were inclined to join the reclining figures.

On this backwater of a road it was like reversing into another century. Rural life here on the stifling plain was slow, ponderous and traditional. We meandered by fields of villagers scything and raking and tossing hay high on to rough wooden wagons, using wooden pitchforks like those we had seen in Poland, their horses dozily swishing their tails in the shade of a tree. At work the menfolk wore peasant clothes and conical black felt hats perched on their heads; women were enveloped in voluminous skirts and printed pinafores.

Their villages sprawled across the dusty road. Children played among the pecking chickens and gaggles of white, waddling geese who stoically ignored them, while women gossiped in tight animated groups, pausing only to stare at us as we glided by.

The houses, like those of Transylvania, were old, wooden and decorative, a few with elaborately carved gables and delicately painted with friezes of flowers and intricate patterns. Each cottage had a well, a small vegetable plot and a fenced compound for livestock; just enough to ensure self-sufficiency where produce could be shared or exchanged with neighbours; quite literally the only means of survival. A fortunate few kept a cow and we often would pass a woman or child walking their beast on a lead like the family dog. In one place – I think it was Grivita – gypsy women strutted among the sombre villagers in loud fiery-coloured groups; lithe girls and haggard mothers perpetually pregnant. Again fresh water was abundant though here on the plains the pumps were of different design: fulcrum-operated poles that lifted their buckets in easier fashion than did those of the capstan and chain models. Seldom did we pass one by without slaking our heat-generated thirsts.

Such was our rate of progress that in spite of the high temperatures and pauses en route we reached Slobozia by late afternoon, the last few kilometres along the busy E60, traffic-snarled and dangerous. This was the main Bucharest-Constanta highway, and it should have warned us of what was to come, but we were confused by an apparent contradiction of road categories on our two maps, both out of date. My Hallwag 1:1,000,000 showed the E60 to be no more than a main road whilst my Romanian tourist map elevated it to a motorway and, after Slobazia, the signs indicated this to be the case. We therefore elected to take the more direct parallel- running Bucharest-Constanta artery 15km south which was numbered a lesser 3A against the other's higher-rated 2A, our maxim being to use smaller roads where practical. In retrospect we would have done better to have stuck to the 2A, motorway or not.

But first we had to negotiate Slobozia where we likewise came unstuck. Willing to sell our souls for a beer we were unable to find a single bar in this sizeable town. Additionally a woeful lack of directional signs found us pedalling painfully along the busy ring road in the wrong direction towards Bucharest and it was some six wasted kilometres before we discovered our error. Renegotiating the town we stole a rest against a statue of Mirca the Old. That worthy was ruler of Wallachia from 1386 to 1418, one of the province's great heroes, who kept the Turks at bay while concluding an anti-Ottoman treaty with Sigismund of Luxemburg, King of Hungary and later Emperor of the Holy Roman Empire as well as King of Bohemia – seemingly a ruler of many parts. For us Mirca's proffered shade from the sun was profoundly appreciated.

We had seen nothing, statue-wise, in Wallachia of the other great national figure, Ianeu de Hunedoara, enthusiastically feted in Transylvania. This might have been because the Hungarians likewise claim him as their national hero. But whoevers hero he was Ianeu was an outstanding figure in an age of leaders larger than life. Ban (duke) of Sererin, Voivode of Transylvania and Regent of Hungary on behalf of the under-age King Laszlo, he led an army of Hungarians, Czechs, Poles, Wallachs and Germans (virtually a medieval Warsaw Pact) against the Turks before dying of the plague.

Strangely, Paul was in a worse state of exhaustion from the day's exertions than I (usually it was I that found the last kilometres of a hundred plus kilometre ride the most deadly) though it was more heat than distance that affected him. On the correct road at last – that leading towards Calarasi, near the Bulgarian border and one which would bring us to the 3A highway we had chosen – we raised camp in a clearing of maize close to an enormous factory complex where not even the rhythmic thud of dynamos could keep us awake.

Well ahead of our loose schedule we saw no reason to break speed records over the final leg of the journey. Already the signposts were indicating our destination and though the urge to plunge into the sea was strong we could afford to take things a little easier. Accordingly we slowed our pedals, rested more frequently in shady nooks, camped for longer periods and remained ever-ready to divert to anything of the slightest interest though the landscape thereupon became as featureless as it was possible to be.

The small straight Calarasi-bound road carried us southwards pleasantly enough to its crossing of the 3A highway near Dragaina but here there was no option but to turn east once more. It was a Sunday and the dangerously-narrow, badly worn tarmac was awash with cars crammed with families and friends released from the humid confines of the Romanian capital and hell-bent for the seaside. All were going in the same direction as us, speeding past our bikes with inches to spare. To add to the discomfort came the odd trailer-towing international truck to buffet us with slip-stream. Alongside the road ran the Bucharest-Constanta railway line upon which I had ridden years before. I fervently wished I could be on it now.

Those last days of the journey were, alas, the least memorable with only the prospect of journey's-end to provide any sort of climax. Occasionally we halted at new privately-run restaurants in which badly cooked meals were off-handedly served at sky-high prices.

Somewhere west of the Danube river and its parallel tributaries we came out of Wallachia and entered the smaller province of Dobrogea, an almost entirely flat land of vast sunflower fields and vineyards. The Muslim minority of Romania are concentrated here, the seat of the Mufti being at Constanta. It is said that the presence of a Muslim Turkish and Tartar population in the country dates back to the fourteenth and fifteenth centuries, when the Turkish armies entered the Dobrogea region, though an organised Muslim religious life began only during the early sixteenth century, when the Ottoman Empire brought large numbers of colonists to settle in the district.

At Fetesti we arrived at a secondary arm of the Danube labelled on my maps as the Brafel Borcea separated from the Danube proper by a dead-straight 17km express highway ending at Cernavoda. From the enormous bridges at both ends hydro-electric workings were visible on all sides guarded by soldiers and sprinkled with no-photography signs. In spite of the stifling heat the smooth-surfaced motorway made easy going with a resting place halfway across in the shade of the only tree for miles around. Cernavoda, which we by-passed, though its river port could clearly be seen, is the western terminus of the Danube-Black Sea canal, the most ambitious project in any of the Romanian former five-year plans and one of the largest, at that time, being undertaken in Europe. The project involved the construction of a deep-water port at Agigea, just south of Constanta, and a link by a 70km canal with Cernavoda to provide a saving of 250 miles for ships engaged in trade between the Danube and Constanta, the country's chief port. From the vantage point of yet another bridge we looked down with interest upon the complex of locks and quays before quaffing a pint in a Cernavoda suburban bar.

Alternating between relaxing in wayside woods and pedalling a few further kilometres we resumed negotiation of the hated 3A highway which reverted to type after Cernavoda, renumbering itself 22C as if trying to fool us. I had been labouring under the delusion that Romanian drivers were more considerate than others in eastern Europe though I had now begun revising my opinion. Certainly all the worst drivers in the country must have been concentrated on that cow of a highway this particular weekend and we were fortunate to survive intact in body if not in mind.

Water replenishment points became non-existent; no further wells or pumps were to be found. A raging thirst had Paul scaling a barbed-wire fence to approach an agricultural sprinkler spewing pulsating jets of water in all directions and I was treated to the spectacle of my supposedly sane son trotting in circles attempting to avoid the jets but catch some of the life-giving liquid in his tin mug outstretched before him. Defeated in this endeavour he finally gave up, returning to the road considerably damper outside than within.

Our last camp was amongst undergrowth on a hillock outside the town of Medgidia, forty kilometres short of Constanta. Some sort of festival appeared to have been in progress as we came through the town judging by the congestion of excited people. We held a ceremonial striking of the tent next morning in the belief it would be the final time we would be using it. A red ball of a sun the previous evening was matched by a similar red ball at dawn.

We departed early in an effort to beat the worst of the traffic, but everyone else had the same idea. However we still managed to reach Constanta centre by mid-morning, ploughing doggedly through its endless suburbs. It was the middle of August; we hadn't expected to reach the city before the end of that month.

Constanta's history goes back to ancient Greek legends though you'd hardly believe it passing through the ugly streets, made the uglier by Comrade Ceausescu since I last cast eyes on them. The city's Greek and later Roman name was Tomis, a word meaning 'sections' or 'slices' resulting from its associations with Jason's search for the Golden Fleece and the story of Medea. Pursued at sea by her father, Aectes, King of Colchis, from whom she was attempting to flee, she cut her small brother to pieces and threw them into the water. Papa stopped to collect the pieces for proper burial on land thus allowing Medea to escape. More factually, the great Latin poet Ovid was exiled here in AD 8, on orders of the Emperor Augustus because of the former's relationship with the emperor's daughter. He must have found life in Tomis bleak after the luxury of the court in Rome and tried desperately to return only to meet constant refusal. The Roman empire's ever-expanding boundaries had brought the original trading settlement founded by emigrants from Miletus under Roman control but later, when that empire was falling apart, it came under Byzantium's rule. Subsequently the Genoese moved in for a century or more before the ubiquitous Turks took control until 1878.

Unattractive as the city has become, much resulting from the late president's fetish for housing his subjects in urban cages, its varied history is reflected in the different buildings and traces of the old port that can be found amongst the dross.

But you have to go and search for them. This I had done a few years before the Ceausescu era when I was investigating the coast from history-impregnated Mangalia on the Bulgarian border to Tulcea and the fascinating Danube Delta, finding many intriguing Greek and Roman remains in and around the then newly-opened resorts.

Paul and I, discarding culture and getting our priorities right, made for the railway station to ensure we knew how to start wending our way home under any steam but our own. Next came a more enjoyable commitment; a re-acquaintance with the delicious waters of the Black Sea. I knew the way to the neighbouring resort of Mamaia, the closest worthwhile beaches, so off we sailed in anticipation of a watery climax to the journey.

Then things started to go wrong. Pausing for a beer halfway to the resort we were approached by an individual intent upon selling US dollars for Romanian lei. "You mean the other way round," I suggested. "No, I give you dollars, you give me lei," he confirmed and quoted a very reasonable rate of exchange.

But we held just enough Romanian currency to buy railway tickets for ourselves and bikes to get us to the Hungarian border so declined his extraordinary offer though unable to hide interest. It was then that he clumsily revealed himself as an undercover police officer, a member of the black market currency squad. His attempted entrapment duties done he left and his plain clothes colleague stepped forward out of a doorway to demand, in the rudest fashion, our passports and wallets. Fortunately the currency I held reposed sweatily against my skin under my waistband but Paul's moneybelt was highly visible. With wads of US dollars, British pounds, French francs, Hungarian forints, Austrian schillings and more strewn over the table for his inspection, he subjected us to a barrage of staccato questions, barking "shut up!" whenever I opened my mouth to reply. I foresaw things getting nasty but the day was saved by the 'To whom it may concern' letter I held from the Romanian ambassador in London requesting that all assistance be given the bearer and his son. Had it not been for that I'm sure he would have confiscated (i.e. stolen) our money, even though there were no black market acquired notes amongst it.

I had met his kind before; minions of the security police, all over communist East Europe, but none knew their ugly methods better than did my fiancée, Anna.

She had known she'd been under surveillance for many months. The sharks called themselves secret police but, whenever they wanted, they were anything but secret, showing a perverted glee in exhibiting their presence and power to anyone unfortunate enough to be on the 'conditioning' list of the STB. It wasn't just unpleasant interviews at their headquarters but this half-open surveillance business that was so unnerving, coupled with the odd 'incident', whether it was in Slaný or Prague.

And it was as she was returning home by train from a shopping day in the Czech capital that one of these 'incidents' occurred. The train was nearly empty and she found a compartment to herself with ease. But hardly had the city suburbs dissolved into a wintry countryside when the door slid open and the two youths she'd noticed following her earlier stumbled in.

Their attentions were as brief as they were objectionable. For a while they said nothing; simply sitting there boorishly puffing on cigarettes with occasional glances in her direction. Then one turned and asked where she lived in a tone of voice that demonstrated he didn't care a fig. She said it was Slaný . They must have known anyway.

As if this brief exchange sufficed as basis of an acquaintanceship, the two brazenly asked if she would go out with them that evening. The request was couched almost as a demand and her refusal was equally brusque. They made it plain that her refusal bothered them little. She then asked them why they were molesting her. Both denied having seen her before though plainly they were aware she had seen them. And they weren't even acting or making any attempt to hide this fact in spite of the denial. The loutish behaviour made no sense; it was clear the two men had been put up to it.

The intruders left the train at the intermediate station of Kralupy. They probably caught another straight back to Prague. What would they report? She was at a complete loss to understand the reasons behind this strategy of beastliness; maybe it was all a part of a new phase in the 'art' of dissuasion' following the rejection of her second marriage application. Whatever it was her future offered a prospect as disagreeable as it was sinister.

At least we got our Black Sea climax. Over what remained of the morning and all afternoon we took turns to recline lanquidly in the gently choppy water with one of us stretched out on the sand guarding the bikes. The filth and sweat of weeks washed off us and the Black Sea assuredly became blacker. It was heaven in spite of the crowded beach backed by serried rows of concrete and standardised hotels in far greater profusion than when I had last been here.

We planned to remain by the seaside a day or two, resting and recuperating. Accordingly we moved off in the late afternoon intent upon finding accommodation in hotel or camping site.

That's when things started to fall apart again. Being mid-August every hotel was bursting at the seams with eastern European holidaymakers and it was the same story with the one campsite seven kilometres away. There was simply no room anywhere. And the coastal strip that ran between the ocean and the freshwater Siut Ghiol lake being a nightmare of brash development there was not even the possibility of raising our tent in some secluded field. The Romanian manager of a Club Mediterranean establishment offered to find us a room in return for an exorbitant sum in hard currency but I didn't much like the look of him. In fact I didn't care much for anything in either Constanta or Mamaia and no doubt things were equally dismal in the other resorts along the shoreline. No, we'd had our long-anticipated swim; it was time to go home.

But maybe we'd spend just one night in the beastly hotel whatever it cost and then catch our train westwards in the morning. I said as much to the man. He looked at me strangely, then made a startling comment.

"Don't you know that Romanian Railways are going on strike from mid-night tonight?"

Chapter 10
The Way Home – The Banat, Romania, and Across Hungary

Suddenly I wanted to go home more than at any time on the two and a half months of pedalling. And now a rail strike to eliminate our intended vehicle for attaining that objective. I couldn't face the prospect of slogging it across the whole width of Romania; only a slightly lesser distance than that of the diagonal course we had already taken. But what was the alternative? Presumably Bulgarian Railways were operating but that country's only other western outlet was a belligerent former Yugoslavia and I didn't think cycling through sniper-infested Bosnia to be a particularly bright idea. Flying from Constanta to Bucharest and on to Budapest or Vienna was another possibility but this would be expensive and the flights assuredly heavily booked. My Cook's Timetable pages showed the last train from Constanta to Bucharest left in 30 minutes, and if we could reach the Romanian capital at least it would be a step in the right direction. But half an hour. We could only make it from where we were on the wrong side of Mamaia if the train left late. Mounting our bikes we raced for Constanta Station through the rush hour, our nice freshly-bathed bodies breaking out into a soak of sweat.

I have to say I completely lost my cool on that ride and it didn't help when my chain disconnected itself and fell off. Hands smothered in grease we battled on, ignoring buses and trolleybuses that hooted and clanged at us in consternation and rage. We lost our way once and when we did reach the station it was to discover several later departures for Bucharest scheduled before the midnight deadline, our timetable listing only main express services.

The subsequent train out was a lost cause; packed to the gunwales before we could get near it; even without bicycles there would have been no hope of boarding. We debated the notion of remaining in the relatively pleasant station concourse until the final departure, it being cooler and less constricted than would be Bucharest Nord. On second thoughts, however, and judging by the apparent pressure of clients using them, maybe we should struggle aboard any train that offered space. With tickets for ourselves but not the bikes (these had to be obtained heaven knows where) we waited, dallying on the open platform enjoying the chill of early evening.

An hour went by and then a completely unscheduled train pulled in. "Bucharest?" I enquired optimistically and was surprised when told that, indeed, Bucharest was the destination. More surprising still was that few travellers wanted to use it – or maybe didn't know about it – so there was plenty of space for our bikes at the end of the corridor of the coach in which we installed ourselves though we were promptly requested to move to another one. To get everything aboard trains meant stripping the bikes, flinging seven items of baggage up into the coach doorway and then lifting the bikes up three metal steps after them. The doors were high above the ground and when the operation had to be repeated three times in quick succession it became an exhausting business.

A busty blonde ticket inspector with a wicked sense of humour launched us into a Dutch auction as a preliminary to the levying of carriage charges for the bikes, following which, highly satisfied with the turn of events, Paul and I sat back to enjoy the 3½-hour ride. Until darkness obliterated the scene we were able to gaze smugly down upon the Bucharest – Constanta highway of our last days of thankless pedalling, relishing the ease by which we were now covering the same route.

The one other occupant of the compartment was a tramp. Or at least he *looked* like a tramp, with unshaven, unwashed jowls and ragged clothing, his few belongings wrapped in a cloth. He stared at us but never smiled. I nodded at him but found only expressionless eyes gazing back in return, not even the most basic kind of human recognition. Paul had gone to sleep on the opposite seat so I tried to follow his example.

We drew into Bucharest sometime after 11.30 p.m. And it was here that our luck not only held but increased. Wheeling and humping our loads to the head of the platform, an indicator board offered the information that a train would be leaving at five minutes to midnight, its destination Timisoara, about 170km from the Hungarian border. But would we have time to purchase tickets and locate the train (no platform number was shown) and, more to the point, would there be the slightest chance of us finding space on it for our bikes and ourselves?

By dint of a struggle I gained tickets for ourselves, not bothering about the bikes; this being too complicated to argue about in two conflicting tongues and among a seething mass of intending travellers. A huge crowd spread across the platform alleged to be the one from which the Timisoara train departed, and by the time we had ploughed some way through the throng, rumour had it that the train would be arriving at an adjacent platform. Like an army of refugees fleeing bombardment everyone surged back to the head of the platform and onto the next one. Three times this mass migration occurred and it was simply the luck of the gods that when the train finally backed onto its allotted platform Paul and I were in the right place when the thing halted. Adept by now at boarding trains with bike and baggage, our drill was impeccable. While I blocked a door with the two bikes, Paul nipped aboard the coach, took the bikes and baggage I lifted up to him before climbing aboard myself. There followed an onslaught of crazed humanity, some already flowing down the corridor from the other end and within minutes our bikes and bags disappeared under a sea of bodies. Paul and I became separated, he winning himself half a lavatory seat on which to rest a buttock in a toilet occupied by six people. Already tired and exhausted, I hardly relished the prospect of a nine-hour stand-up journey but was nevertheless thankful for making it beyond Bucharest.

Both of us had been to the Romanian capital at different times, Paul more recently than I. The place likes to be described as the 'Paris of the Balkans' though the description would not be mine. But I see what it's getting at. There are tree-lined boulevards, pleasant parks and even an Arc de Triomphe halfway up the wide Sasona Kisselef which has Champs-Elysees aspirations. Before World War Two the city had a reputation as an uninhibited spot and seasoned travellers will tell you that by placing your umbrella in a certain position in your hotel room you could ensure a willing companion.

Though politics, war and revolution have lined the face of Bucharest it is still a lively metropolis. The city is ideally sited on both banks of the Dimbovita river, surrounded by woodlands and with no less than nine small lakes within easy reach of the centre. Herastrau Park no doubt remains one of the most beautiful parks to be found in a European capital. On my first visit I stayed with a local couple – cousins of the celebrated playwright Arnold Wesker – who showed me their city with undisguised pride. What Bucharest lacked in the grandeur of many of its European counterparts it made up for with an abundance of fine old trees and acres of flowers.

First mention of the city appears in the charter of Vlad the Impaler in 1459 but excavations have unearthed traces of the time of that worthy's grandfather. Part of the old walls of that period, protected behind glass, I had been able to see in the vaults below the streets and in the gold cellars of the Museum of Romanian History.

The deadline for the start of the rail strike had passed by the time our cruelly overloaded train heaved itself out of the station. Further intending travellers were left behind simply on account of there not being, literally, a toe-hold in any part of any coach. I was painfully squeezed against my bike upon which a couple of fellow passengers lay in contorted postures while a woman repeatedly complained that her dress had picked up a smear of grease from the chain though there was nothing I could do about it. The same woman moaned every time I was pushed against her and even when she was lucky enough to be able to squat on one of our panniers she maintained her lamentations.

However she was the exception; everyone else made light of the situation and we became a close-knit community in more ways than one. My neighbour spoke reasonable English, expounding upon his intention of finding employment in the provinces since there was nothing available in the capital. He possessed a bottle of *tuica* which he regularly passed to me for a swig. The fiery liquor deadened the aches in my legs and I could hardly fall down in a drunken stupor within such a tight-fitting confinement. I comforted myself further by recollecting an earlier rail journey under even worse conditions in India at a time when Indian Railways ran a third-class grade of travel. En route to Delhi on the Flying Mail I was compressed for 14 hours with thirty-six others in a compartment designed for a maximum of eight. My chief concern then revolved around simple survival amongst a sweaty, unclean gel of humanity, including a bunch of distinctly hostile Sikhs.

The night was a long one. Halts were made at Craiova, Turnu Severin, Orsova and elsewhere and at each station as many passengers managed to get on as those who got off. By dawn the crush lessened perceptively and I was able to rescue items of our baggage strewn about the floor, our tent – rolled inside a karrimat – in danger of falling through the aperture of the carriage couplings onto the track below. The sunrise offered glimpses of splendid mountain scenery as the train wound through ravine and gorge.

We reached Timisoara around mid-morning and a bedraggled mob of passengers it was that stumbled thankfully off the train. As well as being capital of the western Romanian province of the Banat, part of Austro-Hungary until 1918, it had, since Christmas 1989, become better known as the city where the revolution that toppled Ceausescu began. A protest rally raised to prevent the arrest of the dissident Hungarian Calvinist Pastor Laszlo Tokes was initially – and brutally – fired on by the army and police until the former discovered the protesters to be not just from the Hungarian minority as they had believed. The soldiers promptly joined the protesters. The following day Ceausescu returned from his ill-judged three-day visit to Iran to address a supposedly well-drilled crowd of 100,000 in Bucharest who began to chant 'Ti-mi-soara' with increasing fervour to a background of the old, then-banned, national anthem. Ceausescu was forced to give up his speech in confusion and police started firing on the crowd; fighting continued all night, spreading across the country. The army changed sides everywhere and the hated president was forced to flee, only to be captured and, with his equally loathsome wife, executed by firing squad.

The Banat is predominately flat which, from a cycling point of view, was fine by us. But it was also hot as we were all too soon to discover when the sun rose higher in the sky. We breakfasted on the usual unbreakfastlike morsels at the station 'bufet' and then moved off to explore the city.

Being within day-excursion range of Hungary Timosoara has become a popular destination for Hungarian-based tourists – mostly Germans – crossing the border to acquire a brief 'feel' of Romania before scuttling back to comparative affluence. An elegant city sporting much Baroque architecture and an impressive opera house fronting a well-flowered square, it was milking a new-found fame to the hilt. A cross marks the spot where the first shooting began and shop windows displayed photographs of the dastardly deeds of mid-December 1989. Devouring ice-creams in an effort to lower our temperature we watched a folk-dance troupe go through their repertoire, lunched rather well and expensively in a 'privat' restaurant, then stretched out in a shady park in a vain effort to make up for lost sleep.

In all we took four days to reach the frontier. The first night we both slept soundly in a wadi, the only indent in a dead flat plain, and rose late to cooler weather with a few drops of rain. Stopping off in villages strung along the highway to Arad for the odd beer and chat with the locals we were to meet some odd characters. One was surely the village pimp since his sole topic of conversation revolved around the procurement of girls for sex and the ease (and cheapness) with which he could arrange matters. Other locals wanted to hear about our

journey for which we received many a handshake and expressions of goodwill.
The road was straight and too busy for our liking but there were no alternatives.
The second night we camped in a field of sunflowers, their big nodding heads
admonishing us as if for some indiscretion. Maybe they knew something we
didn't – like the consequences of the suppurating salami we ate for supper. I
caught an attack of the runs and Paul was sick.

I would have imagined Arad, designated as no more than the Banat's second
city, to be considerably larger than Timisoara; it has the big city feeling which,
to me, Timisoara lacked. Its most noticeable feature is the citadel, built by the
Austrians probably more for the purpose of keeping the townsfolk in check than
to guard the region. It too exuded a Baroque elegance, and is backed, in the east,
by the vineyard and peach orchard-covered foothills of the Zarand Mountains.
The central shops, undoubtedly influenced by neighbouring Hungary, were better
provisioned than any we had seen in Romania and we enjoyed a minor spending
spree, disposing of the bulk of our remaining lei in one 'magazin mixt' after
another. We lunched on an unappetising pizza and did little better at the empty
railway station and its restaurant. But for the strike the station would have been
a hive of activity since Arad is classed as a major rail centre carrying the main
line from Bucharest to Budapest that once was the route of the famed Orient
Express when its easternmost terminus was Constanta.

Dawdling again, camping beside a static watercourse among reeds and
listening to fish jumping for flies, we selected a dirt road the following day on
which to reach Nadlac, a couple of kilometres short of the border. The track, for
that's all it was, made a longer route to that of the main highway but we had
acquired a strange reluctance to leave Romanian soil for the probably duller and
certainly more expensive Hungary. At the village of Seitin we halted for our
daily pint and were joined by a gaggle of citizenry all immensely amicable at
first. But they had become too tainted with the commercialism across the border
for unadulterated camaraderie and, inevitably, this turned to requests for dollars
and cigarettes.

Continuing westwards, zig-zagging from one side of the track to the other to
avoid the worst of the ruts, we set up our last camp five kilometres short of
Nadlac, taking the usual care to avoid prying eyes. Yet again even here, in the
most rural of settings, came three men to scythe the very strip of grass upon
which we had raised the tent. They were Slovaks; a friendly trio who made no
complaint; they simply scythed round our encampment leaving us in peace.

Next morning we bumped our way into Nadlac, made a circuit of the township,
purchased a last tin of sardines as a kind of farewell salute, and, ignoring the
long queues of vehicles lined up at the border post, passed effortlessly out of
Romania.

To be on smooth Hungarian tarmac again was an undeniable relief and went
some way to compensate for the expected commercialism that this former
communist ally of Romania has enthusiastically embraced. Even in those harsher
days the country had been a step ahead of most of its allies when it came to
standards of living and, today, is almost on a par, economically, with its western

neighbours. Our return to 'normality' was to be a gradual process but, Hungary was a big step towards it.

Mako, 23km ahead, was the first town and in it we located the railway station, intent upon continuing homeward by train. There appeared to be a rail strike here too, for not a soul was to be seen, while the station timetables showed a distinct deficiency of services in the direction we wanted to go. Mako, together with its nearest and bigger neighbour, Szeged, possesses an aura exclusive to border towns, the former being close to Romania, the latter to Serbia.

Spoiling ourselves with cream cakes and double ice-creams chosen from a selection unheard of in Romania we pushed on towards Szeged to try our luck at what would certainly be a larger station astride a main line to Budapest.

We came upon the smaller road that, according to our map, ran parallel with Highway 43 to Szeged, when we least expected it while lost in a suburb. It was a perfect little byway; smooth, flat, straight and devoid of traffic. It tripped joyously through harmonious wooded countryside plentifully endowed with onion fields, a vegetable for which Mako is famed. The distance to Szeged was 30km, the route cut by the Tisza river we had last crossed at Tokaj. The day was fine, sunny and warm, and, while waiting for the small vehicle ferry, we immersed our feet in the cool water.

Actually two sizeable rivers unite here, the Tisza and the Maros, the latter having accompanied us since Mako, though we hadn't noticed it. On the opposite bank we stripped off and enjoyed a full-blown swim before cycling into the city.

Just 14km from the Serbian frontier, Szeged is a town of considerable charm centred on a square planted with plane trees, limes, rhododendrons and Japanese cherry. Its streets are lined with classical Baroque houses and there is a riverside promenade where the burghers of Szeged take the air and exercise their dogs on Sunday afternoons. The place was formerly the second city of Hungary and remains the traditional, economic and cultural centre of the southern region of the Great Plain. It is also closely associated with two products indisputably Hungarian: paprika and salami, which add up to a unique culinary trio with Mako's onions.

Trying to find the railway station situated far from the centre was something of a trial; the seeming inability of anyone to speak anything but Hungarian. Expressing 'railway station' in every tongue we knew – German, French, Russian and Czech – produced no more than blank stares while my attempt at imitating the noise and motion of a train had people backing away from me in alarm. Eventually we found it, only to come up against a decidedly uncooperative attitude by the railway authorities when it came to the subject of accompanied bicycle transportation.

And that was when contemplation hardened into decision. We would *cycle* to Budapest; it was only 200-odd kilometres, the weather appeared set fine, the roads good and flat. Bugger the railways and their high-faluting attitude to cyclists. We relaxed on a bench outside the station, devoured an early cold supper and, in the cooler temperatures of late afternoon, set off along the broad E75 highway towards the Hungarian capital.

We made it in two days' easy cycling. On all sides the Great Plain stretched to far horizons through shimmering fields of burnt stubble and maize. The sky was hot, blue, far-reaching, and central Europe extended monotonously westwards beneath it from one yellow village church to the next. We camped amongst sunflowers and partook of highly nutritious – by Romanian standards – hot meals in restaurants that knew no shortages.

We paused only to explore the interesting towns through which the road led. Tongue-twisting Kiskunfelegyhaza filled with prosperous-looking houses (*anything* in Hungary looks prosperous compared to that in Romania) and possessing a turreted town hall with colourful ceramic roofing. Kecskemet, looking old-fashioned but not historical, with mustard-yellow streets paved in glazed bricks, and houses painted ochre, pink, turquoise and mint green. And Dabas, a long, narrow township just off the main highway.

The villages of the Plain were provincial and dusty, strung along the road. At midday what little movement there was centred on the local bar, where bicycles were propped against rails by the door as horses might once have been tied. Inside, past the crates of empties, the men in faded blue overalls who sat beneath girlie calendars paid scant attention to strangers. After Kecskemet we were able to leave the busy E75; in fact we had to, since it suddenly became a cyclist-excluding motorway. In its place we found less nerve-jangling cycling on the lesser-used Number 50 via Lajosmizse, Orkeny, Dabas and eventually Budapest. Between Orkeny and Dabas we passed lay-bys occupied by pairs of mini-skirted, over-painted girls of the oldest profession – a sure sign of the march of capitalism – loitering for custom. Embarrassingly my bike developed a double puncture close to one such pick-up point, the girls eyeing Paul with eager anticipation as they awaited the completion of repairs; our tyre levers, spare inner tubes and tubes of rubber solution spread about the ground. The task accomplished, we fled. Outside Kiskunfelegyhaza, as we made a biscuit-and-chocolate snack stop at another lay-by equipped with picnic tables, a Montenegran family joined us, the gruff swarthy father handing us the fatty jaw-bone of what looked like a camel (but was probably a goat) to pick clean. He watched us challengingly as if daring us to eat and we had neither the heart nor the courage to refuse. At Alsonemedi we were treated to a beer by the first English-speaking Hungarian we had so far met, a coach operator who gave me his card in the hope I could put some business his way.

Our route had led quite close to Bugac, the centre of a former sandy region of some 30,000 acres, the true *puszta*, which provides poets and painters with inexhaustible material. I had come this way years before to watch Bugac present the Hungarian version of the rodeo, an incredibly fine display of acrobatic horse-riding.

With the far-flung environs of Budapest stretching out urban fingers we camped in what was the last green swathe before the city enveloped us. A stifling night it was too; as hot and sultry as the days had been for the past week or more. And the ride into Budapest was strictly an unavoidable necessity with the rush hour all about us.

I wanted to show Paul something of the Hungarian capital so we crossed the Danube on the famous Chain Bridge and made our way up Castle Hill to the

Fisherman's Bastion and St Matthias Church from which vantage point there is a superb view.

Cleverly incorporated into the Bastion is the Hilton Hotel, a modern glass structure that in no way detracts from the pseudo-historic surroundings which actually are only of nineteenth-century vintage themselves. I had stayed in the hotel before so renewed my acquaintanceship. In spite of our un-Hilton-like appearance we managed to gain a meeting with the general manager with whom we enjoyed a pot of tea in a venue far removed from those we had been accustomed to for months. Taking advantage of our tenuous relationship with the manager we put the palatial cloakroom to good use, leaving it, I fear, in a state I would not have tolerated in my own home – but Paul always was a messy washer.

The viewpoint looks down upon Pest across the river, another pseudo-Paris with a set of vaguely Parisian pretensions: wide tree-lined boulevards, a railway terminus built by Messrs Eiffel, a neo-Gothic parliament building (reputedly modelled on that of Westminster), and pompous imperial monuments – many in a state of semi-decay.

Buda is very different. Narrow streets alongside the river bank run through a dilapidated quarter squeezed between waterway and hill while others coil upwards to the Old Town, now largely rebuilt rather than restored having suffered devastation in World War Two and again, to a lesser extent, in the 1956 uprising. The first person to grasp the advantages offered by nature's tongue of limestone plateau overlooking the city was King Bela IV in the thirteenth century whose mind was concentrated by the Tartar invasion of 1241. All that was needed was a fortification around the rim of the plateau and, voila, the perfect defensive position. As we descended to river level the sun glinted on cornice, lintel and ornament with, here and there, a line of pitted bullet scars of the years 1956, 1945 and perhaps even 1919. At least Budapest was spared Bucharest's brief agony in 1989.

Finding our way out of the city was harder than finding our way in. We had now resolved to go the whole hog and proceed to the Austrian border, or even Vienna, under pedal-power, the weather remaining fine and the going easy. Beyond Budaors we turned off onto a minuscule road that led idyllically through a series of tidy villages to a hilly region – one of the few in Hungary – called Gereese. As we camped beside a field of maize, the weather broke and we awoke to an all-too-familiar patter of rain on the fly-sheet. And not only did it rain but it turned bitterly cold; within hours the temperature changed from sweltering to near-freezing. Thunder rolled as we packed the soaking tent and pedalled on miserably through the Gereese hills, the picturesque Downs-like terrain obscured by low cloud.

We hit the Danube again at Nyergesujfalu to join Highway 10 towards Gyor, accompanying a river that had here become a border between Hungary and Slovakia. My sights were set on Komarom, 45km on, for I had a date with a certain railway bridge close to that town. Rain still fell as we set up camp again 10km short but, miraculously, stopped, allowing us to dry things out a little. A nearby factory and the proximity of the main Budapest-Vienna railway line ensured it was not the most tranquil of camping places but the woods ensured privacy.

A misty morning found us in Komarom where, following a bout of supermarket shopping, we repaired to track down my bridge. From the road bridge in the town that leads across the river to Komarom's affiliate, Komárno, on the Slovak bank, we could glimpse it indistinctly a kilometre upstream. But that was not enough for me. Proceeding further along the Gyor road, then turning off it, we tracked it down in spite of twice being warned away by well-wishers who insisted that railway bridges in frontier zones were forbidden territory. And so they were in communist days and maybe still are today. Leaving our bikes, we climbed down a bank to the river's edge, dodged a fisherman, walked a hundred yards along a pebbly beach to stand under the three-span, box-girder structure. My mind flew back to a summer's day thirty eight years before. . . .

I first entered Hungary and set eyes on Budapest the summer some ten months after my inauspicious return from East Germany. That setback had not been allowed to paralyse the efforts of Anna and I to be with each other whether in her country or mine and, straightway, fresh methods of achieving that aim had been instigated. But it was the appearance of another crack in the Iron Curtain that became a focus for my probing attentions. As if the hard currency of the West trickling sparingly into East German coffers through the device of the Leipzig Fair had been a catalyst, other hard-currency-starved republics in Eastern Europe began allowing into their well-guarded domains a limited number of Western visitors.

And it was Hungary that re-started it. As soon as I heard of the first of two tours to be run there by a small London agency I applied for participation and was fortunate to obtain a place since the number of participants was limited to fifteen.

Some weeks later Czechoslovakia succumbed to the tinkle of the sterling cash register but, whereas the Hungarian regime was content to welcome unconditionally their intake of British guests, the Czechs were more canny. Their chosen agency was a strongly politically biased one whose director was the communist candidate for Tottenham and they expected his clients to be of similar political hue.

Upon learning of this further glimmer of light that flickered in the darkness I at once applied for participation in that tour too though surmising I'd have a cat's chance in hell of being accepted. The Czechoslovak regime, it transpired, was going to make capital out of the visit, turning it into something of a political junket. But on the assumption that nothing ventured is nothing gained, I posted off the application form, shrugging off the prospect of a lost deposit, and put the matter out of my mind. With the Hungarian trip a certainty and Hungary separated from Czechoslovakia's third province by no more than a river, that project offered better prospects. With my fourteen companions I left London by train for Budapest.

It was while we were ogling the Danube soon after drawing out of Gyor that I first set eyes on the bridge. There it was, a three-span affair, carrying a spur of the main Vienna-Budapest railway line into Slovakia. But what particularly excited me was the cradle of scaffolding that hung beneath the spans. There, if the gods were on my side, was a way into the forbidden land. The tour commenced with two full days in Budapest at our own devices. A night in the city's faded Astoria Hotel and I was at Keleti Station first thing in the morning with a return ticket for Komarom and a notion I might not be returning.

At Komarom I took to the main road to Gyor, the river to my right; the main railway line to the left. The spur line swung away from the latter and crossed the road and this I followed to within a hundred yards of the bridge. From a clump of undergrowth I scrutinised the structure, noting the soldiers at each end but seeing no border patrols on the shingle beach that bordered the river on the Hungarian side. My vision was now full of bridge, my eyes taking in every detail of the scaffolding around the buttresses and framework of planks that formed a catwalk beneath the ironwork of the spans. The river was too wide to permit observation of much detail on the Slovak side though the catwalk appeared to continue unbroken past the halfway point.

Clumps of poplars lined the Hungarian bank affording additional useful cover. The pier, rising from the trees, loomed close and I registered anew every detail of the splints that encased it, the scalability of the timbers and cover from view. Nobody was working aloft so far as I could see though movement out on the third cantilever betrayed the presence of Slovak border guards on the railway line.

My reconnaissance completed, I returned to the town, purchased bread rolls and a slab of chocolate which I stuffed in my pockets, then hung around until evening. By dusk conditions would be perfect; just enough illumination to see what one was doing and no more. I wore rubber-soled shoes and my wallet contained currency in pounds sterling, Hungarian forints and a small amount of Czech crowns acquired on my last incursion onto Czech soil. Returning to the Gyor road the river flashed a fluorescent greeting as I made once again for the bridge. Approaching cautiously I gained the base of the southern pier.

Overhead the girders offered indistinct and unenticing sanctuary. Only as I began to mount the rough timber framework, hand over hand, did I feel vulnerable, though the ascent was not difficult in spite of the absence of a ladder. I have a reasonable head for heights but in some circumstances am affected by vertigo. I am better in mountains than on man-made structures and here, in the unnatural surroundings of a mammoth Meccano set, I at once felt the symptoms. From above came the hollow rumble of a train amplified and echoing amongst the rusty spars. I began to sweat, not so much from the exertion of the climb as from an awareness of what I was doing.

At the top of the pier I rested on the timber platform formed there, then tackled a stubby ladder that led vertically upwards into the dark recesses of iron intestines. The short ascent almost defeated me. All of a sudden I found myself afraid more of the dark unknown above than of a simple ascent of rungs. Gritting my teeth I crawled from the head of the ladder onto one of the heavily flanged main girders that made up part of the first span. Its solid bulk was reassuring after the frailty of the timber scaffolding and, from it, I was able to gaze around at the fretwork of spars and tubular connecting rods that were the sinews of the bridge.

Transfer from warm insecure timber to cold rock-firm metal, however, gave a discomforting view of the abyss below. Before me a catwalk of planking effectively made an extension to the steel flange of the girder. This precarious path led over the river accompanied by a retinue of spars pinned at intervals to tubular lynchpins that hung from beneath the carriageway a few feet above my head.

On hands and knees I moved gingerly forward, keeping as close to the iron wall as possible and away from the sheer drop on my other side. The spars acted as hand-holds and I tried rising to my feet to lessen the discomfort but enormous rivet-heads pushed me outwards to force me, petrified, back on my knees.

Progress was painfully slow. Within minutes I was smothered in rust dust: hair, face, hands and clothes. I longed to rise and stretch. At intervals I took a breather, extending myself out along the planks to relax stiff muscles. A shimmer below disclosed the unmistakable fact that I was over water. At least it'd be nicer to drown than be dashed to pieces on the ground.

The train took me by surprise. A hollow rumble exploded into a great smash of sound and I cringed in awe. The railway track lay close to my head and the huge invisible monster bore down on me. My eyrie of girders, spars and struts trembled like a living thing as I flattened myself over the catwalk clinging on like grim death. The locomotive's heavy wheels pounded into my head a cacophonous crescendo of sullen fury and the wagons that followed beat a rhythmic tattoo. Then silence, a dead, unnatural silence.

Resuming my deliberate movements, hand before hand, one foot carefully placed before the other left its anchorage, I carried doggedly on, trying to ascertain the distance I had come. Another fifteen minutes could put me on the Slovak side of the bridge. Repeatedly I rubbed my eyes to get the rust out of them.

Suddenly I ran out of catwalk. One moment I had firm timbers beneath me; the next they were gone. A yawning gap lay before me. Yet the framework of scaffolding continued unbroken towards the northern end of the span though no catwalk existed.

Shocked, I cast about me for alternative methods of proceeding further but there was nothing. Not even Tarzan could have made it to the other side. Guardedly, I lowered myself into the fretwork of timber joists below the catwalk with the object of observing conditions on the up-river side of the bridge span and so engrossed was I in this endeavour that I failed to notice the string of barges approaching upstream. The throb of the towing vessel – a squat tug – had impinged upon my ear but I had not interpreted its source. Only when a shout cut through my deliberations did I hastily revert to the catwalk and spread-eagle myself upon it once more. But too late. Plainly my silhouette had shown momentarily against the lesser darkness of the sky while I was clear of the sheltering girder. Now, dimly outlined by the cabin light, I could make out the tug's superstructure and a figure on it gesticulating wildly. For a moment I thought he was shouting at me but from above issued answering voices and a clatter of running feet upon iron plating.

The head of the barge train was almost beneath the bridge and I could distinguish the man's face, a white blob in the gloom. He appeared to be staring straight at me but his attention was directed at the guards on the parapet. I was nonplussed; unable to accept I was the cause of the excitement.

That my advance was checked was made obvious by the cessation of the catwalk. That a graver crisis had arisen took time to register. If the excitement above was a result of my discovery there was but one thing to do; retreat and retreat fast.

I turned about, not without difficulty, and, in a crouching stance I'd dared not use before, I part-crawled, part-loped my way back, all caution flung aside. The void beside me ceased to be a cause of concern, its menace eclipsed in the knowledge of the greater threat. Below, the shimmer of water gave way to indistinct terra firma and the base foundations of the buttress. Shinning down the vertical ladder produced no fears now and my swinging descent of the scaffolding could have had Tarzan green with envy. At the back of my mind lay the notion that any parapet guard wishing to reach river level and cut off my line of retreat would first have to negotiate the bridge approach embankment and find a way down through the scrub from there. This could prove my salvation and provide a few vital seconds to offset the other's ability to move faster and without hindrance.

The pounding of running feet had ceased which indicated that the Hungarian guards had moved off the bridge. At the foot of the buttress I paused for a moment to ensure nobody was already on the shingle to intercept me from there. Fresh shouts came from the bridge approaches. I had judged correctly. The guards, caught in the middle of the structure probably fraternising with their Slovak counterparts, were having to detour away from me to reach river-level. Making off at an angle – not straight down the shore towards the town, the direction they'd expect me to go – I lunged into the scrub intent upon reaching the Gyor road by any route other than that following the railway track.

I came to a stubble meadow and crossed it. Another I traversed by going round its outer edge using the cover afforded by an overgrown hedgerow. Abruptly I came to the road and, brushing the worst of the rust out of my hair, slowed to a walk and proceeded towards Komarom, all innocence and virtue.

The houses of the town enfolded me protectively and I made directly for the railway station, thankful for the semi-darkness that hid my dishevelment. The sooner I could distance myself from the area the better I'd like it. A military vehicle, headlights blazing, drove by at speed and I wondered if it had anything to do with me.

Back at the station I studiously locked myself in a toilet to spend a cramped hour cleaning myself up with the aid of water from the cistern. I was in a frightful mess; hair and hands brown with rust. My only emergence was to study a wall-timetable and then board a late-night train back to Budapest. Nobody noticed that my day-return excursion ticket had expired.

Paul and I had a decision to make. We could proceed to the Austrian border on either bank of the Danube. Which should it be?

The shortest route was via Gyor and Mosonmagyarovac straight to the border village of Hegyeshalom and our map showed a tempting little road running between the former couple of towns. A longer route was that on the Slovak bank with a complex of lanes hugging the river for the first 50km that eventually led to the Slovak capital, Bratislava. From there it was only 30km to Hegyeshalom or about 60 direct to Vienna.

We discussed the pros and cons. I had been to Gyor before as I had Bratislava so, for me, there were no fresh cities to conquer. Gyor I remembered as a large industrial town with a fine Austro-Hungarian centre since renovated after years of neglect. Bratislava was a new national capital, having been promoted from a provincial one with Slovakia's cessation from the Czech Republic – not that it would look any different from what it did then. Paul was for the longer grind and, since we had spent so brief a time in eastern Slovakia on the journey, it seemed but right and proper to make up a little for the short shrift we had given it. Also prices were likely to be lower there than in western Hungary. We cycled over the road bridge in Komarom's heart to Slovakia's Komárno the other side intent upon having a pork and dumpling meal before coming to a firm decision.

Crossing into Komárno gave me a quiet satisfaction. After 40 years I had finally made it to the other side of my bridge.

We never came back.

Chapter 11
The Way Home – South-west Slovakia and Westwards

The pork and dumplings, washed down by good Czech beer, was a treat. It perked us up no end, while a sunny day endorsed the decisions we had taken. Paul's leg had been bitten – or, more accurately, nipped – by a diminutive but raucous dog as we returned from the railway bridge, and I examined the teeth-marks as we finished our meal. The skin wasn't broken so we deemed the risk of rabies to be slight. Bathing the affected area in the remains of our beer we left for pastures new.

Komárno turned out to be a considerably more attractive town than its Hungarian cousin, the venerable river port dating back to time immemorial; we had observed its shipyards as we crossed the Danube. Dallying just long enough to establish the layout of the place we proceeded along the Bratislava highway 63 turning off at Zlatna onto a confusion of lanes, some atop embankments resembling Dutch dykes, along which we found (and lost) our way through minuscule villages bearing names like Klizske Nema, Travnik, Čičov, Klucovec and Medvedov. We were in no hurry and halted for another swim, this one in the equally unhurried waters of an arm of the Danube where an island deflected the main fast-running stream the other side.

The little roads were lined with fruit trees and neat kilometre stones. As in Hungary I noticed many of the road signs were pitted and bullet-scarred as if they had been peppered with shot – which no doubt they had, for both Slovaks and Hungarians are ardent hunters, even innocuous road signs providing an option to wild boar. Here and there were beginnings of hills that came to nothing, simply falling flat again as if the effort was just too much. The fields looked well-husbanded, the villages – again like their Hungarian counterparts – neat and tidy. We were becoming accustomed to the shape of such villages by now. Street verges bedded with flowers. Centres often paired with churches, Roman Catholic and Protestant – but here mostly the former. The inevitable bar and supermarket, each with a retinue of bicycles in a rack outside, and the ice-cream stall surrounded by leathery-faced old women. The houses were mostly single-storey, presenting only a stuccoed side wall to the road but facing long rectangular yards; some still of peasant thatch and whitewash. Newer more urban-type houses with proud gardens of dahlias and gladioli behind clipped hedges and high metal fences fast taking the place of the old.

In a village supermarket I found myself in conversation with a man who spoke English. He wanted to know from where we had come but, his linguistic knowledge failing him, thought we were en route *to* Romania. He laid a paternal hand on my arm.

"Don't go to Romania," he warned. "There is nothing there; only trouble. An ugly country."

"There's the Carpathians and Transylvania," I responded.

"But there's no food, nothing in the shops, and the people are bad. The country is dangerous."

"Have you been there?" I asked him pointedly.

"No, and I don't want to," replied the man with feeling, and not for the first time did I feel sorrow for those whose opinions are shaped by pre-conception.

Beyond Medvedov we delved deep into the inescapable maize fields to camp well away from the river but the mosquitoes found us just the same; their attacks were unrelenting and ferocious, spoiling our supper and driving us into the heat of our net-protected tent.

The elements now started to play jokes again, inflicting icy mornings preceding warm, sultry afternoons. A tent-soaking dew and a freezing mist chained us to our beds that late August morning but farm workers began to appear to drive us on our way. In spite of the cold Paul seemed quite happy to shed his pullover and jacket while I piled on all the layers of clothing I could raise to keep the chill out of my old bones.

Near Gabčikovo we turned onto yet another rural road that led eventually to Bač, astride the main Bratislava highway. Unable to find any suitable restaurant when wanted we purchased pasta, soup, bread rolls and *vánočka*, a Czech and Slovak speciality sweet bread which we found both filling and delicious. These provisions we prepared and consumed beside the road before swallowing up the last kilometres to Bratislava. We could have easily reached the city by late afternoon but, since we wanted a full day to explore it, another night in the sticks made sense. So 10km east of the city we raised camp for what was to be our wettest night of the whole journey. It wasn't so much the deluge from the sky that was the cause but the placing of the tent in a grassy indentation between two ploughed fields. Again our site was the last hope before suburbia took over the landscape, the view across the ploughed furrows being a gaunt row of mostly redundant factories with smoke emerging from just one of nearly fifty stacks – a happy sight for environmentalists; a sad one for Slovakia's economy.

As we were preparing supper an old woman approached brandishing a long-bladed kitchen knife. We viewed the apparition with some alarm but, it transpired, the knife was destined for maize cobs, not us. We were subjected to a discourse in rapid Slovak, a percentage of which we were able to decipher with difficulty. "It's going to rain," were her final words (even I recognised the Czech word 'prší,' meaning 'to rain') and she wasn't joking.

The downpour at least had the decency to hold off until we were installed in our bivi-bags, but it continued all night, our indentation forming a conduit channelling water into it so that, by dawn, we found ourselves reclining in a miniature lake. If nothing more it acted as a most efficient alarm clock, though the donning of wet socks, wet shoes, wet T-shirts and wet everything on a cold, damp, grey morning was a depressing task.

We entered Bratislava in the company of a host of early morning workers long before the shops opened. The ominous sky gradually lightened to lift our see-sawing morale accordingly.

Many a first-time visitor is disappointed by Slovakia's premier city. Expecting a Slovak version of Prague, they discover instead a rather shabby town that seems to embody more of the previous regime's blind faith in modernity than the stormy history of this once Hungarian capital. The narrow streets of the Old Town and the squat bulk of the castle on the hill look decidedly secondary in their crumbling antiquity.

The city was a Czechoslovak one for just over 70 years. Its origin dates back to a Roman outpost on the Danube known as Posonium, whence it derives its Hungarian name of Poszony from the time it was brought into the Hungarian kingdom by Stephen I at the end of the tenth century. Following the Tatar invasion in 1241, the Magyar kings brought in German colonists to repopulate the town. They called it Pressburg, while the original Slovaks knew it as Bratislava after Prince Bretislav. With the occupation of Budapest by the Turks in 1526, and again in 1541, the Hungarian capital was transferred here until as recently as 1835. Only in 1919 did the multi-named city become part of the first Czechoslovak Republic though its yearning for independence was most infamously demonstrated in 1939 when, under the fascist leader Josef Tiso, it became capital of the autonomous puppet state of Slovakia at the start of World War Two. It has now won its national capitalship and independence in more – though perhaps not much more – democratic fashion.

St Martin's Cathedral, a massive but plain Gothic church, was closed. The view over the city from the castle hill was obscured by low cloud which spat driblets of rain. I lost the way – though I'd been there before – to the Russian military cemetery at Slavin ponderously decorated with typically Soviet monumental extravagance. And when we crossed the modern bridge that resembles a grounded spaceship to the other side of the Danube (which is no longer the border with Hungary) it was to find ourselves amongst a depressing suburb, rank upon rank of hideous high-risery of which Comrade Ceausescu would have been proud. Thus our sightseeing endeavours in Bratislava were not one of our more inspiring undertakings. And to cap it all, when intent upon having a lavish but inexpensive meal before bankrupting ourselves in Austria, we could find not a single restaurant among the dross. It was the last straw, so we hurried back to the city centre – only to discover it was Saturday and everything but everything closing on the dot of midday, which was the very time we arrived. I just managed to grab a handful of cheese portions and a couple of rolls in a supermarket before being, literally, chased out of the establishment by an impatient manager wanting to go home.

Heading out towards Vienna, our tails between our legs, we finally obtained our long anticipated brunch at teatime in a village close to both the Hungarian and Austrian borders. Here we were crossing the fag-end of the Great Hungarian Plain over which we had earlier ploughed. A century ago it was wild grassland – except where the great slovenly rivers had flooded to form areas of marsh. Today it is cut into broad rectangles of wheat, maize, sunflowers and paprika. Drainage, irrigation and collective farming have imposed a geometric order broken only by the scattered homesteads.

Our last camp of the whole journey was virtually at the spot where the three countries meet but we raised the tent only to dry it out. In its place we had found a discarded hulk of a van, wheelless and rusting, lying close to a farm and, with the active collaboration of a gang of highly-amused labourers, filled its cope with fresh hay to make a softer bed than we'd known for weeks. We were on the threshold of what was once the West – with a capital 'W' – in a region that was strictly no-man's-land a year or so before. But now the barbed wire and watch-towers were gone; this once lethal strip of terrain finally at peace. Down the road I had seen a sign indicating the motorway to Prague and Bohemia. These days it is so simple to attain such cities and provinces of a former East Europe. Ensconced in the warm hay of our improvised bedroom I remembered the dream-come-true of a whole stolen fortnight I connived in the land behind the wire with the girl upon whom I had set my heart.

Upon my return home from the failed mission in Hungary I was to learn, with undisguised rapture, that my earlier application to join the first group of British tourists to visit Czechoslovakia had been accepted. I just couldn't believe my luck. Someone, somehow, had slipped up both in the Czech Embassy in London and in the corridors of power in Prague, though the fact that a group visa was involved could have had something to do with it. But I wasn't going to lose any sleep wondering how it happened. Here was the biggest break I'd been given in all the period of my crusade and, whatever the degree of parental disapproval might be, I intended taking full advantage of it.

Barely back from one trip and I was off on another, this one to the plaintive cries from my mother and controlled fury from my father. At London's Victoria Station I joined my new and larger group of 'fellow-holidaymakers' who, right from the start and encouraged by their collective security, acted out what was virtually a cartoon characterisation of the 'fanatical Red', their astonishing tirades on imagined repressive conditions prevalent in the United Kingdom becoming louder and wilder with every kilometre into the European continent. The worst of this traitorous bunch was a gimlet-eyed woman enveloped in a bright orange dress whose shrill voice provoked me into heated denial on several occasions but, for the most part, I held my tongue not wanting to be branded a 'reactionary', at least before we had entered Czechoslovakia.

Back again on the familiar territory of Cheb station I glanced about for the police officer of two of my previous incursions. Before he had apoplexy at seeing me yet again I wanted to assure him that my latest arrival was legal but he was nowhere to be seen. In a hurried missive to Anna I had let it be known that I would be at the spa resort of Mariánské Lázně (Marienbad) this very mid-afternoon, praying that she would receive it in time. However, though there was nobody present to greet me on this occasion there was a reception committee of another sort.

Self-conscious in national costume, girls distributed flowers and stilted English words of welcome to this first party of tourists from the 'Capitalist West' to their country since the establishment of the New Order. A drizzle fell and the 'Peace' banners hung limp in the grey forenoon. The thump of a polka top-heavy with brass came from a scruffy army band and, as if to show nothing had really changed in spite of this largesse of a toleration of visitors from the other world, the ring of border guards remained, only a little less conspicuously encircling the contaminated train.

My compatriots had a field day. Bleating treason they treated the curious Czechs on the platform to a catalogue of the alleged miseries of life in Britain, much of it lifted straight out of the pages of Charles Dickens. The orange peril dominated the proceedings as she attempted to explain to a perplexed audience the depth of pleasure she felt to be breathing the free, untainted air of the New Czechoslovakia purged of the monstrous tyranny of suppression and exploitation the British people were suffering at the hands of a wicked government under the influence of the United States of America. Where I could I quietly went around making amends but came under the hostile scrutiny of one of the trio of tour conductors.

An hour and a half behind schedule the now designated 'Peace Express' pulled out of Cheb station to a flutter of banners and flags. It dawdled through the dark pinewoods of the Bohmerwald, the ranks of trees a silent army of sentinels that broke ranks only for the odd cannon-ball of rock out-crop within its timber parade-ground. I re-read my copy of the highly organised tour programme for the umpteenth time wondering how it would be possible to skip some of the scheduled trade union meetings, radio interviews, factory visits and selective sightseeing in Prague, Karlovy Vary (Carlsbad) and Plzen. In less than an hour I would be meeting Anna, not for a stolen few minutes or hours but for the eternity of a whole fortnight.

Within the hour too I would be with this girl who could inspire such determination within me. I shook my head in disbelief but it was no dream. My heart thudded with suppressed excitement. Yet doubt could not be entirely dispelled. What if she had not received my last missive or had been prevented from coming to Mariánské Lázně? But the fact of being in her country on a legal basis for a full two weeks offered comfort, for I could put those two weeks to very good use indeed. The train began to brake at the outer suburbs of the spa.

From the open window I scrutinised the station approaches as if my life depended upon it. A sea of faces swept into view as we drew to a halt. The thump of another band took over the drumbeat of metal wheels and a display of bunting heralded another reception extravaganza.

The faces diffused into a blur as I wildly searched for the only one that mattered. The train jerked to a standstill and in a daze I walked through a gap *in the crowd of well-wishers that opened for me. A bunch of flowers was thrust into my hands. Surprised, I turned to the donor but saw only a stranger. Kind, friendly, simple faces pressed around, asking questions about a world locked out of their lives. They were clapping now, smiling and nodding. I tried to smile back but was haunted by a deepening dread. I began to search for the means by which to leave the group to make my way to Anna's home but, at this juncture, chances were slim with so many watchful minions of the state about. I had told her we were staying at the Zápotocký Hotel. Yes, she could be there. I mustn't do anything premature. Desperately I clutched at straws and moved faster towards the exit.*

Suddenly she was before me. For a moment I was unable to comprehend; my smile was superficial, my reaction slow and clumsy. I stopped abruptly and looked at her as if she was the last person on earth I expected to see. Her mouth was an 'O' of wonderment though the tears were unchecked. Then she began smiling and crying at the same time and the spell was broken. Clasped in my arms her mouth found mine and in the middle of several hundred onlookers we found a solace usually reserved for more intimate occasions.

The audience was delighted and roared their approval, showering us with flowers. Undoubtedly we gave them a demonstration of Anglo-Czech solidarity that no official delegation could ever hope to achieve. One of the erstwhile guides arrived to see what the fuss was about and stood, perplexed and disapproving, as we completed our public, private welcome. Brusquely told to move on as we were delaying a speech of welcome we happily obliged and allowed ourselves to be herded into the official enclosure where local dignitaries declaimed upon militant socialism and peaceful co-existence. Holding hands and whispering together, we heard not a word.

More crowds pressed around the portals of the Zápotocký Hotel and yet another band played boisterously beneath a slogan-laden banner stretched across the road. But inside, in the old-fashioned stone vestibule, a modicum of tranquillity existed allowing us the euphoria of being alone with each other.

Dinner in the pillared restaurant was an excuse for more speeches but, with Anna by my side, was no great ordeal. By unspoken consent she had been allowed to join the group for the meal, a tolerance we were able to stretch to participation in the full range of activities covered by the tour. She had arranged her own accommodation at a lesser but nearby hotel, not being permitted a room at the Zápotocký, least of all share my own.

That evening we escaped from the shallow bonhomie of the receptions, the inane conversation of my countrymen and the inquisitive stares of the Czechs to go out into the ill-lit streets of the town and become just another couple to haunt the shadows.

Mariánské Lázně is one of the most beautiful spas in Europe, graced with a homogeneous architecture and surrounded by a plethora of exquisite parks, an environment surely planned and formed over the decades with lovers' strolls in mind. It was dark in the glades and there were pine-needles underfoot. Copper beeches and maples were tangled with the pines and the cool damp grass beneath them reflected a greenish light onto the domed thermal buildings that pushed up, like huge mushrooms, between the trees.

Back at the hotel, in the seclusion of my room, we delayed, joyously, our final goodnights. Anna stood by the bed. I lay back upon it, arms behind my head, gazing at her in silent adoration. I couldn't speak. I felt only, with my whole body, the bright and serious calmness of her young face. It seemed in fact younger than I'd remembered before, its youth having a fresh and lovely brilliance, and in her eyes the almost shocking assurance that I had noticed earlier. I had nothing to say; she did not speak either. She gave me one short smile and then bent down, putting her face against mine. The skin was very soft and warm first against my own face and then my hand. She let her head lie lightly against mine and I put my hand on her neck and kissed her, pulling her down beside me.

Only the restrictive regulations assured a return to her own hotel for what remained of the night.

The running of the Czech tour bore little resemblance to that of the Hungarian one. The composition and attitude of the participants was the first difference. Those in Hungary were straightforward tourists; on this they were political activists. So far as the tour programme was concerned in Hungary the activities were dictated by historical and geographical interest; here every event held political overtones. In Hungary the trips were voluntary; here they were compulsory. Only two of our trio of Cedok guides could speak English, a fact that surprisingly raised no comment, and their real purpose was obvious from the start – though not to the blinkered majority. Throughout the fortnight we were based upon Mariánské Lázně whence the group was taken by coach to various cultural and industrial establishments to be subjected to heavy doses of propaganda. Though some of the destinations were not without interest their very nature was alien to the British traditional notion of carefree holidaymaking. Our 'off-duty' evenings we were encouraged to spend in Mariánske Lázně's Hall of Culture, there to fraternise 'progressively' with comrade guests of other people's republics.

Into this maelstrom of pseudo-solidarity, political glorification and organised spontaneity, Anna and I were swept by the wave of circumstances. We hardly left one another's side and Anna became an accepted member of the British group. We remained in the background of events though our plight gradually began to dawn on some of the less blinkered and militant participants, generating a growing and genuine sympathy.

However, we were not content to while away the whole period of our stolen days together without utilising some of it in the quest for our dual return to Britain. Here, on Czechoslovak soil, was an opportunity to promote our cause for all it was worth. On the fourth day of the tour the coach took us on the scheduled excursion to Prague.

Playing truant from the group as they gaped obediently at the carvings in the city's Jan Hus Bethlehem Chapel, Anna and I made our way across the *fairytale Charles Bridge to the British Embassy. The blue-uniformed policeman saluted smartly, recognising me as British. I knew his duties included noting the names of Czech subjects bold enough to enter. Already Anna had tasted the acid fruits of such action.*

It was a depressing discussion we had with the pipe-smoking consul. He already knew of the situation and could only re-state the efforts the embassy was continuing to make on our behalf. Results, to date, had been meagre, the only positive 'success' being the hardly encouraging one of a negative reply at the third prompting, the other two having been replied to not at all. But we were promised that the efforts would continue which, really, was all we could hope for anyway.

The central headquarters of the Ministry of the Interior became the next object of our attention and, together, we stormed the thick plate-glass doors guarded by a squad of police toting rapid-fire artillery.

We've come to the wrong place," I observed, executing a smart about-turn. "This is the Ministry of War."

Anna checked my retreat. "They're all like this," she whispered.

To a weasel-faced corporal with a hedgehog for a chin I surrendered my passport for examination and Anna her identity card. Both made substantial reading matter and the good soldier Schweik was a slow reader.

"We want the emigration department," Anna stated simply.

Schweik continued his reading.

"Why?" he asked suddenly.

Anna gave him the general idea.

Much of the day thereafter was spent being shuffled between different personages, departments and buildings. We completed innumerable forms and repeated our party piece to a host of individuals. Gradually, by dint of Anna's vocal insistence, we wore the bureaucratic opposition down, crossing hurdle after hurdle until we attained the minister's secretary.

The mild, middle-aged character to whom we finally presented ourselves hardly inspired confidence. Nor was he the minister's secretary; only one of his secretaries. Having shaken hands and acquainted himself with the facts of our case from a massive dossier he relapsed into a monologue which was half apology and half explanation for the manner in which his department was inconveniencing us. It was as good a bit of government claptrap as I have heard and, in a long, devious manner, meant precisely nothing. Since Anna's marriage application had again been rejected there could be no reason for the state to further consider her emigration. It was as simple as that, though put differently. We were ushered out, entirely dissatisfied with the interview but knowing not how to extend it constructively.

It was early evening before we got back to the Alcron hotel in time to attend the Radio Prague recording session at which my presence had been demanded. The session was behind schedule owing to the absence of British-born wives of Czechs with their expected verbal 'proof' of idyllic conditions within the Czechoslovak state. Only one turned up.

At the end of this miserable performance the group was herded out of the hotel and on to the waiting coach for the drive back to Mariánské Lázně. Our couriers were already in a bad mood in consequence of the upsetting of the timetable and their tempers were not improved when I told them I intended remaining in Prague for the night as we had further business to which to attend the next day. It was their first experience of open revolt within the group and I enjoyed their discomfiture.

"I shall return to Mariánské Lázně in due course," I finished. I wasn't even going to tell them it would probably be tomorrow evening.

"But you can't stay on your own," the tour leader chimed in with growing concern.

"Why not?" Anna lashed back. "I can look after him."

"But it's strictly forbidden," came the stock reply to anything that was not a stock question.

Anna was not to be deterred. "Why should a night in Prague be forbidden?"

The man was becoming impatient. He had steadfastly ignored Anna's unofficial involvement in the group, not even acknowledging her presence. "For you, no, but Mr. Portway is a foreigner and he is registered in Mariánské Lázně If he remains in Prague he will be in trouble."

"But he will register here in a hotel tonight."

A look of relief spread across the leader's face. "You mean he's not staying in a private house then?"

"No. We shall take rooms in this hotel."

The man, mollified, returned to the waiting coach content in the knowledge he had not been party to the sin of allowing an Englishman to spend a night under a private Czech roof. But clearly he was far from happy and I foresaw the likelihood of his attempting to cleanse the group of Anna upon our return to it. Losing, even temporarily, one of his charges had further provoked his unease. Or maybe it was because he was learning that one of his doves was a pigeon.

With a night alone in a city of repression, we tried to find laughter. We drank inferior vermouth at an inferior night club and danced on an overcrowded floor to a second-rate band. But though deeply content to be in each other's company we found no laughter. And the man who stood near our table and followed us everywhere had little enough to laugh at either.

In the morning a sun was shining in a watery sky transforming Prague's Gothic towers, Renaissance spires and Baroque cupolas into a city of magic. Alas, dreams in Prague were all that was left of liberty. In the streets, red banners and placards proclaimed the socialist development, loudspeakers attached to lamp posts blared out martial music and exhortation. The Party was ubiquitous, inescapable. Communist indoctrination began in nursery school at age three. There were party representatives in factories, offices, schools, newspapers, apartment buildings, neighbourhoods. The Party duplicated all forms of management and government from the top down, matching Prime Minister with Party Secretary. About one in fifteen of the population belonged to the Party, the self-proclaimed 'vanguard'. Being a member helped in the everyday concerns *of life like acquiring a reasonable job, a car, better health-care and better education for one's children. Not being a Party member meant putting up with second best, with envy, with a sense of disenfranchisement, with a submerged sort of existence. In Prague dreams were rife.*

After breakfast of ersatz coffee and stale rolls we set out to call on the President. At least that was the intention. Having always nursed a belief in starting at the top and working downwards when aiming for an objective I saw no reason why the principle should not be applied in present circumstances. Stories were prevalent concerning Antonin Zápotocký. Few were complimentary though it was said he played the accordion well when drunk. I'm partial to accordion music so at least he had one thing going for him. As all kings and presidents should, Comrade Zápotocký ruled from a castle. His was that of Hradčany, former home of Czech kings and rising high on the hill above the river Vltava. A number 23 tram passed the door. The sentries were a let-down – no scarlet and gold-encrusted warriors but a handful of peasant soldiers clutching the usual ultra-lethal hardware lounging around the main gate. We walked straight through, ignoring their presence. In turn they ignored ours.

No obliging notice in the cobbled courtyard read 'To the President' but there was one indicating an office. It sold postcards but we decided it would do for a start.

From such humble beginnings we worked our way up, through a repetition of perseverance and stubbornness, to the presidential office, no less, though it sounded grander than it actually was. The guard on the door wore a crease in his trousers and the calibre of weaponry was but that of a discreet pistol. He'd also shaved. If appearances were anything to go by we were attaining the upper reaches of the hierarchy.

A senior clerk tried to put us off until the afternoon. "Two till four are the hours for applying for presidential interviews," he told us.

But we weren't having any of that. Anna explained that I was a British visitor with limited time to spare.

At that the man displayed a spark of interest and transferred his gaze to me in the manner of a farmer calculating the worth of a stallion. He didn't actually poke my withers or look at my teeth; instead he retreated into an inner sanctum. Together we waited in hushed expectation.

The man reappeared. "The President's secretary will see you," he announced and ushered us into the holy of holies.

We entered a chamber of almost palatial quality. A rich unsocialist carpet graced the floor and gentle illumination emanated from an exquisite chandelier. A young man in a dark suit rose from behind a mahogany desk to shake hands and indicate two well-padded chairs.

Anna once more spoke her party piece.

The secretary was sympathetic. He knew of our case, but he still wrote copious notes on a pad as Anna spoke. He even called for a stenographer who wrote some more. But he couldn't produce a president. Nobody, he told us sweetly, could physically meet the President; not just like that, you understand. But he would be made personally aware of matters. The President was a very busy person indeed. Affairs of state and all that. I strained my ears for accordion music.

But the secretary could promise one thing. Anna could make another application and he himself would see that the President gave it his close consideration. And the President, as his doting people were aware, was a kind and considerate man.

With such benign words sounding hollow in our ears, we withdrew and the echoes of our footfalls in the stone corridors were equally hollow. I glared ferociously at a lounging youth pretending not to be a security man.

In the evening we returned to Mariánské Lázně, two sadder but wiser individuals. Perhaps no wiser since Anna had started out with no expectations and I, to be honest, only needed the evidence of my own ears and eyes. The sum total of our accomplishments over the two days had been the granting of permission for Anna to make yet another marriage application which, at least, was something. If that failed we were left with only one course of action. The Elbe below Bad Schandau, the rolling hills near Horní Dvořiště, the bridge at Komarom, and the, as yet, unattempted crossing of the Tatras into Poland all pointed a way out. But a counter hurdle loomed, distant, indistinct, more ominous even than the barbed wire and minefields. Its name was retribution. As our train to Mariánské Lázně sped through the soft Bohemian landscape I became uncomfortably aware of the truth, the bitter truth, that Anna's escape would open an account with the state. And Anna's aged parents and her sisters would remain behind, surety to its settlement.

Darkness enveloped us as the train plunged into a tunnel. Our hands met and clasped tightly. Faith had become our only friend.

It was the weather that, for the remaining days, did its best to shatter the illusion of carefree abandon we attempted to create. Flinging ourselves into the assorted activities of the group, we managed, however, to find something akin to happiness in spite of the unceasing rain which at least curtailed some of the more ludicrous items on the programme. Mostly, we found it prudent to remain with the group – a prudence encouraged by the unsecretive presence of the secret police who seldom left us to our own devices. They were invariably dogging our footsteps, listening and watching. Even the members of the group made better company than these silent, faceless footpads and I was gratified to note the increasing sympathy and indignation our plight was producing within British breasts, a change of attitude quickly noticed by our courier watch-dogs. Yet no effort was made to banish Anna from the alien ranks – perhaps through alarm that doing so would cause even further damaging repercussions.

Our last day together we spent roaming in the stillness of the woods around the spa. We came to a clearing where the edge of a stream was firm and sandy, showing the water had risen and receded leaving the banks dry and white in the sunshine. We halted by mutual consent for it was warm here, remote and lonely. Anna turned to me and began to say something about wishing me luck back in

Britain. She had thrown back the collar of her jacket and I noticed the triangle of her throat, pale under the black edges of the material and the darkness of her hair. Then she ceased speaking, looking at me for a prolonged moment and came close to me.

"I don't ask for it. I'm not holding you to marrying me, you know", she said in a small voice.

I was taken by surprise. "You mean you don't want to?", I replied.

"It's not that, as you know", she went on. "I mean I don't ask it of you unless you want it more than anything else in the world. The situation we are in might continue for years and years, and I would not watn to stand in the way of your happiness if another girl – a more attainable girl – came in to your life". I saw the strain of what she was saying pucker her face.

"Oh God", I exclaimed savagely. I put my cheek against her shoulder and let my lightheartedness drain away. "I do want it. I do want it. I want it so much. You must believe it, please. More than anything else in the world".

She continued looking at me but in a different manner. Her eyes were bright with wonder.

"Then it shall not be otherwise", she said simply.

"What made you offer to release me?", I asked after a pause though I thought I already knew the answer.

She stared at the ground. "You once wrote to me that you would understand if I gave you up", came the barely auidable reply. "It came to me that you might have found someone else".

A stab of shame passed through me. I never realised how much I had hurt her with an earlier letter offering release from our commitment to oneanother, that I had sent in a moment of weakness when I had felt the whole world against us.

There was nothing I could say that wouldn't sound trite and inadequate. Instead I embraced her with all the fervour at my command. "It couldn't be otherwise", I added finally, using her own words.

The fourteenth day of the tour I departed with the group on the midday Orient Express to the West.

Violent squalls of rain welcomed Paul and I to Vienna sending us dashing for cover in shop doorways and bus shelters at frequent intervals. Our first objective was the city's West Station to which to entrust our bikes prior to their rail transportation to Paris. "It'll take five, possibly six, days for them to get there," we were told as we paid an exorbitant fee, with Austrian, German and French Railways each taking their cut. "Why so long when a train covers the distance in little over 12 hours?" I indignantly asked. "It's the Germans," said one official. "It's the French," replied another. But there was nothing we could do about it, though how we were going to mark time in the meantime with our cash supplies running low we had no idea. A hasty totting up of our combined resources revealed enough in sundry currencies to provide for basic provisions for a few days and to pay the heavy levy likely to be charged for bike transportation from Paris to

Dieppe, but sojourning in hotels was out. Except for one. Hilton International had kindly arranged a gratis bed and breakfast stay in their central Vienna pad and to this we guided our faltering footsteps, shoulders loaded with baggage, intent upon obtaining the most benefit from at least one night out of a possible six. Again the rain squalls had us dodging in and out of bolt holes as we struggled through the water-logged streets and at the imposing reception counter of the Vienna Hilton on Am Stadtpark we were saved from being turned away as vagrants only by the tattered remains of the Hilton International letter of introduction I had managed to retain.

I nurse a notion that prolonged luxury can be almost as tedious as sustained roughing it but our initial 24 hours of Hilton high-living was elixir as we wallowed in hot baths and soft beds and consumed a breakfast of a size that should have been entered in a Hilton Book of Records. And upon our gaining a meeting with the general manager that good soul was persuaded to allow us a second gratis 24 hours of heaven, thus cutting down the threatened nights on the tiles to four.

Next morning dawned warm and sunny so I introduced Paul to the Austrian capital, covering, on foot, everything worth seeing from the spurned Danube, through the central Stephansplatz to the out-of-town Schöenbrunn Palace. No other European capital speaks of empire so eloquently, elegantly or pompously as does Vienna. Everywhere gilded imperial eagles gaze down sneeringly from Baroque eyries, reminding those who'd forget that their masters once ran a tract of land extending from Switzerland to the Ukraine.

Reluctant to leave our voluptuous pad the third day until the very last moment we emerged to catch the 2300-departing Orient Express, thus ensuring part of a night's relative comfort on the train. With half an eye I beheld the station at Linz and momentarily recollected events there of years gone by before Munich East Station welcomed us to its draughty platforms upon which we attempted to doss for the remainder of the night. But a posse of railway police decided otherwise. It rained again as we partook of breakfast; a tin of sardines and a saucepan of soup heated up on our cooker in a park opposite the station. Only an early-morning park sweeper witnessed these antics and I could swear he didn't believe what he saw.

Determined not to reach Paris too soon we gave ourselves up to another day of sightseeing with Munich the venue on this occasion. Catching the late night train to Paris would give us a further part-night's soft seat upon which to relax.

The Bavarian capital has one considerable asset for the casual visitor. A majority of its museums, monuments, palaces and churches are concentrated in the Innenstadt – the inner city – which makes it a great place for walking. And since walking is a free pastime we walked, having deposited our baggage in a hotel near the station. From the Marienplatz we wound our way outwards, eventually running to earth a friend of mine, one Uwe Prectl, a senior employee of the Bavarian Tourist Board. That worthy was good enough to entertain us to a substantial dinner – and when it comes to eating, Bavarians don't do things by halves. Full of Schweinbraten, dumplings, Apfelstrudel and Weisbier (white beer) we felt fortified enough to face what further trials might lie ahead as we boarded the 0130 Orient Express for Paris.

Arriving at the French capital's Gare de L'Est we went straight to the Bureau des Baggages to enquire about the arrival of our bikes fully expecting – and dreading – a night or even two at this most inhospitable of stations. But, joy, our bikes were to hand and these we rode, somewhat unsteadily, across the city to the St Lazare Station intent upon getting them to Dieppe in the same boat train we proposed catching ourselves.

A warm – too warm – and sunny day in Paris. Twelve hours to kill but not much money to spend. The circumstances indicated another walking tour since, again, Paul was unfamiliar with the city. One of the streets through which we strolled was the chic Boulevard Haussmann. My mind flew back to an equally balmy day – 17 March 1957.

In the land behind the wire something began to happen, or at least for me it did. It started with a dose of pure vitriol.

I had been back from my successful visit to the Czechoslovak Republic a while when I was invited by Fenner Brockway for a meeting with him in the Member's Canteen at Westminster. Over a cup of tea and a sticky bun I listened in incredulous silence to a catalogue of 'proven misdeeds' attributed to my fiancée carried out over the past couple of years. In short, Anna was alleged to be two-timing me.

The accusations, still fresh from the lips of the Czech Ambassador, and repeated now in a neutral voice by a highly respected member of the British Parliament, poured into my astonished ears. No doubt some of the seeds were supposed to fall upon fertile ground but the picture my mind conjured of senior governmental officials and senior diplomats furnishing reports on the tittle-tattle of a small country town was absurd enough to kill every seed stone dead. Altogether this amazing ambassadorial charade was enacted three times over a period of two months by which time the imaginative powers of the local authorities presumably dried up. On each occasion the unfortunate Fenner Brockway, ensnared in the chain of communication, was the embarrassed purveyor of the poison and the poor fellow was more distressed than I.

Even if I had no immediate explanation for some of Anna's 'indiscretions' the ludicrous proceedings were so clumsily carried out as to be an obvious fake. And I knew my Anna. Our physical acquaintanceship over more than four years might only be measured in days but together we had touched the depths and heights of human emotion.

Upon deeper investigation the flimsiness of the charges was revealed but I awarded the booby prize to the one concerning the late-night debauchery attributed to her and a tall, fair young man in a Prague cabaret hall. Even dates and times plus a wealth of detail was available proving without a shadow of doubt that it was I who was the secret admirer!

The other less specific instances of Anna's apparent infidelity I treated with the contempt they deserved and Fenner Brockway was as pleased as I when this insidious method of counter-attack was finally abandoned.

Then suddenly, from a very different quarter, there burst upon the scene a

*new and much more startling development. My first reaction was plain disbelief.
Worn down at last by incessant clamour emanating from the United Nations,
the British government, the British press and, I like to think, our own refusal to
surrender, the Czech authorities had instigated, it seemed, the ponderous process
of expelling Anna from her homeland. The first news of this revelation came
from Fenner Brockway, then from 'Rab' Butler, and, finally, from Anna herself.
The expelling procedure, outlined by the Ministry of the Interior in Prague,
involved the completion, by her, of a number of formalities divesting her of all
rights and claims on the Czech State after which she would be permitted to
emigrate from the country. The news eclipsed further steps I was actively taking
in support of the 'Polish Plan' as well as Fenner Brockway's revealed intention
to go to Prague to intercede on my behalf.*

*The completion of those formalities was to take many months. Some involved
Anna in Catch-22 situations which had to be unwound; others produced the
necessity of her going before tribunals to acquire statements appertaining to a
range of financial and emigration matters. Frantic and impatient for information
on progress and for things to happen I bombarded Anna with uncoded letters
and made myself patently objectionable to everyone.*

*Possessed of an air-ticket sent by me, and very little else, Anna took leave of
her family. It must have been both a joyful and sad occasion. For her mother,
father, two sisters and brother-in-law it could but produce irrevocably tangled
emotions.*

*On Sunday 17 March 1957, at Prague's Ruzyne Airport, Anna boarded an
Air France Viscount for a one-way flight to Paris.*

*I was at Orly Airport to meet her, of course. The French capital had lain under
a damp blanket of mist that morning which contrasted strongly with my mood. I
had booked a double room at a luxury hotel in the Boulevard Haussmann for
that night and, as if to cap this extravagance and herald the finale to the drama
to be enacted that early afternoon, the sun broke through, warm and brilliant.*

*And drama there was. In the arrivals concourse I waited impatiently. I heard
her flight announced and watched its passengers issue from the customs bay to
be swallowed up by the crowd of people awaiting them; its numbers gradually
dwindled to nothing until it was just me alone. Alarmed, I pulled open the doors
through which the passengers had come only to be restrained by two gendarmes
the other side. But there across the far side of the imigration and customs hall I
saw her. She was arguing with an official.*

*Breaking free from the arms of the law I strode towards Anna, the two
policemen trying to pull me back and shouting for me to stop. A terrible fear
had gripped me.*

*Both the official dealing with Anna and another, more senior personage,
came over to intercept me. He now offered explanations, confirming my worst
forebodings.*

*In near-perfect English, spoken in a soft, competent manner, he said, "I'm
afraid this lady has not a proper passport or documentation enabling her to*

enter this country." His next words exploded like a bomb in my ears. "I regret she will have to return to Prague."

For a full ten seconds I was speechless. Then I walked firmly over to Anna and, tightly holding her hand, turned to face the new opposition.

"She goes back over my dead body," I exploded. "What's wrong with her papers?"

The senior official explained that Anna's travel documents in no way constituted a passport and that neither had she a French visa of any description.

I retorted that, being stateless, how could she hold a proper passport. And whatever shortcomings might exist so far as the document was concerned, it held a legal and valid British entry visa. I could see it with my own eyes.

The official admitted that the British visa did seem to be genuine. But this was France, and . . . .

I interrupted. "Well, if she can't remain on the holy soil of France, why can't she be put on the next flight to London? Why send her back when she can be sent forward?" The gist of the conversation was becoming painfully similar to others I could remember. I felt a flush of shame.

Driven on by reproach I extended my thrust. I wasn't angry any more; simply incredulous. For the best part of five years we'd been fighting the whole Cominform to effect this union between man and a woman. Now, on the threshold of victory, a Frenchman, a citizen of a country in which love and romance were on a par with the Marseillaise, wanted to destroy everything because of some deficiency in the wording on a piece of paper.

The man saw I meant business. He hesitated and was lost. "I'll make further investigations," he promised and moved away to return after a while with two colleagues. Anna and I became exhibits numbers one and two but their attentions were not hostile. The senior official smiled bleakly.

"I think things'll be all right," he affirmed, "but she's not to leave the airport."

We were escorted to a smaller room with discreet bars across the only window. It was the airport detention lounge. The bevy of officials, now reduced to two, withdrew, leaving us alone with each other.

I turned to Anna. "Hello," I said weakly. It came to me that I'd not been given the opportunity to speak a word to her.

And there, sharing an overstuffed leather armchair, we spent our first night together in the Free World. I thought wistfully of the big double bed, empty and deserted, back at the hotel in the Boulevard Haussmann.

For Paul and me the last night of our journey was spent equally uncomfortably on the lounge-floor of the Dieppe-Newhaven ferry. We had been re-united with our bikes at Dieppe harbour, though, through the uncooperative attitude of a disgruntled individual in the baggage car of the boat train, they had very nearly been returned to Paris before we could claim them.

From Newhaven we cycled the last 13 miles home and I hoped it wouldn't be sardines for lunch.

EPILOGUE

Anna and I were married on 5 April 1957, twelve years after we had first set eyes upon one another. The wedding took place under the bright stare of television cameras.

For years following Anna's departure from her homeland we were both excommunicated from that country; a penalty we willingly accepted. But time is both a healer and a changer of fortunes. A relaxation of restrictions, coupled with a natural desire on the part of Anna's parents in the evening of their lives, to see their daughter and their grandchildren, offered reason for occasional and permitted return visits to the land behind the wire.

It was during the first such visit that we learnt of an ominous development. The fact that Anna had left her country in a legally constituted manner had not, after all, prevented the state from taking revenge upon those members of the family who remained behind. Their lives became a constant rift with authority; rights were denied them, and my brother-in-law, Pavel, was removed from any worthwhile job his undoubted ability gained for him.

Irritation – and it was no more than that – emerged also from my side of the fence; surprisingly from certain authorities of my own country. The fact that I had valid reasons for visiting a Czech family of impeccable reliability (i.e. anti-communist) was not lost upon the intelligence service at Whitehall who, furthermore, were aware of Pavel's former employment as a radar and radio technician within the Czech Ministry of Defence. Once again I found myself 'up before the beak' though, instead of reprimand and disapproval, I was to receive requests for information I could obtain on my next visit to Czechoslovakia. The list of items on which they wanted details was formidable but mainly of an economic nature – though tucked away among the contents was a more contentious one concerning particulars about Soviet-made tanks known to be lagered in the military depot in Slaný.

Thus on subsequent visits to Czechoslovakia I obediently kept my eyes open and listened to what Czech citizens had to say about conditions under which they lived. And the 'tank question' hardly had me crawling among their tracks with a tape-measure since Pavel, with his technical expertise, provided the data required. I was also able to pass onto our military attache in Prague data given me one day by an excited Slaný citizen who arrived breathless at Anna's family home with the information that batteries of Russian-manned missile launchers were being secretly installed in a nearby forest – at a time when no Soviet troops were supposed to be in the country. To transmit this tit-bit of intelligence I visited the British Embassy whereupon, on arrival at the office of the military attache, I was bade remain silent, a note being passed to me which indicated that I was to write down my message while discoursing in general upon less vital matters, a course of action I found excruciatingly difficult to carry out. Seemingly it was known by the attache that his office was bugged, which provided a convenient vehicle for the transmission of dis-information to the listening ears of the STB.

Back at home Anna and I were visited by a civilian-attired colonel of Intelligence who pumped us dry of the smallest details of our combined lives and I was 'invited' to report to various offices in London to discuss further 'matters of mutual benefit'.

But it was the ugly situation in which Pavel, and to a lesser extent his wife Mary, found themselves that became the chief concern. During our initial return visits he confided in me his increasing fears for their future and elicited a promise that I would come to their aid should by some twist of fortune the circumstances turn in their favour. I concurred, of course, though aware that, to generate these circumstances, it must be Pavel who would have to initiate the first move.

We met, my brother-in-law and I, on the sun terrace of the Hotel Kontinental, Rijeka, in Yugoslavia, one sundrenched afternoon in late July.

The warmth of Pavel's handshake spoke more eloquently than his limited English of his pleasure – and relief – at seeing me. An exchange of coded telegrams had brought me a thousand miles from England and him more than half that distance from Czechoslovakia. For Pavel the journey was to shape the destiny of his life, and I was one of the props – a vital prop. He said he knew I would come but the relief was there all the same.

For more than 20 years Pavel had been dreaming of leaving his country for the security of the West. He had paid for one attempt to turn the dream into reality with the nightmare of a year's imprisonment. Since that time, though a highly skilled technician, he had drifted from one menial job to another. The fact that he had 'Western connections' – a sister-in-law who had emigrated to England – was, in the official files, a further mark against him. But the connection worked for him too and, with the worst excesses of Stalinism past, his wife Mary was occasionally allowed to visit her sister. Pavel had to remain behind, a living guarantee that she would return. Yet Pavel knew that within the few short weeks when his government irregularly allowed Mary beyond the gates lay his only opportunity for both of them to find freedom. He turned his eyes southwards to neighbouring Hungary and, beyond, Yugoslavia. There lay a fellow socialist state of a paler shade of red and, more important, possessing a common and less lethal border with the West.

At first he could not synchronise his own and Mary's movements. Either Mary was refused an exit permit to visit England, or Pavel's application to visit Yugoslavia was delayed until her safe return. Later, restrictions on travel to *other Eastern bloc countries were eased. By careful planning and with the help of a trusted companion, Pavel managed to reach Yugoslavia without the immediate knowledge of the Secret Police. And earlier that July Mary had gone to England. The combination of these factors was a stroke of luck. Seldom was the STB careless in the execution of their vigilance. In fact, as far as Pavel was concerned, it happened only once in 17 years. But it was once too often.*

We left Rijeka together in Pavel's small car and, threading our way past the hulks of half-completed ships, ascended the tree-clad heights behind the town. The heat of the sun was beginning to die, and we had two hours in hand to attain a cross on my map, 70km away, that I had designated to be Pavel's crossing point into Italy.

The day before, with Tony, a Maltese friend who spoke Italian, I had reconnoitred the area behind Trieste, and, in so doing, had come across Monrupino. From the church that perched atop the dramatic little hill that towered over the village, the border looked innocent and tranquil. An Italian peasant, noting our interest, had pointed out the line of the frontier curving along the middle of the valley that lay before us. Our eyes had taken in a watch-tower near a rural checkpoint and another on the brow of a hill. But dusk or darkness and an abundance of trees and scrub could hide a trespasser. There were, allegedly, no minefields and little barbed wire, though border guards patrolled at frequent intervals. With Tony watching from Monrupino church, I would, from the other side, accompany Pavel to within a few yards of the border, create, if necessary a diversion and the job would be done. I would then return to the car and alone make my way back via the main checkpoint at Sezana to Trieste, picking up Tony en route and then await Pavel's eventual arrival at our hotel.

With this scheme in mind, Pavel and I drove to Vogliano, the tiny hamlet close to the border on the Yugoslavia side opposite Monrupino. This was to be our base for the operation. It was not easy to find, for my Italian Touring Club map was inaccurate. We came upon the hamlet from behind when we least expected it and were suddenly faced with the local checkpoint – the one Tony and I had seen the day before. Hastily we reversed, turned, and drove back to the cluster of houses that had hidden the post from sight.

We left the car beneath a tree and locked it. Taking advantage of the remaining daylight we decided upon an open reconnaissance of the area to locate a well-sheltered section of the border where we could hide until dusk or darkness. A track ran westwards, roughly parallel with the border, and we took it. On our left, the silhouette of Monrupino church stood out starkly on its mound against a blood-red sunset. Somewhere up there amid the granite walls Tony would be watching and waiting.

Abruptly we came to another cluster of houses. But something felt different. The street was empty though we sensed hostile eyes upon us. An old man, sucking an ancient pipe, surveyed us morosely from a doorway. A lame dog skulked by to turn and bark defiance – the only noise in a community of silence.

Round a corner we glimpsed a striped barrier. We sheered away and took another track leading away from the border. A shout brought us to a halt. A policeman, buckling on a pistol belt, emerged from a house. He asked us what we were doing, then, not understanding our reply, examined our passports and gave us to understand that we had strayed into a forbidden zone and must leave immediately.

Halfway back along the track, out of sight of the houses, we slipped into an orchard and located a hiding place in tall grass very close to the line of the border. We lay down to await the darkness and had been there only a quarter of an hour when we were abruptly confronted by the policeman. His suspicions must have been aroused by Pavel's Czech documents and by our strange movements. Quietly he had followed to catch us in this most compromising of situations.

We were ordered to accompany him back the way we had come and, with him in the back seat, were bade drive to the earlier checkpoint. In the customs house we were questioned in turn, our wildly differing replies being thumped out on a typewriter. A series of telephone calls were made, presumably to higher authority. My own answers to the questioning were intentionally vague and, to my relief, the questions ceased when a home-going Italian, dazed by a surfeit of slivovice, ran his motor-cycle full-tilt into the frontier pole.

In all we remained three hours in the customs house, watching darkness blot out the tantalising view of Monrupino. I thought of the unfortunate Tony patiently waiting. It was quite dark when an officer arrived and we were taken – me in a police car, Pavel driving his own under guard – to the township of Cezana. Here, in the barrack-like surroundings of police headquarters we were questioned again but more thoroughly for several hours. Upon a whim I strongly expressed my own dissatisfaction at being a persecuted tourist and declared my intention of reporting the fact to my embassy with a view to curbing the influx of Western visitors to Yugoslavia. The ploy was wildly successful. In a flash the attitudes of our oppressors changed. With an almost grovelling apology we were handed back our passports and released.

I left Pavel at a local hotel and, taking his car but arranging to return in the morning, drove back to Trieste. It was too late to collect Tony; he would have found his own way back to Trieste by now. To my agreeable surprise, little interest was paid to the Czech-registered car at the border, a point I noted in support of a germ of further ideas revolving in my mind to effect Pavel's bid for freedom.

The following day, back in Yugoslavia, Pavel and I gazed across the expanse of tree-shrouded hills, our eyes roving up and over the double crest. My heart sank at the formidable task that I had set my brother-in-law. He himself was plainly aghast. The early afternoon sun beat down with cruel intensity – an added challenge to the unknown hazards of the frontier that ran along the reverse slope of the second crest.

I had chosen the place after a long study of the map. Wooded hills far off the beaten track seemed to offer the best way out. With a troubled heart I left Pavel on a forgotten dust road somewhere between the hamlets of Vallegrande and

Pliscovizza di Madonna. But it was essentially a one-man job. Tony and I would meet him in the Italian hamlet of Sgonico on the other side. We would wait all night if necessary. Pavel plainly hated my leaving, and I hated myself for the brutal way I was pushing him into further danger. But it had to be done. Either that or surrender. In the driving mirror I watched him, a sad forlorn figure swallowed up in a cloud of dust.

In Sgonico, a mile and a whole world from the opposite side of the border, Tony and I waited, comfortably ensconced in a vine-sheltered albergo. But the waiting seared my soul as the doubts piled into it. Had I sent a man to savage captivity? Had I failed his wife who likewise waited? Had I failed my own whose faith I carried? And fear grew in the fertile abyss of my torment.

In the afternoon I walked deep into the border area as the urge to share Pavel's burden of danger stirred restlessly within me. Later a storm broke with violent suddenness. Tony and I finished our umpteenth beer and watched the lightning lash the roofs of Sgonico with vivid hate. Thunder rolled. Yet no rain came to Sgonico that night, but we could hear its angry hiss as it fell on the trees in the hills. There was no sign of Pavel so Tony and I returned, crestfallen, to our Trieste hotel as dawn pierced the sky.

The telegram that reached me mid-morning lifted a great load off my mind. It was not until later that I learnt how Pavel had fared the previous day. In the heat of the afternoon and on into the refuge of evening he had struggled through the dense undergrowth. Drenched in sweat, he clawed his way up and over the first crest, only allowing caution to retard his progress near the summit of the second. For two hours he rested, listening for the sounds of danger and preparing for the final thrust. With nightfall he moved forward again. Suddenly he heard men and dogs close by. His eyes, accustomed to the gloom, had picked out a telephone cable which he followed; a foolish action, for it led to deeper danger. Then, close to a watch-tower that reared above him, all sounds and shadows were obliterated by the deluge. The storm was not only protection but a warning. To ignore it was madness. Pavel decided to tempt providence no further and, soaked to the skin, slunk back whence he had come.

At least Pavel was alive and still at liberty. But he was not free. The direct assault on the border was paying no dividends. A more subtle method would have to be employed. My mind flew back to what I discerned as a lax attitude to cars passing through the border checkpoint.

It was Tony who came up with the final solution. We had already discarded the concealment-in-the-boot-of-the-car idea. The odds were too high. And we could all go down, car included. But a doctored passport? There lay an outside chance. In support of such a possibility I had brought with me two identity photographs of Pavel, a blank passport identity slip and three of my cancelled passports that a considerate Foreign Office returns to their owners upon expiry of validity. I never thought I'd have to use them but now they offered salvation.

Back in the hotel we went to work. An inkless ball-point pen, a penknife and a tube of glue were our tools. And, as the scorching sun proclaimed mid-morning, between us we produced a minor masterpiece. To replace the description page with the slip fitting Pavel's distinguishing features was simple; pressing the indented Foreign Office stamp from one of my old passport photographs onto that of my brother-in-law so that it fitted the portion of stamp set in the valid document was not.[4] The task nevertheless completed all we had to do was glue things into place – but not until the valid passport was used by myself to go and meet Pavel back on Yugoslav soil again to explain the new plan. At the border it was the usual procedure; the passport was stamped and I was in. I met Pavel at his hotel and, over lunch, outlined the idea to him. He fell in with it at once.

The passports of outgoing travellers were not stamped by the Yugoslav border officials, but the ingoing stamp was verified and the passport carefully scrutinised. It was International Tourist Year and to suit the occasion no visas were required. The Italians only glanced at passports and took the registration number of cars.

Back in Italy Tony's nimble fingers and talent for forgery (he worked in a bank) soon had my passport suitably 'adapted' for Pavel. Then hiding it in the car and utilising his own passport at the border he drove back into Yugoslavia, deposited the car and doctored passport with Pavel and returned on foot.

Again the waiting and the doubts. Would some smart Alec recognise the car or the driver? I had passed through the checkpoint a dozen or so times within the last 48 hours. Twice the car had stalled while its ruptured exhaust made a memorable noise. But if the car was becoming a familiar sight would a different driver be noticed? And Pavel himself? Would he be recognised by one of the many policemen who had seen him under interrogation two nights previously?

Pavel spent the long afternoon washing the travel-stained car. A clean car was a less conspicuous car. As he polished the bodywork he contemplated his emergency action should things go wrong at the last moment.

Tony and I were thinking of them too as we moved up to the Italian barrier. If Pavel, waiting in his car at the Yugoslav border post, was recognised he was to put his foot down hard on the accelerator and crash through both sets of barriers. Tony would yell a warning to the Italian officials, and I was to place myself directly in the Yugoslave line of fire. I didn't think they'd shoot. I had pathetic faith in International Tourist Year.

It was five to ten at night. 'Zero hour' was ten, but Pavel was to delay until a couple or more cars had formed a queue on his side of the border. With a few cars in front he would have opportunity to look before he leapt.

The minutes crawled by. I watched one, two, three cars come through. Then a gap. Only one Yugoslav was on passport duty, but two others hung around. A machine-gun slit in a concrete blockhouse leered at me. Another car came into the yellow sphere of light 50 yards away. Ten o'clock. The car passed through. Tony and I moved close up against the Italian customs house. The palms of my hands were sticky and my mouth was dry.

Suddenly, like a star turn in a cabaret, Pavel's car was transfixed in the yellow spotlight. I watched him hand the passport to the Yugoslav official. The man flipped through the pages, glanced up at the driver, then spoke. I saw Pavel

---

4. This is no longer possible; the FO having re-designed the relevant page of the passport.

nod. A moment of eternity as nothing happened. The passport was handed back with a brief salute. The car leaped forward – and stalled. In a daze I heard the starter whirr and the engine catch. The Yugoslav turned at the high-pitched screech of the punctured exhaust, but the car was at the Italian border. I barely saw the brief formalities that followed. It didn't matter any more. Pavel was free.

In those ecstatic moments when the three of us stood transfixed with wonderment and triumph, we all learnt the meaning of that most maligned of words – Freedom. Pavel perhaps most of all, but Tony and I were also to feel its priceless quality as the cars came trickling through the barriers, their drivers unaware of the drama that had taken place.

But freedom is a fragile commodity. It has to be nourished and kept alive with infinite care and guarded with passionate devotion. And as we journeyed with Pavel deeper into the free land of Italy, he was to fall victim to the guardians of this liberty.

To complete the miracle we aimed high. I would take him home to Britain right there and then. But her representatives on Italian soil could only shake their heads, albeit a little shamefacedly. The Consul in Trieste, the Consulate General in Milan, the Embassy in Rome, all said no. There are no short-cuts to freedom.

Hotels closed their doors to the man who had no country, and we had to resort to the subterfuge of the forged passport even to get him accommodation. But help was at hand in the guise of the First Secretary of the British Embassy who, with the co-operation of Rome's chief of police, allowed us a week to work the oracle. Taking over a hotel telephone exchange, I made contact with every person of influence I could raise in Britain. But without success. On the eighth day, like Cinderella at the Ball when the clock struck midnight, the 'black maria' took Pavel away to begin his six-months 'sentence' at a refugee camp. Defeated in this subsequent project I drove Pavel's car back to Britain – only to have it impounded by customs at Dover.

Upon learning of Pavel's successful defection, Mary had applied for and been granted asylum in Britain. She now waited, understandably apprehensive, for the final release of her husband.

To obtain authorisation for him to come to Britain was no mean task. A work permit was just one of the keys to the multi-locked door and these were extremely hard to acquire. Additional to this hurdle the security services began casting aspersions upon Pavel's integrity. How, they wanted to know, had he evaded the increased surveillance of the Czech Secret Police? And why had the Yugoslavs let him go as well as me when we had been arrested in that country? The inference was that he might be an STB 'plant'. I saw their point and my dismay became despair when they almost had me believing him to be a spy. But I persevered and, one by one, the hurdles fell.

In the meantime Pavel languished for months in an assortment of refugee camps throughout Italy experiencing no great physical hardship since, while in Rome, we had applied to the Pope and the Vatican for aid so that sustenance had been forthcoming in no small measure. On the sixth month a posse of undercover agents from London descended on him to check his credentials (which they did by encouraging him to talk freely following a surfeit of brandy) and, finally, he having repeatedly declined offers of employment in Sweden and Germany, came an interview at the British Embassy in Rome and the issue of a British visa.

A week later the doors opened. Furnished with a one-way rail ticket to Dover supplied by myself Pavel took leave of the not inhospitable land of Italy bound for the near-unattainable shores of Britain.

For Anna and myself these events offered fitting conclusion to and deliverance from a seeming eternity of strife. Back in Czechoslovakia, Pavel and Mary were not to escape retribution as the price of their defection. Each was awarded a prison sentence in absentia; their property confiscated by the state. Nor did I get off scot-free, my crime being 'aiding and abetting illegal emigration'. While the republics of Eastern Europe bestowed heavy penalties for unauthorised departure from their soil, Britain was – and still is – charging heavily for admittance to hers. But for Pavel, reunited with his Mary, and today a proud Great Briton, the price was the bargain of his life.

Today all this is in the past. In the final decade of the twentieth century the borders of eastern Europe are once more negotiable; anyone can cross them 'without let or hindrance' by aeroplane, train, car, on foot – and by bicycle.

Endpiece
by Sir Henry Beverley CBE, OBE
Director General, The Winston Churchill Memorial Trust

One of the ideals most firmly expressed by Sir Winston Churchill was that men and women from all walks of life should be able to travel overseas and learn about the life work and people of other countries. In this way, and as a result of personal experience gained during their time overseas, they would make a more effective contribution to the life of this country as well as generating international relationships. Christopher Portway's epic journey exemplifies the endeavours that the Winston Churchill Memorial Trust has supported over the 30 years of it's existence.

The Trust was established on Sir Winston's death in 1965 to perpetuate his memory: the concept of the travelling fellowships having met with his approval before he died. Each year the Council of the Trust selects different broad categories within which British Citizens of all ages and from all walks of life may propose study projects of their own choice. Travelling Fellowships are awarded for original and relevant projects allied with qualities of character, enterprise and a sense of responsibility. The scheme offers the 'Chance of a Lifetime' to many who would not otherwise have such an opportunity.

100 Fellowships are offered annually and, since the formation of the Trust, over 2,900 Churchill Fellows have been selected from some 80,000 applicants. Those selected travel to all corners of the world as representatives of this country and in the name of Sir Winston Churchill. They and their achievements, constitute a growing and living memorial to the great British leader and world statesman.

Christopher Portway tells a remarkable story fully demonstrating the character, thirst for knowledge, the humility and service which made Sir Winston such an inspiration to mankind.

Bibliography

Travel Books:
Dew, Josie, *The Wind in my Wheels*, (Warner Books, London).
Farr,Michael, *Vanishing Borders*, (Joseph, London).
Harding, Georgina, *In Another Europe*, (Hodder & Stoughton, London).
MacKenzie, Andrew, *Romanian Journey* (Hale, London).
Murphy, Dervla, *Transylvania & Beyond*, (Murray, London).
Portway, Christopher,*Czechmate*, (Murray, London).
Scott-Stokes, Natascha, *The Amber Trail*, (Weidenfeld & Nicolson, London).

Travel Guides:
Eastern Europe (Fodor, London/New York).
Eastern Europe on a Shoestring (Lonely Planet, London).
Eastern Europe (Berkeley, London/New York).
Hungary, A Traveler's Guide (Helm, London).
Hungary (Berlitz, Oxford).
Hiking Guide to Romania (Bradt, Chalfont St Peter, Bucks).
Poland (Lonely Planet, London).
Rough Guide to Poland (Harrap Colombus, Edinburgh).
Russia & the Baltics (Fodor, London/NewYork).
Scandinavian & Baltic Europe (Lonely Planet, London).
Where to go in Romania (Settle Press, London).
Cycling in Europe (Pan Books, London).
People to People – The Baltic Republics (Cannongate Press, Edinburgh).

Maps: (From Bartholomew Ltd., Edinburgh).
Bartholomew's *Lithuania, Latvia & Estonia* 1:850 000,
Hallwag's *Hungary* 1:500 000,
Hallwag's *Hungary, Czechoslovakia, Poland* 1:1000,000,
Hallwag's *Romania, Bulgaria* 1:1000 000,
Collins *Road Atlas Europe*,
From Springfield Books, London, Freytag & Berndt's *Slovakia* 1:5000 000,

Books by the same author.
Non fiction:
Journey to Dana (Kimber, London).
The Pregnant Unicorn (Dalton, Lavenham).
Corner Seat (Hale, London).
Double Circuit (Hale, London).
Journey Along the Andes (Oxford Illustrated Press, Sparkford; Impact Books, London).
The Great Railway Adventure (Oxford Illustrated Press, Sparkford; Coronet Books, London).
The Great Travelling Adventure (Oxford Illustrated Press, Sparkford).
Czechmate (Murray, London).
Indian Odyssey (Impact Books, London).
A Kenyan Adventure (Impact Books, London).

Fiction:
All Exits Barred (Hale, London).
Lost Vengance (Hale, London).
The Tirana Assignment (Hale, London).
As John October, *The Anarchy Pedlars* (Hale, London).

INDEX